History of Walton County

The Discovery, Wars and Development of Florida's Emerald Coast

By John Love McKinnon

Published by Pantianos Classics

ISBN-13: 978-1-78987-342-9

First published in 1911

John L. McKinnon

Contents

First Epoch 7

Chapter One - Sketches Pertaining to Walton County's History 7

Chapter Two - The Finding and Settling of Walton County 10

Chapter Three - Col. McKinnon Receives Letter 14

Chapter Four - Col. McKinnon's Last Visit before Moving Family 23

Chapter Five - The First Gin, Grist and Saw Mill 32

Chapter Six - The Origin of the Euchees 38

Chapter Seven - A Council Called by Neill McLendon and the Chief 40

Chapter Eight - Goes on Search 46

Chapter Nine - The Euchees Depart from Walton 52

Chapter Ten - Neill McLendon Getting Ready to Leave 54

Chapter Eleven - Settles Near Waco 56

Chapter Twelve Walton's First Sensation, or Sam Story's and McLendon's Exodus 58

Second Epoch 59

Chapter Thirteen - The Indian War 59

Third Epoch 65

Chapter Fourteen - The Creek War in Walton 65

Chapter Fifteen - Intervening Times Between the Two Wars 70

Chapter Sixteen - Ferocious Animals 76

Chapter Seventeen - The Great American Bald Eagle 84

Chapter Eighteen - The Negro in Walton 91

Chapter Nineteen - Physical Improvements 98

Chapter Twenty - John Newton, the Teacher 100

Chapter Twenty-One - Medley in their Physique and in Attaining Aims 102

Chapter Twenty-Two - Newton the Knox Hill Teacher 104

Chapter Twenty-Three - School in Center of Valley 105

Chapter Twenty-Four Fourth - July 107

Chapter Twenty-Five - Lessons Outside of Books 110

Chapter Twenty-Six - A Man of Few Words 115

Chapter Twenty-Seven - A Man of Prayer 117

Chapter Twenty-Eight - Contraband Books 119

Chapter Twenty-Nine - His Home 121

Chapter Thirty - He Marries 122

Chapter Thirty-One - Churches 129

Chapter Thirty-Two - The Ringing out of the Old and the Ringing in of the New 132

Chapter Thirty-Three - Dedication Day 133

Chapter Thirty-Five - The City of Our Dead 138

Chapter Thirty-Six - Mary Gillis 140

Fourth Epoch 145

Chapter Thirty-Seven - The Civil War 145

Chapter Thirty-Eight - Reenlistment — Two Companies 148

Chapter Thirty-Nine - Leaves Camp Walton 149

Chapter Forty - On to Vicksburg 152

Chapter Forty-One - Battle of Chickamauga 153

Chapter Forty-Two - General Joseph E. Johnston's Battles and Retreats to Atlanta 156

Chapter Forty-Three - General Joseph E. Johnston is superseded by General John B. Hood, Who Goes in Rear of General Sherman 160

Chapter Forty-Four - The Battle of Franklin 161

Chapter Forty-Five - Lady Sympathizers 164
Chapter Forty-Six - To Johnson's Island Prison in Lake Erie 165
Chapter Forty-Seven - Walton's Soldiers at Home 172
Chapter Forty-Eight - The Ashboth Raid 175
Chapter Forty-Nine - Committee Sent 178
Chapter Fifty - Reclaiming Property and Settling Deserters 180
Chapter Fifty-One - The Carpetbag Negro Rule of Reconstruction 182
Chapter Fifty-Two - Sorrow and Progress 187

Fifth Epoch 188

Chapter Fifty-Three - The Projection of the P. and A. Rail Road 188
Chapter Fifty-Four - De Funiak Springs 188
Chapter Fifty-Five - The Florida Chautauqua Established 191
Chapter Fifty-Six - Schools 194
Chapter Fifty-Seven - Churches in De Funiak 195
Chapter Fifty-Eight - Walton's Daughters 196
Chapter Fifty-Nine - The Monument 199
Chapter Sixty - Gov. David S. Walker's Tribute to Walton's Daughters 202

First Epoch

Chapter One - Sketches Pertaining to Walton County's History

Walton County originally embraced that territory lying between Black Water River on the west, Choctawhatchie River on the east, Alabama on the north, and the Gulf of Mexico on the south.

This grand old County, large enough for a state, with its primeval forests, beautiful bays, winding rivers, and gushing springs, was formed November 28, A. D. 1828, with an area of 2918 square miles. The first census was taken in A. D. 1830, and showed a population of only 1,207, not quite a half man to the square mile. O, how lonely these individuals must have felt in this wilderness of woods! The name "Walton" was given to this territory in honor of General Andrew Jackson's efficient aid, Colonel George Walton.

November 28, A. D. 1842, Walton County gave birth to Santa Rosa County, giving all of her territory west of Yellow River. And January 8, A.D. 1848, she contributed 435 square miles out of her northeast corner and west of the Choctawhatchie River, to form what is now known as Holmes County. This leaves the Walton County of today, with 1,384 square miles, quite a large county yet.

Now, it is this territory of the Highlands of Western Florida, the very foothills of the Blue Ridge, lying practically between these rivers, the Mexican Gulf and Alabama, this land thus hedged in, and its people, that we propose, in the main, to speak of through these pages.

In writing this history we feel that it is due to the memory of the aborigines, our Scotch pioneers, and for the wholesome benefit of their descendants, who may feel that they have eclipsed them in learning and in the true ways of life in these advanced days of thinking, of education, and of fashion.

We will venture to say just here that there are but few bits of territory to be found anywhere that are so pregnant with readable history, if properly brought out, as this little, once isolated, Walton section. Lying here, as it were, in the protecting arms of her bounding rivers, with these loving daughters keeping faithful watch, with her head lying in the lap of Alabama, that says, "Here let us rest," while the great Mexican Gulf, at one time, humbly washing her feet with its gentle waves, to make them pure and white like snow, and at another time dashing her angry waves in maddened fury upon her, with hollow murmuring that sickens the heart and threatens destruction. Listen! Jupiter is enraged now, the coruscations of his wrath leap over the deep, the pent-up winds are loosed from their caverns, and old Neptune is riding in glory on the surging waves and through the angry breakers. What a picture! Hugged on either side in the loving arms of unsleeping protection, her head at rest, while her feet are being trampled upon by cruel waves threatening total destruction. Unique though this picture may seem, yet we find that it symbolizes the history of her people.

This little land, in its people, has had the strongest protection and the most gracious plenty, the sweetest rest in peace, and the most heart-wringing sorrows and cruel surges in war. There are episodes of the home-love and of the chase, episodes of peace and of war, and if they fail of being brought out, you may still be sure that they are here.

Who Were the First Settlers of Walton County?

In the years A. D. 1808-09-10-11-12, there was an English ship named "Scotia" that made regular trips from Liverpool to Wilmington, North Carolina, and New Amsterdam, bringing passengers. The greater portion of the emigrants that came from the different parts of Scotland stopped in Wilmington, especially those that came in the year A. D. 1810, for these were all Scotch from the Highlands; and in these years the Scotch and Scotch Irish emigrants came over by the hundreds to North Carolina. A few of their relatives went to Canada. We know of no radical cause for their leaving their native heath. Some say "They left to escape the halter." There was no persecution, either in Church or State at that time, to cause them to emigrate. They came fully impregnated with the Calvinistic doctrines and the love of country, and the liberty that ever burns in every Scotchman's breast. They had Scotch friends and relatives here that were identified with the first settlers of North Carolina. They had glowing descriptions of the country and its liberties; and this gave them a longing for this better land. These emigrants would often call for blessings on the good ship that brought them safely over the waters, and would speak of the "Scotia" as their "May Flower." - the second "May Flower."

Now, it was from these Scottish emigrants and their descendants that the first settlers of Walton County came. In studying the general history of this county, we will find three men standing out prominently in their respective spheres, — one born in Isle of Sky Scotland, one in North Carolina, and the other in Pennsylvania, — one a foreigner, one a Southerner, the other a Northerner, — the first two by extraction Scotchmen, the third a Puritan Yankee, — the first two were first cousins, the third with no kin south of the Mason and Dixon line, — the first and the last with a classical education, the second one with a common school education but with a great deal of good, common sense. They all three commenced their life's work in North Carolina, — the first a farmer, the second a general surveyor of lands and stock raising, the third a practical school teacher. But they were all together on one essential thing — they were religious — all staunch Presbyterians of the old Scotch Covenanters' type or of the old Calvinistic order. So this solves the mystery of how this strange combination of men can be seen marching up and down through this little land, making history up to date; especially when the Southern born Scotchman and the Yankee never met, — the farmer fin-

1. Guy Davis. 2. A. D. McKinnon.
3. Dr. C. E. McKinnon. 4. Col. John L. McKinnon.

ishing his work and leaving more than a decade before the teacher came to begin his, but leaving the stockman surveyor on hand to introduce the teacher to his work.

Now, the prominent leader of the three, in starting our history, was Neill McLendon, the "Pathfinder," (or Neill McClellan. as he was sometimes called in Texas), Colonel John L. McKinnon stood for the military and civil trend, and John Newton represented the educational interest, — while no one prominently, but all, generally and faithfully, represented the religious, agricultural and commercial advance. All this will be brought out more prominently as we move along.

Chapter Two - The Finding and Settling of Walton County

In the spring of A.D. 1820, Neill McLendon of Richmond County, North Carolina, a born pioneer, in the glow of manhood, full of health and strength, a leader of men, with advanced thoughts and ideas, the very soul of integrity, alive with energy and courage, — this man, — this typical Scotchman, who could never see any danger in the way of anything that he wished to accomplish which he didn't feel he could over-leap, — this remarkable man, this Trailer, became restless in the old North State and longed for a newer and better country, — a cattle, hog and sheep range, — a home where he could have "more elbow room" and breathe purer air.

He had read of Florida, "the land of sunshine and flowers," of its towering pines and spreading oaks, its green pasturage, its great bays, lakes and rivers, abounding in fish, and of the mighty gulf that lashed its shores. He longed to have a plenty of everything, so in that early spring morning he sprang from his bed, got ready, with his wife and family, his brother Lochlin and his family, and his brother-in-law, Daniel D. Campbell, an unmarried man, and one John Folk and his family, and started out with their teams in the direction of Pensacola, through that zone which was opened up through South Carolina, Georgia, Alabama and Florida, by removing, through treaty, the unfriendly Creek Indians westward.

After many adventures by the way, which, if recorded, would fill a little volume, they reached Florida near Bluff Springs, and rested for a while along the banks of the Escambia and Black Water Rivers. They were much pleased with that beautiful country. They went up and down the lands between those two rivers, looking at the lay of the country and pretty streams, but it was not exactly what McLendon wanted, or was hunting for. He visited Pensacola often, and made many friends among the Spaniards, especially among the officials and merchant men. He had a great tact of winning friends among those whom he met in every grade of society. While he was in plain dress, and coarse, or abrupt in manner, he had a good kind heart, had many winsome ways to draw men to him. It might be said of him, "He was a plain blunt man that loved his friends." He told the merchants, whom he had met there, the kind of country he was looking for and must find. An old doctor heard him, and joined with the merchants in telling him of the new country up the Choctawhatchie Bay and River that was hemmed in by the Gulf and rivers. They informed him that there was but one way by which he could reach this hermit place, and that was by boat through the bay and intricate channels of the sounds and narrows along Santa Rosa Island. They told him that, while they had never seen this country, they had most bewitching descriptions of it from the Chief of a friendly tribe of Indians called Uchees; that they had lived there for years and years and they had never heard of any of the tribe going on the war-path through all these years. These men pictured this Indian Chief, whose name was "Sam Story," as a most wonderful Indian, full of born integrity, with a kind, warm heart in him, punctual to meet his obligations, who made a most acceptable chief, governing well his tribes; that he came regularly five or six times each year to Pensacola in his market boats. bringing both fish and dried game for sale; that he would be in about the last of the next week, and if he would come in then they would introduce him to the Chief, who would tell him all about his country and how to get there, but they felt sure that the only way was by the Chief's trading boats and their piloting through the narrow channels. McLendon was well pleased with what he learned from these Spanish merchants, and went to his home on the Escambia to rest and dream of the ideal country in prospect.

When the appointed time came to go to Pensacola, he went promptly. This stout, brawny, typical Scotchman, in the very prime of life and strength, met and was introduced to the tall, agile, Indian Chief, just a little worn with age, with high cheek bones, a prominent, receding forehead, flashing eyes, and a wide mouth that spoke in muffled tones about his great hunting ground, and of McLendon's welcome up there. As the Chief talked, — and he talked well both in the Spanish and English tongues, as well as in his own dialect — McLendon's friends could see the benign smiles play upon his face. All could see that there was, or would be, friendship between the two, that there were things common in their natures that might lead to something good. The Chief said to McLendon "Come and see," told him the best way for him to come, — was to go back to his home on the Escambia and go up the river to a certain point, and there he would find an Indian trail leading from the Northwest toward the Southeast, and if he would follow that trail it would lead him to his headquarters on the south bank of Bruce Creek (opposite what is now Euchee Anna). This place is now known as the "Old Place," being the first settled place in the County, the home, for a while, of the McLendons, and the one long cherished home of Colonel McKinnon in Florida.

So, in a little while, this home-seeker, when he had arranged some things in his Escambia Camp, put his brother Lochlin in charge of the women folk, had food prepared, and a lot of bullets molded for his long Buchanan rifle, took a good night's rest, got up with the dawn, and started for the home of his newly made friend, "Sam Story." He was accompanied by his brother-in-law Daniel D. Campbell, whose sister he had married, and who is the father of Judge

John L. Campbell of Chipley, Florida, and of our Dr. Daniel L. Campbell, who is with us here in De Funiak Springs today, — and that John Folk.

This trailer had no trouble in getting on the right trail, and keeping on it. With their guns and packs on their backs, they followed this dimly beaten path, wading, swimming, or pontooning the creeks and rivers that fell across their way. This trail led them right along where DeFuniak now is, and by the little round lake, or spring, that was later called the "Open Pond," and on across Indian and Bruce Creeks to the Chief's quarters. When there, they were gladly welcomed and royally received. Sam Story had returned home from Pensacola, so they lodged with him. They were served with strong black coffee, fresh Indian cornbread, beaten in a hand mortar, fresh game and jerked venison hams, which they ate with a relish after their long journey.

The dress, manners, and general appearance of the young natives were no greater curiosity to these white men, than the appearance of these white men were to them. Most of them had never seen a "pale face" before. These Indians were all dressed in the skins of animals, nicely prepared in tanning. The women were gorgeously arrayed in beads and turkey feathers in their headwear. The young braves were much taken up with the "pale faces" long guns. Sam Story had quite a large family of tall boys and girls and they seemed to be above the other families in knowledge and manners. The other families seemed to realize this and gave them due respect.

After two days rest, the old Chief, with his young braves, took his white friends out to show them his fine hunting ground. All started well equipped, to be gone several days. They went up and down the land from one end to the other, along the Gulf, the bays, lakes, springs and rivers. Before the look was half over, all save McLendon, saw enough and were worn out and returned to the quarters to rest; but the old Chief and McLendon went and went from daylight until dark, through broad savannas of rich grass, through river swamp, and cane brake, admiring the beauty and utility of the country. As they went they gave no thought to the reptiles that crawled at their feet, nor to the wild beasts that reluctantly moved out of their way. This man came to see, — he saw and was captivated. He came back to the station refreshed instead of worn out. He knew now, pretty much all about the country he came to see. He was pleased beyond his expectation. As he walked on the rich green grass amid the forests of lofty pines, they seemed as Elysian groves to him. When he laid himself down at night around the camp fires to rest, he said "This is an Eldorado enough for me."

While they were resting and recuperating for their return, they were shown around the quarters, the tanneries, the circles of the green corn dances, and the fields where they raised the corn for the dance. This field was a good size corn field in the midst of the dense swamp of Bruce Creek, with only a trail leading to it. Here was a rich green field of Indian corn growing, with no fence around it, — there was no need of a fence, as there was not a domestic animal in all this region, except their little Indian ponies with their long manes and tails. It may be well to say here that this field is on the "Old

Place" and that Colonel McKinnon cultivated it for a number of years after the Euchees left, and let it grow up in timber and cleared it up again and cultivated it in his life time, and that one of his sons has this same field under cultivation today, and raising on it good stuff, and it is known today as the "old Indian field."

The old Pathfinder was pleased the more when he saw what fine corn could be grown in this beautiful country. He saw at once how independent one could live here, and this was the paramount thought in his mind while on the search. He did not conceal from the old Chief how well he was pleased, and this pleased the chief, especially when he found that he wanted to come, because their late association drew them closer together. He gave him his tomahawk and told him to blaze out such lands as he wanted, without any reservation for himself. Now, we look at this as the very highest type of pure genuine love, especially as it exists between the red man and the pale face, equal, I may say, to any on record; equal to that which existed between William Penn and Roger Williams and their red men; yes, to that of Captain Smith and Pocahontas. And the beauty of this is that McLendon knew how to appreciate it, as will be shown, and he was modest in choosing, taking homes for himself and brother adjoining the Chief's; and a little farther down on the creek and bend, homes for the rest of his friends.

Now these three men were the first white men to come into this territory, seeking and finding homes. All things having been satisfactorily arranged for their new homes in this wild country, and having gained a pretty good idea of the lay of the land by tramping up and down through it, they are now ready to return to their camp home on the Escambia. They advised with the Chief as to the best route to reach their new homes with their teams and families. He, being thoroughly familiar with the contour of the whole land, advised them to move well up the rivers, and they would surround the heads or find fords across their prongs; and following these instructions, and the knowledge McLendon had of the country, they would have but little water to contend with along the way. So with their guns and packs on their backs, and well provided with food for their way, through the red man's hospitality, they took leave of their new aboriginal friends, and went with quick steps and glad hearts back to their families along the same old Indian trail which they came.

After an absence of one month, with few incidences of worth, along the way, other than like those they had when going, they reached their dear ones, to find them all well and heartily rejoicing at their safe return, for said Mrs. McLendon, "You stayed so long, and we heard so much, after you were gone, of small bands of hostile Indians massacring whole families of prospecting parties, and of the cruel reptiles and savage wild beasts in the way you went, it made us awful sad, and we were fearful that we would see you no more; sure we are glad to welcome you back, my dear." Then said McLendon, "Don't you know there is never a lion in the way of those seeking good for themselves and others? Why, we never saw a living creature along our way, save one lone, black, black crow, and he spoke to us in the kindest language that he knew, and flew away to tell his friends of our coming." These adventurers rested and talked several days with their families about what they had learned while gone, about the beauties of nature undisturbed, — nature in her happiest moods.

Chapter Three - Col. McKinnon Receives Letter

McLendon wrote a long eight page foolscap letter, full of truths, to Colonel McKinnon in North Carolina, about the new country he had found. This letter was read and appreciated by all of his Scotch friends and their friends. They knew it was just as he said it was; there was little that was pessimistic in the letter, and his optimistic ideas were all based on facts that he gave. This letter set the minds and hearts of that people on fire. We wish we had that letter as it was written, that we might interject it into this history, believing, from what we have heard of it, that it would be more satisfactory to the reader than anything we shall be able to produce.

It was some little while before these emigrants struck camps to move to their new homes. They went several times to Pensacola on business and hoping to meet Sam Story. Finally they met up with him there, and at his instance, they brought in all their moving that they could possibly dispense with on the way, that he might take them up on his market boat and give them light wagons to come across the country. This proved to be a most excellent arrangement, and another illustration of his born unselfishness. In a little while after these arrangements, these homeseekers, in their light wagons, with plenty of prepared food for the way, started out northward, circumventing creeks, or passing over river prongs, through fords, bearing eastward, until they had reached the watershed that divides the waters flowing into the rivers and bays to the southwest, and those flowing in the rivers to the southeast, and then turned south and southeast and reached their destination with comparatively little trouble. Again, they with their families are welcomed by their new friends.

After a little rest, they settle down on their lands, and with the tools they had provided in Pensacola, they go to work and soon they build, out of round logs, comfortable bungalows to shelter their families. Then they enter the forests with their axes to fell the trees and clear away the brushes to make bread, — they had already learned that there would be no trouble about meat as long as their old Buchanan rifles could be kept in ammunition.

To say that these families were now happy in their new homes would be but putting it mildly. They thought, no doubt, that this would be their earthly home for all time, — and this was true of some of them. They felt too that they would soon have their friends and relations around them in this goodly land and there would be no more moving around, — this also was true to a great extent.

When Colonel McKinnon received that descriptive letter, he read it with great interest and was pleased. The letter urged him to come at once and bring some of his laborers and certain tools to prepare a home before bringing his family, and gave him the Chief's and his own best ideas as to how to reach them. The Colonel was a practical surveyor and a good localist, and his business had brought him often through South Carolina, Georgia and Alabama, as far down as Columbus and Montgomery, so these advantages would make the route practically easy for him. In a little while he made ready for the trip. He was unmarried then, but married on his return, April 26, A.D. 1821, and before his second trip to Florida. He procured his younger brother, Daniel L, McKinnon, who stayed in his home and faithfully took care of his interest there until he moved to Florida. He owned a large reliable bay stallion horse named Jack. He procured a strong two-wheeled vehicle, which he called a "gig," — suppose we would call it today a "road-cart." All things arranged, he took leave of his family and friends and started out with Jack and his gig and a trusty negro man named George, to find his friends and to make a new home in Florida. They did not travel on the same route that the McLendon party came, but went a good bit farther toward the east and struck in about where Geneva, Alabama, now is, and came on a few miles west of DeFuniak Springs, striking in at the "Faye Place" where the Freeport and DeFuniak road now leads, and around the heads of Bruce and Mill Creeks, on to the "Old Place," where he found his friends hard at work, who were as glad to see George and himself as they were to find them.

That first evening and most of the night was spent in wholesome talk about the old home folks and the new country. Their journey from the old North State was, upon the whole, a pleasant one, with many adventures of interest, especially from George's view point. This was a great trip for him, and he, in the passing years, would often entertain the younger generation for hours with his stories of wonder on that trip. But there is so much to tell we will have to leave this unwritten. They found no one along the way who could give them better ideas of how to go than they had themselves. After they got across Pea River a little way, they met in with three Euchee hunters, who gave them directions how to go around Bruce and Mill Creeks that they might get with their gig to the Chief's headquarters.

After a little rest the old pioneer took his first visitor, in quest of a home in the new land, to the old Chief, and introduced him as his near relative and friend. This was enough for the Chief; he extended his red hand, — but not red with blood — took hold of the white hand of the new comer with a hearty grasp and a welcome shake. He handed him his tomahawk, which was never stained with the blood of a pale face, and told him to go into the woods and blaze out a home for himself where he liked. What wonderful friendship and marked unselfishness already existed between these two heroes of peace! And it will be well for us to note the powers of these virtues as they exist here in the very inception, the very germ of the colonies that were to come, because we will show that these virtues had their counterpart in the pioneers that came.

Friendship is a beautiful and sacred relation between those who understand each other. It implies a community of interest, perfect confidence, mutual support, and an exchange somewhere of that which stimulates life. But self-interest and Christ-likeness have little in common. This is the boast of the worldly, the self-centered, the stingy soul, — "I look out for number one." The love and common interest expressed among these early settlers for each other's welfare is a friendship sufficient to awaken the minds and make the hearts of their descendants thrill with pleasure and flush with pride.

Colonel McKinnon located his trusty servant, George, in a log cabin which he made near his friend McLendon and arranged for his provisions. He left him to help his friends fix up homes and clear up lands for the coming year's crop, then he went, piloted at one time by McLendon alone, and at other times accompanied by the Chief and some of his braves, and leisurely surveyed the country, in the sense of looking it over carefully, for he had nothing to work with except his sun dial, which he used as a compass to travel by, and his watch which he carried in his pocket all his days in Florida, which he claimed never varied from the right time, — he kept it in proof with his sun dial. They went up and down every creek and river, around or over every lake and spring, over every sand hill, and through every savanna, through the dense swamps along the creeks and rivers, making rough pencil sketches or maps as he went, and dotting down things of interest as they passed along.

He went on a trip with Sam Story and his crew in their market boats, roughly constructed crafts. They took shipping from a landing on the Choctawhatchie River in the bend made by Bruce Creek and the River, called then "Mushy Bend," but known now by the more classical name, "Mossy Bend," on account of the pendant moss that swings to and fro in such beautiful gray hanks from the trees. This landing was called, and is now known, by the name of "Story's Landing," named for the old Chief. They went down the river, out into the Choctawhatchie Bay, and through it, into the beautiful streams of water, the Narrows and Sound, and on through Pensacola Bay to the town of Pensacola, where he remained several days, making friends among the Spaniards, which continued undisturbed for a half century. The produce sold, — stores for the trip and merchandise for the friends in the home procured, they set sail for Story's Landing through the same waters which they came, visiting many of the bayous and inlets on either side as they returned, and having quite a lot of rare sport in fishing and hunting along the way. When they reached Story's Landing they were met with the Indian ponies to pack out the merchandise to the homes. When back, they made a reckoning of the time spent on the trip, and they found that they had been gone nearly two months, and this, too, without wasting much time on the way. So much for the rudely constructed Indian market boats of that day. That trip could be made now in two or three days.

Now, the Colonel having explored the land and surroundings to his satisfaction, made choice for his future home, the fertile hammock lands on Bruce Creek to the westward of the McLendon's and Indian fields and quarters of the Chief. Sam Story now had the Colonel just west of him and friend McLendon on the east. The Colonel was very much pleased with the country, the aborigines, and his trip to Pensacola. Only those who have listened to his description of this country in detail in the latter years, or that of any of the early settlers, can have a correct idea of its beauties and glories. He held nothing back that would show his friends here and the Chief, how well he was pleased, and his purposes in the future. He showed George where he wanted him to clear away for the home and field, when he got through with such help as he was to give his friends here, which would occupy his time through the incoming spring. He saw that he was well provided for in the hands of McLendon, so he made ready to leave for home.

He hitched up Jack to the "gig," took leave of the red man, the black man, and his pale face friends, bade adieu to his home in prospect, left the land of sunshine and flowers, for his home in the old North State. As he drove off, McLendon called to him, approached him, and said, "See here, John, be cautious and don't encourage any trash to come here, there is plenty of room in other places for them. We want families to come who have tact, from any nationality, who know how to treat rightly their fellow human beings of any race or color." We have reason to believe this caution was given consideration. We were reminded of this advice by an incident which occurred not many years ago down in Euchee Valley.

Some of the "old time" colored people in the Valley felt that they wanted to worship in a Presbyterian Church organization as they did in the "ante bellum" days. They applied to our Presbytery, and a commission was sent in due time who found the way clear, and organized the Church with quite an intelligent set of colored people. They elected for elders an old time conscientious Christian man, full of good solid sense, — the other was a bright, ambitious, sensible young man, the son of a "good-old-before-the-War-slave." When the meeting broke up and the people began to leave, the young elder called the old elder aside and said to him, "See here, Uncle Cal, let us go slow in this church business, let's don't take in the trash." "Look here, my son," said the old man, "it is our duty to go as fast as we can and get in as many as we can into the church and see to making them better men and women." "That may be so," said the young elder, "but there is plenty of room in the other churches around for the trash." We do not know what effect this young elder's thought had, but it is well to say here, that their church has built up slowly and they have ever had an intelligent, educated, preacher to break the bread of life to them, a graduate of the Presbyterian school at Tuscaloosa, Ala.

After short stops in Alabama and Georgia on business, the Colonel reached his home, having been gone eight months, to rejoice with his anxious dear ones and friends in a reunion that was dear, after being gone so long on a trip that seemed to them so full of danger. They had only heard from him once while absent. In a letter which unfolded to them the description of the new country which lay so fresh enfolded in his mind, he confirmed all that McLendon had written and gave more. He was like the Queen of Sheba, "The half had never been told."

This, in substance, is what he had to say, viz.: "Truly it is the land of sunshine and flowers. No wonder that the bold Spanish adventurer, standing upon the prow of his caravel on that Sunday of Palms, when he first caught sight of these lovely shores, exclaimed 'Linda, Florida, — fair land of flowers.' This bold Spanish adventurer and devout Castilian, beheld in her a fit emblem of the day. The aborigines know better how to take care of their country than the white man does. They never allow the fires to run wild and burn up their range. This is why they have so much beauty in flowers and utility in such abundance in stock feed. The piney woods lands along the up-hills and ridges are generally sandy and do not appear to be productive; fine wire grass for grazing purposes at your feet, and the tall moaning pines above your heads are what you see. The pine lands lying along the creeks and rivers seem to be more productive. There are some hammock lands on the creeks and rivers as rich in soil as there is any use for, will grow anything. The branches, creeks and rivers are splendid streams, the best watered country I ever saw. The rivers with the gulf are great barriers against depredators. The rivers can and will be made navigable. There are a great variety of lakes and springs, varying in shape, size and depths. One of these springs is upon the top of a hill, sending forth the purest, limpid waters, perfectly round, and just one mile in circumference. The aborigines say there is no bottom to this lake (DeFuniak Springs). A little way further on in a northwest direction you find the double lakes (Lake Stanley); twenty-four miles further, and on the Alabama line you come to a large lake several miles in circumference (Lake Jackson); twelve miles northeast of the round spring on the hill you come to the other large lake in the piney woods, covering more than a section of land (Lake Cassida); go in the same direction, four or five miles, near the Alabama line, and you come to a boiling spring in the piney woods, covering a small area, but sending forth a large stream of cold mineral water, — there seem to be two mighty boils, separated by a ledge of rock, supporting this spring; some claim that it was just one great boil and not two, that the ledge of rock that appeared to separate them extended only a little way down, while others claim it extends to the bottom and formed two distinct boils (Turner Spring)". It will be well to note here that this spring became, in the days to come, a great health and pleasure resort and many came here to be recuperated. Colonel McKinnon came here with his family and friends many summers for rest and pleasure. On one occasion while a number of them were bathing in the spring, the discussion came up as to whether there was one or two distinct boils in the spring. The Colonel being an athlete in water, stepped upon the spring board and said, "I will dive down and see if I can't settle this question." He gave a spring, bounded up in the air, came down head foremost into the upper boil, and in a little while came up through the lower boil, amid the shouts of the crowd, bearing the mark of his triumph in a long deep cut down his back that he carried with him to his grave, which was made by a sharp projecting rock that caught him as he sprang up through the lower division. This settled the discussion for a while, but in another generation it came up for discussion again and on one occasion, while quite a crowd was present, and in bathing, some one told what the Colonel had done. Some expressed a doubt, and Angus M. McKinnon of Geneva, Alabama, a grandson of the Colonel's, who was a live didapper in the water, was moved to exclaim, "I know there is but one boil," and leaped into the upper opening and came up out of the lower boil without a scratch, his companions cheering him, saying, "You beat your grandfather, — now we know there is but one." This was not the only time that he performed this water feat, but on several other occasions he gratified his friends by the performance. These two are the only ones we ever heard of that did go under that ledge.

James McLean

A little to the south of this spring, and a little further down, you reach a beautiful spring near the banks of what the Indians called "Big Sandy," which mingles its waters with those of the blue spring and with the limpid waters of this great creek (Ponce de Leon Spring). Now as this spring came to be quite a resort, especially for the young people after pleasure and love making in the woods, it will be well to interject this thought here, — Anthony Brownell from the upper part of the country, built what was then a large hotel: a neat double-pen, round log, house, rooms 18 ft. by 18 ft., with a 12 foot hall between, nice shed rooms on one side and a 12 foot gallery on the front. He had patronage, but the war came on and broke up his enterprise, and he sold out the plant and the building fell into decay. In a short time one of the old Scotch pioneers, James McLean, purchased the lands and left the spring to stand surrounded with its natural growth and to be free to the families seeking health or rest, to build booths or bungalows for summer rest, and to the young to have their innocent pleasure in picnics and fishing. When the Pensacola and Atlantic Division of the Louisville and Nashville Railroad was projected by this spring, many were the parties that approached Mr. McLean, offering him fancy prices for the spring to build large commodious hotels and bathing houses, to make a summer resort for health and pleasure seekers. But the old Scotch pioneer, notwithstanding he was not immune to want, shook his aged head, with its curly, silvery locks hanging down toward his shoulders, and said "No, no, I want this spring to remain in its natural state, without a vine or a tree being disturbed, as long as I live, at least, for the benefit and pleasure of my friends."

There was not a word further said, they saw that he meant just what he said, and that was enough. The old hero of service, love and unselfishness has passed over the river and is resting in the shades of the trees and drinking from the river of life that has its source from beneath the Throne of God. And today, that spring, in its primeval beauty, is rushing out its cool waters from beneath the shades of that great oak which has stood so long upon its banks, serving as a leaping place for the boys to jump into the spring. But now this old oak tree is bending over, as its owner did, with the wear and tear of life, and soon it will lay down in its cold watery grave and will be borne away to larger waters.

Four miles further down Big Sandy, and not far from its mouth, we come to a mammoth mineral spring, with different surroundings; in the edge of the creek, and river swamp, with great cypress trees standing around its banks as sentinels, with gray moss hanging in streamers from their limbs. This spring would float the biggest war vessel in the world. It empties its waters into the Choctawhatchie River that is two miles away, through a stream which is six feet deep and 80 feet wide. It flows from beneath two ledges of rock, it is at least 50 feet to the first ledge, and can't say how far to the second. The waters are perfectly transparent. When we floated over its bosom of rolling waters in our Indian canoe, we felt as though we were floating in the skies. This is one of the wonders of the land. Now we must remember that these rivers, lakes and springs, yes, and the creeks and branches too, are all teaming with fish of all sizes and species, — the bream, shell-crackers, the speckled fish, fresh water trout, and we must not forget the white sucker, that is equal in flavor to any shad that swims in the Peedee of our State, or in the Oconee in Georgia. And there are ever so many other varieties of table fish. I was astonished at the large sturgeons and mammoth alligators or crocodiles. There seemed to be a plenty of reptiles, the sly moccasin and bold rattler, but they seemed to be willing to give us the right of way. Now, as to the birds that fly in the air and roost in the trees, for beauty, variety and song, these surpass any description I can give. The woods are filled with their melody day and night. The game birds move around in bevies or flocks. At night the happy mocker, perched up on the highest limb, leads the chorus for the night, the whip-poor-will in the distance chimes in with its plaintive lays, while the horned owl from the swamp joins in with his deep bass voice, joining in the chorus with the other birds. The dawn is ushered in by the strutting gobbler, with his commanding" voice, answered by the deep baritone voice of the long-legged and long-necked sand-hill-crane, that ever keeps watch around the ponds and lakes; and the co-mingling of these voices which sounds at one time like distant thunder, but in the main very much like the voice of our long-eared animal in one of his merriest moods. This morning song of discord awakens all animate nature to action, and as the sun steps up the steeps of the skies and throws its golden rays athwart the land, the heavens are filled with a stream of melody and love by the merry songsters — the lark mounting up the heights, while the merry mocker is still on hand as the sweetest singer. There are ferocious animals that roam over these woods with daring pride, — the great black bear, the sly wolf, the prowling panther, and the saucy catamount, and its cousin the wild cat. The Indians do not seem to mind these, they have no domestic animals for them to prey upon, so they say, "They do not bother us, and we will let them go." The game or food animals are plentiful, the deer, the squirrel, the opossum, and the coon. I saw deer feeding together there in companies of fives, tens, and as many as twenty in a drove, like droves of cattle in our pastures. On our approach, to see them bound over the hills and plains with their white tails thrown over their backs, to me, this was the prettiest sight I saw on the trip. There is no monotony along these creeks and rivers, the lakes or the springs. And the monotony of the plains and ridges is broken by the presence of these wild beasts and singing birds. There are only two approaches opened to this country, a land approach from the north, through which I went and came, the other by water, a commercial approach from the south. This water way opens up a market that is one hundred miles to the west. I made this trip with my Indian friends and I am not ready to give you a description of its beauty and grandeur along the water courses that we passed through. It is enough to say here that I was pleased with both the trip, the men and market of Pensacola. Now, there are families and small tribes of these friendly Indians scattered all up and down the Euchee Valley, and all over the country by the water courses. There is a small tribe camping at that gem of a mountain, the very antipodes of that gem of a round lake — beauty in loftiness of height from the valley — beauty in lowliness of depth from the hill — beauty in sand — beauty in water. This mountain looming up from the valley, like Pikes Peak from the back-bone of the Rockies. (?) stands there as a monument and guide for the lone Indian. And while it lifts up its awful form (?) toward the clouds; at its base runs one of the sweetest murmuring little rivers, equal in beauty to old Scotia's Bonnie Doon. This mountain is nine miles southwest of the round lake and is called by the natives "Sandy Mountain." Then too, Sam Story has a station at what he calls Rock Hill, used sometimes as his headquarters. There is a packed circle there for their green corn dance. This station is kept by quite an intelligent little tribe of Indians (let me say by way of parenthesis that Mr. F. Q. Tervin has now a trough dug out of one of the large boulders on this hill in front of his well, using it for watering purposes, which he says he hauled from Sam Story's camp, in which he fed his little Indian ponies more than a century ago. He has every reason to believe that it will last for centuries to come, as it doesn't seem to be any the worse for wear through the ages past. It is a complete unique trough. From this same hill my father took rock to build his furnaces to boil sugar cane juice into syrup; and on one occasion when he was breaking them up into suitable pieces to be worked, he gave with his sledge hammer, a three foot square boulder, a blow that split it centerly through, and in the very center there was found a good sized frog in a home that conformed to his size and shape, and it was as slick as and of the color of slate. The rend did not disturb his house any more than opening a pair of bullet molds disturbed the bed of the bullet. It was like putting the two palms of your hand together and separating them, — the hollow is still the same in each hand. There was a red streak that ran straight through the rock and it was through this the rend was made. These bits of rock were kept on exhibition for a number of years. It must be remembered that these boulders are what we call sand rock. We have read of Shakespeare's toad living on the "vapors of a dungeon," but never before nor since, did we see or hear of a frog living for ages in the center of a three foot boulder on vapor or anything else. This was certainly a strange freak of nature, and we leave it for the scientists to explain.) Now, you see, we have a land with light, sandy soil, gray mold, and stiff river swamp lands. We can have a country with caves and natural bridges, with valleys and plains, with hills and mountains, a country abounding with game, birds and food animals, a country whose streams abound in the greatest varieties of fish, a country whose climate and health are not surpassed by any on the globe, a country whose aborigines live by the chase and are not thrifty in field work, yet, who are pacific, kind and obliging. Now, what more can we hope for in a country? You say you can but be pleased with the topography — with the contour of the land, with the soil and the water, with the climate and health. Then you say, 'you have heard so much about the treachery and revenge of the Indian that you can't see how you could feel safe in that pent up home with them.' And you say, 'you would not be surprised at any time to learn that they have massacred the whole McLendon party.' Nine times out of ten the treachery and revenge has its birth in the minds and hearts of the white man. This is true in the settling of the colonies and in our states today. I verily believe that if we treat these Euchee Indians right, we will be treated fairly by them. But you see this big Indian is still in the way. he is the "lion in the way." 'Shall we go or shall we not?' This was the question for weeks and months and years, until several years had passed away. During these unsettled 3'ears Colonel McKinnon went once each year to look after his interest in the Florida country, staying from six to eight months at a time with his friends. So the way became quite familiar to him and Jack. And on every return he was better pleased. And during these Waiting years, George had, with what help he gave him, while on his visits, gotten ready quite a comfortable home for his family and a good sized field for his bread, and he began to feel pretty independent on that line. On these visits he always found his friends, especially the ladies, anxious to meet him and learn of their kin and friends in the old State. "When will they make the break and come?" They were so lonely! But as the years passed, and they became better fixed up in their new homes, the loneliness passed away and they were becoming more and more satisfied. On the Colonel's second trip to Florida, he fell in by the way with two parties who had heard of his report of the new country and were seeking it, Libius Hunter and his nephew, Dempsey Jones, from Newburn, North Carolina. These came to the Colonel's home in North Carolina, expecting to go with him on his second trip, but he had left before they got there. His young wife told them that he would be detained on business at a certain place in Georgia and they might overtake him there. They went and found him, and they came on the way together. These men were pleased and well received by the settlers. When the Colonel returned they remained prospecting.

They selected lands at the very head of the Valley. They returned to North Carolina and came again with their families and made good settlers.

Chapter Four - Col. McKinnon's Last Visit before Moving Family

On the Colonel's last visit to the new home, just before he brought his family, on arriving, he found George in trouble. A white tramp squatter, — an uninvited guest, found his way in and went to the field where George was clearing land, and drove him away, telling him he was nothing but a negro and must get out of there. George explained to him that he was doing this work for, and by the direction of his master, who was in North Carolina, that he would soon come with his family. He used ugly words, told him to get out and leave the country. George reported to McLendon and he said to him "You just wait a few days and your master will come and attend to him." The Colonel came and took in the situation. The next morning he sent George to work in the field and said to him, "if Williamson comes to stop you, tell him that I have come, and if he orders you away, you leave without saying anything to him." George soon returned and reported that Williamson met him with his gun and told him if he found him on that place again he would shoot him. The Colonel, with his long Buchanan rifle on his shoulder, and George with his ax, went to the field and there was Williamson at work on the land.

George said, "Master walked up to him quietly and asked, 'Is this Williamson?' He said 'Yes, this is me.'

'What are you doing here?' 'I am clearing up land to make bread.' 'Don't you know you have no rights in here?' 'I know that I have,' replied Williamson with emphasis. 'You know you haven't any rights in this field, neither has such a scoundrel as you any place in this land, so leave at once.'" Williamson jumped for his gun, George said, "When he turned around with it in his hand, master had his all ready to shoot, and he was looking Williamson straight in the face, and was looking daggers at him too, and he said 'Williamson, don't you raise that gun another inch. Turn your back now and walk off, and if you look back while you are in my sight I will put a bullet in you, and you must leave this country too." George said "Dem big blue eyes of master's told him he mean juss what he said, and he went, and was no fool needer, like Mr. Lott's wife." Williamson was seen no more in that country, and the settlers thought it a good get-away. Now, it was Uncle George that told me this, he told it to all of us children lots of times, and he would say, "Now if you chilurns don't believe this to be juss like dis nigger tell you, juss go and ask old massa and he will say, that nigger tells the truth." Our father never did mention this incident to any of us. When I had grown to be a pretty big sized boy, I asked him if he didn't like to kill a man by the name of Williamson, He just turned to me and said, "Who told you that I did?" I said "Uncle George." "George remembers too much." Then I said "Pa, did you ever have a fight?" He answered me roughly and said "No, fools and dogs fight." This was strange talk for me then, for about that age the big talk among the common people was about the bully, the one that could run the fastest, jump the farthest, and the best fighter. But as I grew older I could understand my father's answer to me, and how he now looked on the bully, — fighter.

The Colonel spent on this trip three or four months in arranging home matters for the coming of his family. He had fully made up his mind before he left them that they would come with him the next time. All things having been put in as good order as they could at that time, he took leave of his friends and George, with the understanding that when he would return his family would be with him. When he leached his dear ones in the old home, he found them active in making ready for the move. In a little while, quite a number of families were ready to go. — the ice is broken, the lion is no longer in the way. The emigration commenced in a fall of the latter twenties in caravans of five or six families moving together. Those that left that fall were the first to reach the new home and greet their anxious, waiting friends there. Quite a number of Scotch families in small bands of twos and threes, together, left at different times, one and two years before, but did not reach the McLendon party in several years afterwards. Some of them went too far to the west and stopped in Alabama, a good many of them reached the Conecuh River. Others went too far to the east and stopped in Georgia, some of them getting as far down as the Chipola River in Florida, but the most of these came on in two or three years afterwards, bringing others from these States with them. The emigration spirit was astir in South Carolina too, and many families came with, or about, the time of those from North Carolina. These emigrants were from six to ten weeks on the way, much depending on the weather and trouble by the way. Now, the way opened, the ball put in motion, emigrants from these States roll into Walton County by families, bands, troops, and caravans, for several years, and we may say the emigration from these states continued, more or less, diminishing in the latter days as the years rolled by, up to the Civil War. We had some to come to us by way of Pensacola direct from Scotland. We have prepared a list, as best we could, giving names of families in the order of time in which they came. It is impossible to give the exact date of so many emigratings, but we can come pretty near this order of coming. In running over this list let it be remembered that there are a great many families of the same name related to each other, and others who are no kin, that came at different times. Sometimes the father and family would precede the son and family two or three years, and vice versa. And then there would be those of the same name no kin at all, and from different States with a difference of several years in coming. Hence, the cause for a repetition of the same names. We insert this list here, not thinking that it will be of interest to the general reader, but will be to the descendants of the pioneers.

The list of the Pioneer Families in the Order of their Coming to Walton County.

The McLendons	The Douglasses	The Koonces
The McSweens	The Evanses	The Coles
The Campbells	The McIvers	The Reddicks
The Andersons	The Howells	The Crawfords
The Folks	The McRaes	The Tyners
The Albins	The Crawfords	The Bullards
The McKinnons	The McPhersons	The Oates
The McCaskills	The Scotts	The McKinnons
The George (colored)	The Neals	The Johnsons
The McGilberries	The Walkers	The Hendersons
The Hunters	The Moores	The Biggs
The Ramseys	The McCarters	The Meigs
The Joneses	The Hatchers	The Harts
The McQuaigs	The McInnis	The Wards
The McCarters	The McGinnis	The McRaes
The Hendersons	The Johnsons	The Clarys
The Mallets	The McCulloughs	The McCranies
The McLeans	The McSwains	The McLendons
The Robinsons	The Monroes	The Smiths
The McDonalds	The Andrews	The Johnsons
The McCallums	The McCoys	The Edges
The McKenzies	The Kings	The Lees
The Rectors	The Tuckers	The Coonces
The Purcils	The McCrimmon	The Harrisons
The McLeans	The Bowers	The Bells
The McLeods	The Robinsons	The Berrys
The Pippins	The Landrums	The Millers
The Gillises	The Fishers	The Crofts
The Gunns	The Broxtons	The Turners
The Caswells	The Vaughns	The Brooks

The Grices	The Geoghagans	The McKenzies
The Gaanies	The Browns	The Henrys
The McFarlands	The Wrights	The Crawfords
The Chamberlains	The Coleys	The Seamans
The Tervins	The Parishes	The Smileys
The Cawthons	The Kitrells	The Seamons
The Flurnoys	The Stanleys	The Newtons
The Cockrofts	The Oglesbys	The McMillans
The Youngs	The McFaddins	The Cooks
The Claries	The Wards	The Gales
The Brownells	The Andrews	The Lewises
The Hunts	The Blounts	The Branans
The Infingers	The Watsons	The Carrols

Where They Settled

Euchee Valley proper is twenty-five miles long and will average twelve miles wide. It commences a little to the southwest of the town of Euchee Anna, on Bruce Creek, at the foot of the Red Hill, and takes in all the rich lands down along either side of that creek and extending six or eight miles up the mouth of White and Big Sandy Creeks, and northward as far out as to what is known as the Ridge, and eastward as far as Douglass' Ferry. The rich lands of Mossy Bend belong in this valley, but they are generally spoken of as separate and distinct lands.

All of these Scotch pioneers that came from the several states settled in and along this valley. Allen McKinnon, cousin of Colonel McKinnon and the McLendons, settled in that part of Walton that was given to make Santa Rosa County, and raised a large interesting family of boys and girls who are now living near that section with nice families and in good business. The Landrums and Fishers settled first in the Valley then in Milton, and then the Landrums returned to the Valley. Some of the Monroes too, went to Milton. The McQuaigs, some of the Gillises, Neals, Morrisons, McCallums, Vaughns, Brownells, Oates, Broxtons, Hunts, Geohagans, McKenzies, some of the McLendons, Hunters, some of the Millers, Smiths, Parishes, Stanleys, McFaddins, Turners, Kerlees, Kitrells, Oglesbys, Carrols, Andrews, Neils, Watsons, Albins, settled in that part of the County given to make Holmes County. Some of the Andersons, McQuaigs, McLeods, Bowerses, Caswells, Evanses, Ramseys, Howells, Wrights, Branans, McCoys, Browns, Caries, Infingers, settled on Alaqua Creeks.

The Mallets, Rutans, Hatchers, Harrisons, some of the Crawfords, Youngs, Stanleys, Millers, Rooks, Berries, Crofts, Harrisons, Wards, McCulloughs, Reddicks, Davises, settled on the Choctawhatchie River and bay country near Freeport.

The Cawthons, McSwains, Harts, Woods, Meigs, some of the McCaskills, McCrimmons, Cockrofts, some of the Eddies, Steeles, Claries, Wrights, McCranies, settled on Yellow and Shoal Rivers.

Of the above list of families settled in their homes, all of the Macks, and five-sixths of the others, are either Scotch or Scotch Irish, as you may discern from their names.

Now, these are the families, and of these, in the order of their coming, are the pioneers that came to Walton in and between the years A.D. 1830 and 1860, the commencement of our Civil War. And these are the families too, together with those who came since, to be listed later, that had more or less to do with the making of Walton County history. It cannot be said in truth of them "They left their country for their country's good." They were of the very highest type of manhood and womanhood, with but few exceptions, — the uninvited ones. It is hard in grouping men to have all good, and to fail to mention both the good and the bad would make an incorrect, partial history.

Among those families that settled in the Valley, there were two Douglasses, five Campbells, six McDonalds, five McLeans, four McCaskills, and there is hardly a name in the list, that makes up the Scotch pioneers, that was not represented by from three to six families; and these families raised up many sons and daughters to call them blessed. And as the generations go by, these sons and daughters are raising up children in numbers to the perfect satisfaction of the Rooseveltian ideal.

These pioneers are here in the new land, ready to build up new homes. They come from a highly civilized country, and as a rule are educated, some well-educated, as indicated by the well bound Latin and Greek lexicons and classic books that grace the libraries of their descendants. Every family brought their English and Scotch bible, and an altar is erected in every home.

Many of them brought colored slaves of the highest type of the negro. They brought no domestic animal save the dog, the cat, the mule, and the horse that pulled the vehicles that brought their moving and themselves. Their weapons were the long Buchanan rifle, made by a man by that name in the country from which they came. Every man was armed with one of these, — muzzle loaders of course.

Here they are with the plow, the ax, the spade, and the saw to build homes and prepare farm lands and to open up a new civilization in the very midst of friendly aborigines. Here they are in the midst of nature's boundless resources, in streams, in forests, in soil, in grasses, in game, and in climate. Now the burning question is, while they come seeking to develop the resources of this land, will they look wisely to their conservation? Will they do both? Can they develop the dormant resources and conserve them too? These are economical questions to be considered. The aborigines gave them wonderful lessons in conserving. They handed down to them natural resources that they had kept intact, untarnished through the ages past, and these too, growing better and better as the years roll on. What lessons from the unlettered nations to the learned comers, fresh from the heart of civilization! Will they give heed? The sequel in the years to come must tell the story. Can you find, can you imagine, a colony settling in any country under more favorable auspices than those now being located in this favored land? With forests abounding in magnificent stately trees of many varieties, types of the frigid and types of the torrid in this mild mid region, mingling their foliage together. The lofty pines with their acetalious foliage, as so many eolian harps, making music with the winds. The great spreading oak with its acorn food, the elastic hickory and its species with their meat food. The beech and its cousins with their rich masts, the persimmon with its delicious fruits; the tupelo gum, the poplars, the cedars, the great magnolias with their palm shaped leaves in green, and blossoms of white, filling the air with their odors, — trees of ever so many varieties, trees furnishing the best wood for building, for furniture, for wares, and for ornamental work, trees for home and foreign commercial purposes; and streams of water to move them on, or for power to manufacture them by. The vines entangling the wild woods, teeming with many varieties of juicy fruits, the berry, black, blue, red and purple, inviting from limb and bush; the game cantering over the hills in every direction; the birds of every feather filling the air with music, making all around gladsome; the rich grasses that carpet the earth, and tender cane inviting domestic animals to come and feed on them. What an overflow of nature, resting as it were in a mother's arms of protection! Then too, here is a good open, commercial highway, a water way, a protected inland way, God's way; and while it is a very much watered commercial way, it is and will remain as free as air, to the poor, as well as to the rich, as long as the stars stand. Through this pleasant, beautiful way, the delvers in this goodly land can transport by sail or stream their produce in unlimited quantities, with but little cost as long as time shall last. Through the many, many months and years that I steamed up and down through this inland waterway, I never passed through it without being reminded of God's goodness in providing such a cheap convenient, commercial way, especially for the poor of our country, to go up and down in almost perfect safety in their little gondolas and market sailing boats. We passed over the bosom of these waters in the bright, calm days, in the dark fearful nights, when the lightnings flashed all about us, and the thunders spoke in sullen wrath, while the old ocean through the Mexican Gulf rolled her mad mountain waves, one after another, as though they were coming to destroy us, and either one of them, if they had been able to reach us, could have swallowed us in a moment. But that little strip of white sandy land a little bit above sea level, in some places not more than a quarter of a mile wide, but stretching sixty miles down the coast to Fort Pickens (Santa Rosa Island) the workmanship of God's hand, spoke to them, "Thus far shalt thou come and no farther." So they had to pour out their wrath there, lashing and beating the white shores, while we glided on in quiet peace and perfect safety. In making this trip one can but be reminded of God's love of beauty, for here you will have one of the most picturesque scenes in all nature. Senator C. W. Jones, returning from Washington City came this route on his way to Pensacola. He got on board the steamer "C. Fisher" at Freeport, Florida. We passed along down through the bay, came along by the side of this beautiful island, crossed over the bar and were in what is known as the Narrows. It was a bright clear sunshiny day, and the wind was high. He and I were on the hurricane deck of the steamer Fischer where we had a splendid view of all the surroundings; on our right was the main land with the genuine old live-oak, with their reaching limbs bending in every direction; there too was the great magnolia dressed in velvet green, with its white blossoms as so many white birds perched on its limbs to rest; the Narrows that we were floating in with its transparent waters, showing us the sandy bottom of the crooked channel, was not more than one quarter of a mile wide; then comes the island on our left with the tops of its white mounds thatched over with green scrub live-oak; on the other side of this island was the great Gulf rolling up its waves breaking on the shores. As we steamed on, the Senator drank in the beauty in silence; presently the channel lead us along close by the island, to what is known as the "Ladies' Walk," the most beautiful spot on the island, long hills or ridges with valleys between, leading towards the Gulf; these are as white as the drifted snow, and not a sprig of any living vegetation about them. At this moment the sun was going down, brightening up the West, with its golden beauty; as it cast its soft shadows over these white ridges and valleys, making one of the most charming pictures in nature. The Senator could keep silent no longer. He exclaimed, "Is it possible that I have been living in Pensacola all these years and never knew of this grandeur in beauty? I have just been up the St. Johns River into Indian River and never saw such grandeur in nature as I see here. True, its broad waters were grand, and its banks teaming with the golden fruit, but you can't have such a panoramic view as this. You can't take in at a glance such varieties, such effulgence in beauty as we have now before us. It is the pen that has made the St. Johns what it is, and I prophesy a day when these shores will be teaming with wealthy beauty lovers." I have always felt that if there be one that passes through this inland waterway and is not moved to feel that God is good — God is power — God is wisdom — that one must be oblivious to His attributes.

The new settlers have not only this splendid commercial waterway, but they have navigable rivers on either side and between, running southward into this waterway; and their southern shores are indented with navigable bays and bayous and mouths of creeks or lagoons that run well up into the interior through which they can float in boats their products, to get on this high waterway that leads so direct to the commercial city of Pensacola. There were no Internal Improvement Acts, or river and harbor bills reaching down this way by which these rivers could be opened up for navigation; nor was there any need for their being better than nature had left them, for the kind of boats they had to use for navigation. The whistle of the steamboat had never been heard in all these waters, and they are settled convenient to the already open streams.

Neither was the sound of the iron horse, that great civilizer, the railroad engine, heard rattling through these woods, for there was no need of its work. These pioneers demonstrated years ago in their commercial intercourse with the world, through these waterways, that God-made roads were better than man-made roads. But it seems that it was not until today that the world is appreciating this great fact. This grave truth was clearly demonstrated in that great National conference called to meet at the White House by President Roosevelt, which was the outgrowth of the recommendation of the Inland Waterways Commission, that he had appointed the year before, a convention to consider the question of the conservation of the country's natural resources. To this conference there came by invitation the Governors and their conferees, the Captains of Industry as represented by such men as Andrew Carnegie, the Iron Master, James J. Hill the genius of railway expansion, John Mitchell, labor leader, and Dr. I. C. White, geologist; the Senators and Representatives in Congress; the Supreme Court, the Cabinet, and of course the Inland Waterways Commission; and the specially invited guests that included such statesman as Bryan, Johnson, and Judge Gray. The coming together of these representative men for conference made it National in a peculiar sense. And we believe that its results will show that it was the initiative of the greatest good to our nation. And that the good results will carry down with them through the coming years, the shining name of President Roosevelt as a great benefactor to our nation, in commerce, as well as in peace and war. It was clearly brought out in this conference that there was an uncalled for prodigality in our natural resources, which are our national resources; that railroad transportation had become too expensive, burdensome, and wasteful in natural resources, even in transporting its own material for constructive and repairing, and that a cheaper waterway must be provided to conserve the rapidly failing resources in timber, coal, and oil for building and fuel purposes. They tell us that in Washington's time there was a conference something like this called, and by his influence an Interstate Waterways Commission was appointed by Virginia and Maryland to consider interstate commerce by the only means then available, that of water; and when the representatives of all the states met in Philadelphia for what was in its original conception, merely a waterways conference, yet when they had closed their deliberations the outcome was the Constitution which made the States into a Nation. We hope this conference will finally result in the canalization of our whole country from the Lakes to the Gulf, from Ocean to Ocean, in the speedy opening of the great inland waterways on our eastern and southern coast, and the one down the Mississippi Valley that they propose, and prove to the world that God's roads are better than man's. This work accomplished as proposed, then will the generations of today see as these pioneers proved, that they never did need in Walton any transportation other than our waterways improved.

Surely these early pioneers, settled down in this Utopian land with such rich natural resources handed down to them from these primitive peoples, ought to have been contented and have gone to work with a right good will. And they did. The ring of the ax is heard in every settlement. Comfortable homes are built; fields are cleared, and fences built, for they saw that it would not do for them to let all this good range go without domesticated animals to feed on them, to bring in revenue. So the families sent out their best traders to go here and there, some back to North Carolina, some to Alabama, and others to Georgia, to procure range stock. And soon the low of the cow, the bleat of the sheep, and the squeal of the hog were answering back to the yawn of the cat. the crow of the rooster, the neigh of the horse, and the bark of the dog; all these bringing the hoot of the owl, the bark of the fox, and the doleful howl of the wolf, just over the hills. The ones that succeeded in bringing the most and best cattle were the ones that were soonest the owners of big stocks. There was but one thing in the way of rapid increase, and that was keeping the savage, wild beast from taking them, as will be shown later.

It was interesting to hear these first settlers tell how they got their start in stock. The most of them paid money. Others gave an old horse or mule which brought them out and had no use for in a while; others gave dried and buffed deer skins, while others gave tame fowls; and some gave their rifles, trusting to get others soon. The pioneers who came later, as a rule, brought some stock with them.

In a few years' time, these pioneers made quite a lot of improvements in the way of making homes and farms. The lands were productive and responded to their energy. Bread food and vegetables were the main things that occupied their minds in the way of products. For many years there was not the least trouble for the one who had a rifle and knew how to shoot straight, to get what meat he needed out of the wild woods. They soon imported the sugar cane, which they learned was indigenous to this soil and clime. They ground out the juice with home-made rollers made of the hardest wood, principally the live oak. These were to be found all along through the Valley, three or four small families owning the outfit together. One of these mills was located in Mossy Bend by an excellent spring in an oak and hickory grove; they did all the grinding for all those who lived in the Bend for thirty years, grinding for not less than that many families. They would commence grinding in October and grind until Christmas. This, as were the others, was a great resort for the young people to spend their evenings, exchange jokes, swap knives, play games, have candy-pullings, and court sweethearts. Many happy matches were made around these cane mills under the soft light of the autumn moon. And it is delightful to know that these sugar-mill meetings are still enjoyed to some extent by the youth of Walton today. So accommodating and congenial were these neighbors, that there was never a jar in their work. The only rivalry was to see who could get the most young people to come the week they were grinding, to have the most fun. They observed their turn to grind as systematically as the mill boy takes his turn today for his grist. These mills keyed up close enough to press the juice from the cane, despite all the lubricating oil that you could apply, would make a squealing noise that could be heard for miles. This, no doubt, was grating on the delicate aged ears, but let me tell you of a truth, it was sweet, sweet music to the anxious ears of the young peoples, who longed for its coming in the bright October month. Those who longed at first for the sweet Cider pressed from the juicy apples in the old State, soon found more than a substitute in the cold juice from the cane. This juice, in the early years, was evaporated, or boiled, in the common dinner and wash pots, into a syrup and sugar. As the years passed on. there were great improvements, both in mill and kettles. The three-roller cast iron mill took the place of the two-roller, and the eighty and hundred gallon flared kettle took the place of the dinner and wash pots. For some time the simple hand-turned mills and the Indian hand mortars were used to grind their corn into meal — a stationary bed rock of flint. eighteen inches in diameter, a runner of the same dimensions, with an aperture in center for corn to drop through, fastened directly above, so that it could be raised up and down as the meal needed to be coarse or fine. This runner was manipulated by a wooden rod fastened above and placed in a small hole near its edge, and the Indian squaws would sit down and turn this upper rock around and around by means of this pole, and make good meal.

It was but a little while before this people saw that they must have clothing other than the skins of animals to wear, — these, they thought, were too much out of the line of civilization. They cleared up cotton patches and put in the seed and soon learned that they could grow cotton of a better fibre than that of the old State. The most of them brought with them their "Scotch spinning jennies," and the large rimmed spinning wheel was brought in, and the old time loom, and they soon had clothes of their own making to wear. There was no way of separating the seed from the cotton but by the fingers, and this was the work of the long evenings and of the old Scotch women.

Chapter Five - The First Gin, Grist and Saw Mill

In the early thirties, Colonel McKinnon built a cotton gin to run by water power on a stream near his home, — the first that was built in Walton, — and had a grist mill attached. These mills did good work for the people for a number of years. The dam that held the water that moved the machinery is still intact and as firm as the hills. He never tried to keep these mills up after the War, after his negroes were freed. A man by the name of Albin built a grist mill on a larger creek one and one-half miles west of the "Old Place," but it didn't amount to much, it was too poorly constructed for the stream that it was on, and it was soon gone.

In a little while afterwards Alexander McLeod, father of our County Judge, D. G. McLeod, got Allen McKinnon of Santa Rosa County to come and build a saw mill to manufacture lumber on the same stream and just below the Albin mill. It was a substantial piece of work and stood for years. This was the first saw mill in Walton County. It was an upright saw. This took the place of the hand rip-saw, where one man stood in the ditch below and the other one on a scaffold above, pulling the saw up and down through the log by main strength and awkwardness. There was a good grist mill attached, and this enterprise was a great financial success in the new country.

The pioneers begin now to build for themselves better houses. Frame houses began to take the place of the round log buildings. At one time this plant was a little gold mine. In the fifties Colonel McKinnon bought this plant and gave $4,000.00 in gold for it; this was a round price for it, but everything seemed to be on a boom then. After the war he sold it for less than half that amount, and I suppose it could be bought today for less than half that amount.

A More Definite Settling of Some of the Earliest Scotch

We have already seen that Neil McLendon settled at the first by Sam Story in his summer quarters near the "Old Place." When the Chief moved to his winter quarters, near his landing in Mossy Bend, Neil McLendon moved down near him, out on the ridge where his brother Lochlin settled at the first. It was near what is known as the Cross-roads, not far from the church and graveyard. He remained here as long as he lived in Florida. He left the home he moved from all to his brother Lochlin. John Folks settled down on Bruce Creek about half way between the two brothers. Daniel D. Campbell married Nancy McLean in February, 1828, — their license is extant today, — and he settled in the Valley near Euchee Anna, where he lived all his days in happiness and peace, and raised a large family of boys and girls. Colonel McKinnon lived all his days on the "Old Place." He called the hill on which he built "Pleasant Hill." The Indian field and George's clearing gave it the name of "Old Place." He became the owner of all the lands that the Chief and the McLendons claimed and raised a large family of girls and boys all to be grown. In all the years of his life, he never entertained for a moment the thought of a move. What capital in contentment to begin with! When he was being raided upon in the latter years of the war, his son and friends came and insisted that he would move up into Alabama, away from the raiders. He answered in the most positive tones, "No, not as long as there is a shirt left on my back. I worked for and paid for this place, — I fought for it, and if there is a spot on this green earth that I have a right to stay on, it is this, and I am going to stay right here." And, of course, he did, and was about as well off as those who refugeed to Alabama. Angus McDonald, who married Mary Anderson here, came from South Carolina, by way of Conecuh River, after stopping there several years with his father and other relatives, came and settled near the Valley Church, then moved near Euchee Anna, and then to Mossy Bend, where he lived until his death. His brother Peter settled near Knox Hill. Their father came to see them from Conecuh in 1850 and died while on a visit at his son Peter's, and was buried at the Valley Church. Alexander McCaskill settled just east of the Valley Church. After his death, Finley McCaskill, his son, (called 'White Finley," being an albino,) lived there until he died; and Alexander L. McCaskill, a relative of theirs, bought the place and lived there until he died, and the place is now owned by Laird. Donald McLean (called "Baldy" on account of his bald head) settled below old Knox Hill, near Yellow Bluff. Yawn, or John and Lochlin McLean, and Archibald McDonald, settled near Euchee Anna. Daniel S. McLean (called "Chunky" on account of his build) settled east of Euchee Anna. Daniel Campbell (called "Corn Campbell" on account of his making such quantities of corn with his great bunch of negroes) lived the first year near Lake Casidy in Holmes County and then he bought the Dempsey Jones and Hunter places on the Ridge, improved them, and settled there. All these were settled for life in these homes, and their sons and daughters, as they married, settled around them. Angus Gillis came out before these, and like Calonel McKinnon, he improved a home for himself in the rich hammock lands about the heads of Big Sandy Creek. He went back to North Carolina, married Catharine Campbell, daughter of "Corn" Campbell, and came on his bridal tour with his father-in-law to the new country, and lived on this place that he selected and improved, raised a large family of sons and daughters and stayed on that place until marriages and deaths reduced them to the original two, and then moved down to the Val-

Angus Gillis

ley near the Church, and died at a ripe old age, his faithful wife soon followed, and they sleep side by side in the old Valley burying ground. Archibald McDonald, Daniel Robinson and Hugh McLean, and the McQuaigs, settled permanently near the Valley Church. Lochlin McDonald, the father of John K., Peter K. and Daniel K., settled in Mossy Bend. Alexander Douglass and his mother left North Carolina before these, but he did not get here until two years afterwards. He stayed on the Chipola and made a crop there, and then came on. He was the first emigrant that crossed at Douglass' Ferry, and had to stay there some time, on account of a swell in the river, before they could get him over. It was he that surveyed "that wonderful high water route" through which you can come in the highest water from high bank to high bank on either side and cross the main river, floating down it from either way. It is really an ingenious route. He lived at the "Old Place" for a few years and then moved to Douglass' Ferry, which was named for him, he having established it, and made it a popular crossing place for travelers going East and

West. He died of exhaustion, swimming his cattle from reed-brake islands in the river swamp to high safe piney woods, during the high waters of the "Lincoln Freshet."

Now we have some idea where the early settlers were located. Now, it has always been strange to me why Walton's first County site was for a while at Alaqua. It is true there were quite a lot of good people settled on the Alaqua Creeks on good lands, but nothing to compare with those around the Valley, and at that time it was a very much out of the way place, not even convenient to the Bay people, who were but few. Judge Exam's home, — the first Circuit Judge — was there, and some say this was why it was there. In a little while it was moved to Euchee Anna and remained there until it was moved to DeFuniak Springs.

Euchee Anna was named in honor of the Euchee Indians and the grandmother of Colonel Angus D. and William C. McLean, Esq. She was the first white woman to live in the town. The combination makes a very euphonious and endearing name to many of us. The rich lands around are being pretty well dotted about with settlers. And it is strange to say that many of the best lands were not taken for years and years afterwards. Good springs had much to do in making settlements. Excellent families were these, or the most of them, at least. But coming from a country of stinted natural resources, many of them seemed to think and act as though there was no chance of lessening the abundance here, and without thinking, they went about like vandals, slashing and destroying as they went, as though it were their only mission. And when advised to be more conservative, they thought the advice absurd and would remark flippantly "there will be plenty of range here when you and I will be sleeping in the grave," as though it was our only mission here to look out for ourselves. The great trouble was, the curse of fire turned loose, to destroy the rich luxurious range, which would, if they protected it as the aborigines did, last for generations after generations, and fatten millions and millions of cattle, sheep and hogs from year to year. Then, there was the indiscriminate shooting down of game just to see them fall. The Indians took great pains in showing the very first comers how to protect the game, range and forests, and these settlers took great interest in learning how, following their advice. They pointed out to them the great destruction that unbridled fire would do in a little while to the range, killing the rich berries and the low bush sweet apples that were so nutritious to animal life, the deer and gopher apples; how it would stunt the grass after a while and give place to worthless scrub oak that would soon kill out the grass altogether. They would tell them the best time and how to kill game for table use, so as not to diminish increase, but augment it, assuring them that the game had grown better and better with them, as the years passed by and never fell short only through disease. These earliest settlers not only appreciated these lessons, but showed it by going to work strenuously to put them into practice. They would often take their forces from the fields and work for days fighting fire, cutting it off by short cuts between creek and other water protections, to stop the spread and save the grass and rich cane along the titi branches. One would think when they would see such hard work from their earlier neighbors, this would make them more cautious, but with some it seemed not to move them. They would tell them how the aborigines had taught them the value of the range in its natural state, and how they had kept it in its splendid condition, growing better and better all the years. But they thought it ridiculous that an uncivilized Indian could be capable of advising the civilized white man. These men would tell them how it would displease their Indian neighbors to see the game and range destroyed. All this had no effect upon them. The idea, the talk, of these later settlers, in regard to the conservation of nature's abundant resources was very displeasing to the early settlers. They had learned by observation and experience the value of protecting these resources, and expostulated with these careless roamers from time to time, with but little result in good. They felt that they had good helpful friends in the red man and wanted to retain them as such. They had shown themselves friendly and helpful in so many ways that they were drawn very close to them.

The Chief had a very interesting family of sons and daughters far in advance of the masses, both in appearance and in intellect, and they were respected as such. His whole tribe of women were proverbial for their chastity, their rare virtues. His oldest son was named "Jim Crow," a tall agile, stately, manly fellow, dressing in the best prepared skins and furs of his race, gorgeously attired in the gewgaws of their own making, highly polished shells, beads, and the richest plumes of birds, and all the fancy things that the races are so fond of. Another son was named "Swift Hunter." His third was called "Sleeping Fire." His two oldest daughters were twins, one named "Leaping Water" the other "Quiet Water," and the baby daughter was called "Round Water." The pioneers claim that they were named respectively for the gulf waves that leaped and broke on Walton's southern shores, her greatest spring (Campbell's Spring) and her round spring (DeFuniak Springs).

Jim Crow Takes a Wife

When Colonel McKinnon brought his family to this new country, his wife had quite a handsome servant girl, more than two thirds white blood in her; she was of low stature, plump build, blue eyes, of a rich dark, transparent complexion, with long coal-black hair. She was what was called then, an intelligent, fine looking house "yellow girl." Her name was Harriet. Jim Crow, the Indian prince, several years her senior, was smitten at first sight with her beauty and lively carriage around the home, and as the days rolled by, he became more and more enamored with her beauty. My father and mother tried to discourage his advances, fearing that such a union might in time result in an alienation of the good feeling that then existed between the red man and the pale face, especially of that between himself and Crow's father. Then, too, there was a commercial view to be considered in such a union. But the more they tried to discourage him, as is ever the case in true love, the more the flame kindled and the closer were they drawn together. At first Harriet disclaimed any idea of loving him, and they were satisfied she spoke the truth, for she was not treating his advances at first in a way that showed even the respect that was due his kind treatment, and they felt assured that she had no real love for him, and that "his genuine" love was, as it were, wasted on the desert air, and felt relieved. But finally his manly appearances, his gewgaws in dress, won her to him, and she consented to become his wife, if her mistress and master would consent. He lost no time in approaching them with his pleadings, and after deliberating over the matter for some little while, and consulting together in full view of the facts and the surroundings, they reluctantly consented for her to become his wife, under certain well defined conditions, which he never attempted to overleap. He is one happy "big Indian now." He wanted their union to be after the manner of their tribal marriages, in the Chief's big tent of skins and furs. So, on the following Sunday they were arrayed after their fashion in the rich gewgaws, peculiar to their race, and as fantastically in every way possible. He, by his attendants, was escorted from his headquarters to that of the Chief's great tent which stood near Story's Landing. She, with her attendants, one of her relatives and his three sisters, was escorted to the same tent, where they met in front of it, with its walls all rolled up. Here they joined hands and with their attendants marched around the tent several times, while vocal and rude instrumental music made glad, merry hearts, and as they passed through the pre-arranged aisle in the center of the great tent to the great center prop pole, there they separated, the bride going to the left of the pole and the groom to the right, and met again beyond the pole and stopped for a moment, side by side, with their attendants on either side. The music ceased and they two joined hands while the great chief pronounced a short ceremony in his own tongue. Then the music started up with joyful melody, and the two contracting parties jumped a broom which lay just before them, and they became man and wife according to the Euchee custom.

A cottage was built for them at the end of the row of the negro quarters, not far from the home dwelling, where they lived together very agreeably for a good while. This union never interfered with her domestic duties in the least. My mother said she never had a more agreeable, a more helpful, servant around her than he; that he took more interest in keeping things up around the home than all the other help that she had; that he had a thoughtful mind to provide, and a generous heart to divide his best with others; that coming from the chase, her table was always provided with the best game, even if his had to be scant. When he was around, the very best fish were on her table, as often as she cared for them; that he was ever respectful, honorable and generous, that they were far better pleased with the union than they had hoped to be, and instead of falling off, he became more and more agreeable all the time he stayed.

He knew how to meet the negroes in the quarters. He was not at all too familiar with them in association. He realized his superiority over them and maintained it, and they treated him with marked deference. There was always a marked difference observed between the house servants and the field hand, without much jealousy. Harriet was not a regular cook, just a housegirl. Her first cooking was in her own home for Jim Crow. The house servants were taken from the better class of negroes and were better trained and dressed. Jim Crow was in full sympathy with his father and the earliest settlers in the conservation of the range, the forest, and its game, and often expressed a fear that the waste in these woods would necessitate a change to a newer country for his tribe, which he looked forward to with great dread. And in the course of time, as the white man's civilization spread in Walton, the red man's rights were trampled upon, ignored. It became apparent, even to the casual observer, that there must come a change soon. And the question much discussed was, will they go voluntarily to another country, or will they, like their race has ever done, contend boldly for their hunting ground until their garments are steeped in blood, falling back from the onslaught of the pale face through tracks of blood, and only when their ranks are so depleted that they are not able to make a stand? And the discussion of this question involved another — where did they come from, — who are they?

Chapter Six - The Origin of the Euchees

The early pioneers had learned from the Chief in the beginning that their fore-fathers came from the silver shores of Mexico long years ago, that they could not count. That they left on account of exterminating wars among the tribes there: that they got tired of blood and turned their backs on the bloody West and their faces towards the East — the rising sun — in search of peace and rest; that they left those inhospitable shores in frail barks and coasted along the southern shores, the Great Spirit leading and protecting them in safety to this goodly land; that they had been preceded here by a race of that same blood thirsty, exterminating spirit that they left in Mexico, that in the final battle here only a little handful, mostly women and children, of the vanquished remained to tell the story; and these were soon incorporated into the Euchees and their identity lost. The conquerors that survived after burying their dead, went to the West.

These dark red faced wanderers must have passed through Pensacola Bay before the tall, one eyed Panilo de Narvaez, Captain-General of Florida in 1528, stopped there with his five rudely constructed and equipped vessels from the East. This story of the aborigines was pleasing to those among the pioneers who loved peace and dreaded war. But coming from Mexico, many feared they might be from that great Muscogee race of Indians from whom sprang that bloody, revengeful, spiteful, race, — the Creek Nation, which was such a terror to those whites north of them. But their history shows that they must have descended from one of the best lines of the civilized Aztecs or Toltec races, for they certainly had many good natural inbred traits. We really think their story of the "Kilkinney Cat Fight" among the tribes that preceded them here is borne out in the excavations of the great mounds scattered through this bay country, notably mounds back of old Camp Walton.

In 1861, the first year of the war, when the "Walton Guards" were stationed on the Narrows at Camp Walton, we found great mounds back of the camp, thrown up and all covered over with great trees to their very tops, the live oak and water oak mostly. At first we took those to be natural hills, the product of some cosmic upheaval, but upon closer investigation we found that they were too uniform to be the work of a quake in the earth. So we went to work with ax, pick and spade to pry into them, clearing away the great trees and throwing off the earth from the top. We had gone but a little ways, say 18 inches, when we found we were entering a great charnel house, the home of the dead. There lay great skeletons of men in perfect preservation, lying on their backs, hands crossed in front of their bodies, with heads towards the west and north as they crossed each other, and were filled in between the bodies with a four inch layer of preserving matter, a mixture of lime and some other mineral substance. These were mostly all giants and warriors, killed in battle, as their broken skulls and thighs and arms, as well as the saber cleavage or bludgeon shatters showed. We took the largest of them and set them up with wire joints and placed them in standing positions in a house built for the purpose, until it was filled, and they showed up like monsters stripped of flesh.

We were struck at the wonderful preservation of their bones and the perfect undecayed teeth in their jaws, while they, through the use of years, had been worn to very near the jaw bone, yet they were there without decay. This preserving mixture for bones that they had must be a lost art. This larger mound must have been officers or warriors of high distinction. The lesser mounds did not show the heroic spirit or the gigantic build that was found in the larger one.

We put the trees to their botanical test to gain a knowledge of the times of these heroes. While these trees were hoary with age, they could tell us nothing about the dead bodies they shaded through the day and kept watch over through the night. They easily proved an alibi by the old decayed stumps about their roots that had been old before their coming, and we could not tell how many acorns had fallen and grown up into trees before their day. These could tell, only of their half century watch, and as many years have passed since they have been relieved off of guard duty in the old camp. This largest mound must have covered over an area of an eighth of an acre. It was built sloping in from the base to the top that was flat. Its shape was something like the bottom segment of a great cone, twelve or fourteen feet high. We were very particular in taking these skeletons out, and took from the southern part of the mound, leaving the northern half undisturbed when we left there. After we got the building filled, we became careless, visitors came and plundered them for treasures with no thought of keeping them intact. This matter was well written up by the intelligence of the Walton Guards, to try and learn something of the history of these wonderful warriors and their desperate battles, and what became of the residue.

No Spaniards in Pensacola had ever heard of such giants or of such a battle in these regions. Sam Story's traditional report, handed down to him by his fathers and corroborated by what we found in these mounds, is the most feasible story of these skeletons, and what became of the residue of conquerors after they had buried their dead; and of what remained of the little handful of the vanquished. That this exterminating battle must have been fought a little while before the red founders of Walton, the Euchees, came to these coasts: and long before the time Panilo de Narvaez stopped in Pensacola Bay in 1528, is very reasonable.

What we find in these mounds gives us a very faint idea of how many were slain in this battle; where it is evident in the main that only the most distinguished officers' and warriors' bodies were cared for in the mounds. We must understand too that the slain of the victors and all the slain of the vanquished or annihilated must have bleached and decayed on the battle fields over which they fought and fell, and the numbers slain in these battles must have run up into the thousands of thousands, for that bay coast is one great charnel house. This splendid exhibit of these skeletons of great giants, preserved as they were through centuries, the aborigines of our land — called many visitors to Camp Walton, who returned to their homes wondering how it was possible for the bodies of these dead warriors to have remained so long in our midst without being discovered. That exhibit today would be worth hundred of dollars in any museum or dissecting college.

When the field batteries from Fort Pickens came up in the night time and parked behind the mounds on Santa Rosa Island, opposite our camps on the main land, together with the man-of-war that had been lying, at anchor in the gulf, opposite our station, keeping watch over us for months, opened up a bombardment just as our companies stood in line for roll call, before it was light in the morning, shelling us out of home, that house that held so many of these relics caught on fire and burned up with the shanty buildings. We left for Pensacola soon afterwards and had no time to gather up more. The United States Army men came and dug up more and wrote up the whole matter, but there was too much on hand for either of us to ferret out any intelligence at that time, so the effort perished.

Chapter Seven - A Council Called by Neill McLendon and the Chief

In the early thirties it was evident that Sam Story was becoming uneasy and troubled about the way the new comers were treating the forest and game in his dear old hunting grounds and that Neill McLendon was in full sympathy with him in this matter. They called a council to consult as to some course to pursue, to which Colonel McKinnon and several of the very first settlers were invited. The old Chief was the principal speaker and it was straight talk, great brains speaking through an honest, loving heart, to old proven friends, and with a purpose of winning or helping new ones. He said "We have spoken often one with another about the way the late comers recklessly and without benefit to themselves, tear up and destroy our beautiful hunting grounds and cruelly shoot down the game, not for food, but for fun, as they say, and leave them to decay on the hills. They give no thought to the season or conditions of the game when they take them. They would as readily shoot down a young doe just coming in, as an old one, or a young thrifty buck as an aged old stag, full of sweet firm meat, softer to be jerked for market or stowed for winter use or travel. I saw two of these hunters coming up from the bay with two large hams and the skin of a great stag; they said they left the balance in the woods, they did not care to fetch it so far as they could get plenty nearer home; that they killed it mainly for the hide. It is the same with other game. Some of them readily shoot down the soft-eyed doe while giving suck to her dear pretty little fawns. Many of these comers have placed double guns on one stock which shoots many small or larger bullets, in the hands of their sons, and these youngsters are playing havoc with our sweet songsters and plumage birds. They take the little shrub people, the high perched mocker that gladdens the mornings with its varied notes of melody, the high-flying air birds that tarry but a moment in a place, they go into their rookeries with their guns in the late evening hours, under the cover of night, to kill the shrub-loving whip-poor-will that softens the still hours of the night with its sweet plaintive notes, answering in sweet cadences the call of its mate at the other end of the jungle. They give no more quarters to these merry makers than they do to the blue-jay, or any bird of prey. I tried to show them what a blessing these little feathered people would be to them if they would spare them; how they fill the air with gladness, how they destroy the thousands and millions of insects that feed upon the grasses and the trees that are such a blessing to man and beasts, and saves them from destruction. These lads laugh me to scorn, and with a nod of the head they pass me by saying, 'what a fool old Indian.' Let me tell you, if I were to place bows and arrows in the hands of my boys and they were to use them that ugly, I would put the last one of them under taboo. I told you from the first that while I never intended any other weapon to go into the hands of any of my tribe, other than the bow and arrow, I thought the long rifle, with its clear, gentle crack, in the hands of good men, might not prove hurtful in our hunting grounds, when wisely used. But it seems as though these late comers, come with the loud, roaring double gun in stock, to scare and destroy in any and every way they can think of, without a thought of those that are to come after them; they seem to think their mission is to destroy. They use their guns to kill the fish in the stream for sport, and they put traps in the creeks to entrap them and let them spoil in their homes through age. They come, they waste, they destroy, the good of the land. They seem to have no future before their eyes. And well do you know in these last days they have fallen upon the engine of the greatest destruction of all. They turn loose unbridled the dogs of fire to lap up with their blazing tongues this beautiful range, these great canebrakes, which give such tender, sweet, and strong food to the beasts that roam through them, and these cruel, angry flames leap up in their mad wrath to the tops of our highest trees stripping them of their foliage and even claiming some of them. They make no effort to restrain them or cut them off in their sweep over the range. It is all right with them so that they are not entrapped in the flames. Only once in a half century did these flames get loose from us, and we took them in before they had gone but a little ways. And since the coming of these late ones there has been ever so many of these turnlooses. How often have I seen you and your forces working hard to beat back these ravages of fire, and as often did we come to your help to hinder them. But the more do they turn them loose to destroy. I talked to a company of hunters the other day and tried to explain to them the damage they were doing to themselves through fire, and asked them why they would turn loose such a cruel creature of the bad man to ruin themselves. They answered that they wanted to burn up the snakes, the poisonous rattler that was a terror to them. I showed them that the cunning venomous rattler and his kind had holes and dens to crawl into and be safe from such enemies as fire, and that the one stag that these fires would soon perish out, would kill more rattlers in one year than their fires would kill in a century; that I had often watched them jump upon them in their coil, or on the go, and mash their life out of them with the rapid stroke of their fore-foot, before the rattler could make a strike. And I showed them the many other ways of the damaging effects of loosed fire, but it seems to have no tendency to restrict them.

And let me tell you, my true friends and brothers, you faithful, tried, friends of the red man, you who understand and appreciate his wise, proved plans of keeping intact the country and its resources given by the Great Spirit to use and to hand down to the generations to come, there is no greater enemy to these resources than unrestrained fire. It is the greatest evil of our land. You and I have tried every way we know, peaceably to stop it, and have failed. We have let it go too far, it is getting worse and worse as they come in. There is no way to stop it without a fight, and this world is too big for us to stop here for a fuss. (Now, this is straight talk from an honest heart. If the U. S. Government will only take hold and stop this promiscuous ravages of fire in our woods — in less than fifty years we will have our land reforested and sodden — teeming with the abundance of berries, fruits and flowers that we had here three-quarters of a century ago.) Let us seek for another country, we can't hope for a better. Let us turn toward the East, toward the rising sun. I have been over that land and there is good country yet toward the east and south, along the Gulf and the Atlantic coast. Some Euchees from the same line of my tribe settled on the Atlantic coast along the Savannah River in Georgia, and some of them came as near to us as the Apalachicola River. Come and let us go together and seek out another country. As I said before, we can not hope for a better land. I can never forget these flowing rivers, these rippling streams, abounding in fish, these open plains and hills with their tall pines waving over them, and troops of deer watchfully feeding through them, the midnight hush of these great hammock lands, with nothing to disturb the silence save decayed falling limbs from the trees, and the hoot of the great owl and the merry songsters of the feathery tribes that cheer so much my old heart, as it beats slower and slower as the days go by. It is hard to give these dear things up and the peace they remind us of. Our fathers were driven from the great West years ago in rude boats, coasting along these hospitable shores, and found this place of rest and plenty. In their memories of the West, we do not want to turn our faces towards the setting sun, where the tomahawk is ever drawn to strike in battle and the bow and arrow are never unstrung, where the sun and the moon go down in blood as the days come and go. But rather let us turn towards the rising sun of peace to find us another home, that we may keep from the ravages of selfish men, who care nothing for those who come after them, a country that we will be faithful in from the start, and let no man come in with high hand to destroy their own good and the living for their posterity. We can do this if we be positive and commence in time. There is no other way in peace out of these conditions for us, but to find a new home, and we can readily do this.

I will put my tribes at work in putting our market boats and the long gondolas in order, while we search well to the East along the southern coast as did our fathers, and they will be ready on our return to move. The able ones we will send over land near the shores, while the others, with their effects in the boats, will coast it along under our protection from the land to the new found home.

There is one great fact that stands straight up in the red man's face, — he must go if he would have peace. We have let slip our chances for peace in this good land, and we must go to another where we shall find it and keep it well guarded from the start. Go we must. There is no other way for us to do. Now, come and go with us. We have so many ways and ideas in common. We understand one another so well. Come and go with us 'and we will do you good.' 'I have done. What do you say?"

Neill McLendon Speaks in Council

Neill McLendon spoke outright, pointedly, and said, "I fully agree with the great Chief. He has spoken words of wisdom and of love in our ears that should move our souls. We have lost our opportunities of conserving our resources by being too slow to act and too gentle when we did act. Had we been as prompt and as positive and as severe, in dealing with these depredators at the first as John (Col. McKinnon) was with Williamson when he ran George from his work, and kept it up, these conditions would not exist here today. Carelessness with fire is to be our ruin in this wonderful country. I came upon a company of young hunters who had just placed fire in a large cane-brake in our range, asked them why they did such a wicked thing to destroy the nutritious cane and sweet grass that made fat on our cattle, and the game animals. They said 'we wanted to hear the reeds pop, and there will be plenty of grass and cane here as long as we will live, and after they burn, new grass would spring up that would be better for the cattle.' I used all the power in me to show them that the continual burning over the range would ruin it for cattle, hogs and deer, that the berry and the sweet low bush apples would be killed out altogether, and a useless scrub oak would spring up in their stead, and there would, in a little while be no winter range for cattle to browse over and keep fat on. But all this talk was like casting pearls before swine. They went away laughing in their sleeves at my foolish talk, as they thought. I did not stop here. I went to their fathers and told them all, but found them as well set in the idea of burning the woods for fun and fresh grass as their sons were, pointing me to the rich fresh grass around their homes that was keeping their cows in good milk all the summer. And when I pointed them to the poor range it would make for the winter, in comparison with the unburned, and how it would destroy the many varieties of huckley berries for hogs and chickens and the little birds, they would reply, 'there are plenty of rough woods just a little ways off, if we find them best.' And I find that this is pretty nearly the idea of all of these late comers; they seem to be honestly set in their opinions, that there is no harm in giving up the range to the ravages of the flames, and that this land of plenty will continue to bring plenty without protection for ages to come, or during their days at least, in which they are mostly interested. I don't care to be crowded in so and see our common rights trampled upon as we see here. I have made up my mind to get out of here and would like to go with the great Chief and share his protection and generous hospitality, but I don't care to go farther East. I want to go where there is plenty of room, where I can't be crowded or elbowed out. (Let it be remembered that this is the same Neill McLendon that Miss Brevard in her School History tells us about leaving here seventy-five years ago to get "elbow room.") I am not afraid of the bloody West, the savages there, I know how to meet them now and how to turn them down. I was about ready to go to Texas when I fell in with this good friend, and was lead to this delightful land of health and plenty, of sunshine and beauty. I, with my dear ones, shall make ready to go West at once. I, too, hate to leave this delightful country, these tried, true friends. I know John (Colonel McKinnon) will go with me, or come when I write him."

Colonel McKinnon's Talk in Council

Colonel McKinnon said, "I am in a condition to appreciate fully all that each of you have said, for I have had these same experiences, and even more, with these self-centered, self-knowing, belated comers. I have begged them to use their guns more sparingly, and not to be careless with fire. I have pointed out to them the folly of killing out the game, — the seed corn in the wild woods, that supply our tables with meat, the merry birds that keep cheering melody all the day long, the birds of plumage that decorate our forests and waterways, with living, active beauty. I, with my forces, have made ourselves sick with heat, stopping fire that they carelessly or wantonly dropped in our range, to save it for winter feeding. They give a respectful hearing to these pleadings and admonitions, but it seems they soon forget, or can't realize any good in them. These depredators are comparatively few, when compared with our better people, and they are not what you would call bad people, they have good hearts in them. They are deficient in what we call culture. They have never learned to appreciate beauty and worth in nature, or how to conserve them. They have not been taught their personal obligations to coming generations, that they ought to provide for them. Why, I came very near having a personal encounter with two men just the other day for shooting up a bunch of laying turkeys in the range, they claiming they had as much right to kill in one season as another, to kill a laying hen as an old gobbler, that there would be plenty for everybody as long as they would live. I gave them a bit of my mind on selfishness. They cooled down, and I hope they will think over it and be better. These men would as readily shoot down one of these grand gallinaceous birds of the range, leading a brood of little ones to feed, or brooding on a nest of eggs, as to kill a carnivorous bird of prey in our wild swamps. I am aware that a few such men unrestrained can do a great deal of harm. But, on the other hand, we, outnumbering them as we do, can organize and educate them, at least their children. We will have schools, churches and laws. I think I can see them giving away now to public sentiment. Were we to leave and find as goodly a country as this to the East or West, we would find this same sort of don't care people coming in on us there, and we would have these same things to contend with. The land is going to be possessed. The star of empire or emigration is moving westward and southward and we can not stay it in its course. Let us untie from this star, drive our stakes down here, sure and steadfast. and hitch to it, and ride out the storms that come. Let us fight it out on these lines. Let us seek to make these men better, instead of running from them, to draw to the front the good, and drive out the bad. If we are sure we know the better way, and I think we do, there rest solemn obligations upon us to bring others in this way. Behind these ugly, thoughtless, depredators, and in the glow of these splendid commercial advantages which are ours, I see the more resplendent light of education in morals, in religion, in tastes, in culture, and in character-building in its broadest sense, before which petty encroachments and wanton wastes, must give way. I have a fine herd of cattle multiplying in the woods with but little care. My hogs keep fat the year round about my home. My bunch of sheep are doing fine, but for the wolf, but I have to keep a shepherd after them for protection. It will be hard to find as delightful a place to live in as this, a place as easy to earn a livelihood. I have felt all the while that I was settled for life. I don't see how I could leave when I am as well situated as I am. I hate to see you and yours go in the face of such bright prospects, such promising rewards. We are in the majority and know how to conserve nature's resources, how to protect public rights, and we can come together and create a public sentiment that will show others how to see and respect public interests, as well as private rights. Then, too, we will soon be under legislative laws and order. We will send representatives to our territorial legislature, who will help enact proper protective laws, and we will see that they are properly enforced. Then, these men, whose motto is, in the Latin language, "carpe diem" (Seize the day) in the sense of letting every day provide for itself, and every man and generation look out for themselves, will be forced to an education that will teach them that we are in this world to serve and respect others, as well as ourselves. It can't be long before we will be admitted into the sisterhood of states and be under the sovereign protection of a State, as well as under the sovereignty of the United States. So we have everything to encourage us to cast our lot here in this goodly land, and nothing much to drive us away." On A. D. 1845, Col. John L. McKinnon and D. G. McLendon were elected as representatives to the Constitutional Convention that met at St. Josephs, Florida, when the State was admitted into the Union of States.

The council ended here. These men understood each other fully, and we doubt very much if there were ever three men in council that were more determined and unmovable in the way they set their heads than these three men.

Mr. McLendon said that the world was too big to have a man in his way, at his elbow, every time he turned round, and went at once to Pensacola, got a man by the name of Captain Dodd, who knew something about sailing and a little about the ship carpenter's trade, sawed out by hand with rip-saw. lumber, and kiln-dried it, to build a boat to take him to Texas. In eight or ten months it was ready to launch at Story's Landing.

The old chief said that he did not want to live among a people that had to be made to look out for themselves and others, that knew nothing but waste, and cared nothing for the days ahead, and. leaving his tribe in charge of his son, the prince, Jim Crow, he went at once with four of his sons and five of his tribe's men, to the East, following closely along the south coast, hunting a new home for self and tribe, where they might live in peace and plenty, as in the days gone by.

Chapter Eight - Goes on Search

They went as far as the Everglades and over to the Atlantic coast. He had, in his younger days, gone with his father as far as the Everglades. After a search of six months, they returned, the old Chief very much exhausted with the trip, and it was thought by some, not very well pleased with what he saw. They reported that they had found a few places better in a few things, but lacking in many other things that this country had. They settled on no particular place to go to, — if they did, they kept it to themselves. The old Chief, worn out as he was by the trip, made himself active in getting his tribe together and ready for the move. He called them in from all their camps and quarters to the high grounds in the thick hammocks around Story's Landing.

On one of the bleak days of the chill November month, in the early morn, there came a messenger to Colonel McKinnon's home with a message from the old Chief asking him to come at once to his quarters. Mrs. McKinnon sent word that her husband was away from home, that it would be some time in the night before he would return, but as soon as he returned he would go at once. She asked him if they were going to leave right away. He said "O no, he wants to see the Colonel on business, the Chief is not well enough to go just now." When the Colonel reached home that night and received the message he said to Mrs. McKinnon, "I must go, I expect they are going to leave tomorrow." When he was told by his wife that the messenger said that they were not going to leave soon, that he wanted to see him on business, "Well," said the Colonel, "it must be on that matter between Jim and Harriet. Do you know that during the time his father was gone to the East, Jim often talked to me, expressing a fear that his father would get a place that he would like better than this, which might separate him from his Harriet and baby? He went as far as to ask me on one occasion," in the event his father did move from here, if he would get two buxom maidens to serve in the place of his wife and baby Eliza, if I would be satisfied with the exchange?" I explained to him how impossible it would be for me to hold property in the Indian maidens, that they were free born, as free as he or myself. This seemed to undo the poor Indian. I was sorry for him. He loves them dearly, and I am the more sorry for him because I feel that it is love unrequited. I really don't believe, from what you tell me, that Harriet loves him much. He came to me since his father returned, and, with tears in his eyes, said 'well, we must go. Will you set a price on wife and baby? I will see my father and if we can't arrange to meet it here, I think if he will go to Pensacola, he can arrange for it there. I don't see how I can go away and leave them, if the rest do go, and go they will, I know.' I told him I would think on it and do the best I could and let him know in a little while. He certainly got close to me. He is a good, honest, clear spoken man, and I want to avoid a separation, if they both really love each other." Mrs. McKinnon said, "Yes, you told me all this. Harriet doesn't love him as a husband, as he loves her as a wife. She admires him and is proud of him, and he is so good to her, but I never did believe she had any real love for him. I asked her today, after the messenger left, if she wanted to go with Jim to the East, and she answered promptly and unconditionally 'No, ma'am, I do not. I will live with Jim Crow if he stays here, and he talks to me as if he is going to stay, if his tribe does leave, but I will not leave you and go with him and his tribe, to, I don't know where. I will not leave my brothers and sisters, and master says he thinks my mother, so dear to me, that was left in South Carolina, will come out here in a few years, and I will be then where I can see her.

I am sure not to go farther away from her." (Her mother and family did come.)

"Well," said the Colonel, "this settles it, and settles it without embarrassing us. But I can't see why he was so urgent for me to go at once if they are not going to leave soon." But he decided to go. Friendship demanded it. Services in days passed, on the part of the Chief, called to him to go. In the late midnight hour he rode into that dense forest, that a dark, drizzly night had made as black as Egyptian darkness, a night made hideous by the grating notes of the little screech owl, and the bellowing of the great alligator, that made the earth tremble, and the water spout skyward, as they plunged from the banks into the murmuring Choctawhatchie. As he neared the quarters, he saw a great circle of little camp fires in front of wigwams. He knew then that the tribe, consisting of more than half a thousand, had been gathered for the exodus. In the midst of this circle of fires was the Chief's palatial tent, made of material that was impervious to water and to heat.

He dismounted and hitched his horse. The outside watchers met him as he approached the tent, and without asking a question, lifted the folds of the tent and ushered him in. By the dim light of a taper that rested on a small rustic table, not a lamp or a candle, as we would have it, but a long conical shaped wick that had been soaked in oil and coated with wax, he sees the form of the old Chief in his big rustic arm chair, in the center of his tent, his head resting against the center pole or prop of the tent. His couch was close by him. At his left sat Neill McLendon. As the Colonel approached him he asked "How is it with you tonight?" The Chief, raising his head from the prop, said "It is not with me at all as it has been in the days gone by." Pointing him to a seat to his right, he continued: "They tell me it is an ugly night outside, as it is a sad one to me inside, but I am glad you came. I have been wishing to see you for several days, as this change comes on. I have much to say to you men. I promised Jim Crow that I would talk to you about arranging for his squaw and baby, — no, I musn't say squaw, he doesn't like that, he wants us to call her his wife. The poor boy says he doesn't see how he can go away and leave them and wants me to see you and try to arrange with you for them to remain together." "Yes," said the Colonel. "Jim Crow and I talked that matter over, and I promised him to do the best I could, and knew any arrangement you and I could agree upon would be satisfactory to all parties. But Harriet said today that she could not leave her mistress and all of her kin. She is looking for her mother and family that was left behind in South Carolina to come on in a few years, and if she goes East, she knows she will never see her again. She says she prefers staying with us to going into the unknown." "Well," said the Chief, "that settles this matter. I am sorry on Jim Crow's account that it had to be settled this way, for he loves her with all his heart." He was silent for a little while and seemed to be in a meditative mood. The Colonel broke the silence by asking "What seems to be the trouble with you?" He said "I expect the Great Spirit is calling me and I will have to go. I think now he was calling me all along the way, as I journeyed toward the East in search of a home, for when we would come to a goodly land here and there along the way that would make us homes, disadvantages would arise and something would say within me, there is a better hunting ground for you than this, and so it was, until we reached the Atlantic. And while we passed by many good places, but none so good as this, we have returned without settling upon any sure one to go to, so I feel now that this was the call of the Great Spirit, and the better hunting ground for me is over that last river." The Colonel said to him, "Do you think it will be well with you over there?" He brightened up and said, "I can't say; I am going under sealed orders, and don't know what I shall find there. If I meet your Jesus, the Son of the Great One, I shall claim Him as my friend and tell Him that it was you men that told me about Him, and the Father, and ask Him if it was His Spirit that was calling me over. I trust that it will be well with me over there." Neill McLendon spoke up and said, in his confident tones, "If it will be well with any of us over there, it will be well with you." The old Chief, with face aglow with smiles. and with a trembling voice, said, "We have spent many happy days in the chase and roaming over these wild woods, and in our swift canoes that moved over the clear waters like things of life, but It seems now the parting time has come, we are to be separated far away from one another. It may be as far as the East is from the West, as far as the skies are above the earth." Then he leaned his head back against the center post as at the first, appeared a little tired, but was quiet, and seemed to sleep sweetly. The night was well near spent. There is a hush within and without, a stillness peculiar to the deep forests in the night time. Then comes the rush of the morning out of this stillness. The old Chief started up, he groaned and fell back. It was a groan of the body prompted by the spirit. This brought his large family and men of counsel to his side. The spacious tent is filled. We placed him on his couch and he is at ease again. He rolls his great eyes around and looks in the faces of the watchers standing about his couch. He takes the hand of Jim Crow and is propped up on his couch, and says to him, "My son. I bless you as the Chief of these tribes, in my stead; be faithful and lead them in the paths of peace and plenty, and not in the ways of waste and want and contentions. Do honor to the name of your fathers," and turning his eyes toward those who were with him on the home search to the East, said, "These will show you the good hunting grounds, choose well for them and yourself, and you all be faithful followers and be blessed." Then he turned his eyes and said, "My white friends, good-bye. I want to be buried in a coffin deep down in the ground after the manner of your burying. I want my bow unstrung and arrow and tomahawk placed by my side." and turning his eyes towards his faithful squaw and children he said, "I am passing through the swollen river to join those that have passed over to a better hunting ground. Good-bye." And then he closed those benignant eyes in peace. — in death.

    The folds of the great tent are lifted and the glorious sun, coming from its chambers in the East, throws a flood of light over his sleeping body, through the open branches of the great trees. Thus ends the wonderful life of a great man, not in book lore, but in natural knowledge, — not a hero in war, but in peace, — not a diplomat in the affairs of great matters, but a wise manager in the affairs that pertained to his little kingdom by the sea. In his death we have the foregleams of immortality, that beyond the grave, behind the shadows, is the bright light of immortality, telling us that the soul shall not be left in the grave to see corruption.

These white men present, left him in the hands of his mourning tribes. On the following morning Colonel McKinnon, the McLendons and other white friends, with Uncle George, made him the coffin, took it down, put his body in it, as he requested, dug his grave under the shades of the trees in the hammock land, close by the road that lead to his landing, let down the coffin to its place in the ground, placed the rich mould over him, and at his head they put up a wooden slab four feet high made of fat lightwood, with this simple superscription upon it,

"Sam Story — Chief of the Euchees."

And his grave is with us until this day. I have stood by it often and read the simple superscription.

Campbell, in his historical sketches of Florida, has much to say in praise of his hero of peace, Alexander McGillivra, the educated Scotch Indian, Grand Chief of the bloody Creeks, the descendants of that great Muscogee race of Mexico, to whom the war-hoop was music. He says that this Indian and half Scotchman Chief was the most remarkable man to whom Alabama ever gave birth, and the most extraordinary man to whom Florida has ever furnished a grave. Judge Campbell's mind seems to be much perturbed at the way William Panton, of that rich commercial firm of Panton, Leslie and Company in Pensacola, treated him in his death, when he had professed such great friendship for him, and for whom McGillivra had done so much to increase his fortune, turning the whole trade of the Creeks to his firm for years. He says he ought at least to have erected a brick monument over his remains, reverently protecting it up to the time he left Florida so that this generation might be able to direct the footsteps of the stranger to his tomb. He was buried with Masonic honors in Panton's garden. The identity of the spot has defied diligent investigation, and generations unconsciously desecrate his dust. He tells us too of the bitter thoughts of the Creeks when they knew that he slept in the "Sands of the Seminoles" and not on the banks of the beautiful Coosa, which he loved so well; where he was born, where he had presided over councils and made "paper talk" for their good, and where his hospitality was ever ready, alike for the distinguished stranger and humble wayfarer." Judge Campbell has convinced us that Alexander McGillivra was an astute statesman and diplomat, that he did much for peace among the nations in his quadruple dealing with them. It is said on good authority that he held a Brigadier General's commission from Great Britain, from the United States, from the Spanish Government, and from his own nation of the Creeks, all at the same time. Beyond a doubt he received salaries from all these governments and we may say a good commission from the Panton Co. for the trade he turned to them. Sure we are ready to concede that he was a remarkable man. None but a wonderful man, a highly educated mind, could bring about, in that quadruple way, such marvelous results. He sought after peace and he thirsted for money. His great heart was full of love for mankind, but it was overflowing with cupidity. He was often under dark clouds but they would roll away to make room for others to come. We have no doubt but that President Roosevelt in his "Strenuous Life" would have crowned him as a great hero.

Sam Story, the friend of the Scotchman, and who never claiming to be his equal socially or intellectually, was never under even a transitory cloud. He always stood out in the open, and everybody understood him. He loved and was ever ready to help his fellow man. He adorned the natural, the simple life. He was peace personified. Pacific Isaac was never more yielding and self-sacrificing that he, yet he had the bravery of an Abraham buried deep in his broad bosom. Judge Campbell well says, "The defense of such characters must rest at last upon the final judgment of their own people, their own nation, upon their life work." So judged, Sam Story will hold a high place in the hearts of the lovers of peace and the conservators of the beauties and utilities of nature. This child of the wilderness, nursed in the lap of nature's bounties, schooled in the college of the natural, offers rich lessons to the disturbers of peace, the depredators on nature's bounties.

The old patriarch's friends have nothing to bewail them as to his last resting place, for their appreciation of his worth, prompted them to give him a grave where he asked it, in the groves on the banks of the beautiful murmuring Choctawhatchie that he loved so much and was so loath to leave, a grave around which the merry warblers, sitting on their swinging limbs, will make music through the day, and the night birds sound their dirge notes through the long nights. His grave was marked with the most lasting material the country afforded.

When the last great Day shall come, and the trumpet sounds, Walton will open a grave in which there will be no shrinking back from judgment, but a leap to the plaudit, "well done." Wagner, in his "Simple Life" would crown such an one a "hero of peace and conservation."

Hedging in His People

The writer years ago, when a representative to the Presbyterian General Assembly that convened in Dallas, Texas, remembers hearing a report made to the Committee on Foreign Missions by an agent of the Pan-Presbyterian Churches, who had visited all the missions that belted our globe. In that report he said. "I, with two of the stationed missionaries on the Western coast of Africa, visited a tribe of Africans, well in from the coast and well hedged in from intruders by natural boundaries. They were there in their primitive state. No French trader or Catholic Jesuit had tampered with them. The local missionaries that lead me to them had located them a little while before, but did no missionary work among them. They had some knowledge of the Supreme Being, but offered sacrifices to Him after the order of righteous Abel's fleshly offerings. While they needed much help to the knowledge and worship of the true God, yet they had laws, or customs, and manners, in their government, and many rare virtues that would have done credit to many of our civilizations. Of course they had many crude and ugly habits that ought to be corrected. These same missionaries cited us to other tribes not far from there that had been made worse by contact with civilized French traders that claimed to be missionaries. Instead of being made better, they adopted their vices that tarnished their own inherent virtues."

Now, these hedged in African tribes remind us very much of these pent up Euchee Indians on the Choctawhatchie and show us that God is wise and good, and how He can preserve His oracles through dark ages.

Chapter Nine - The Euchees Depart from Walton

Notwithstanding their old Chief had everything practically ready for their departure Eastward, they lingered for three weeks around the grave of their father, their departed Chief. Smitten at heart, they bewailed his death, so unexpected to them, and performed funeral rites all the days while they lingered. Then the new Chief, Jim Crow, came and took an affectionate leave of his wife and little daughter, Eliza, sorrowing most of all that he would be with them no more. My mother said that Harriet did her part well in giving him an affectionate farewell, and for a week showed sadness over the parting. Jim Crow, in bidding my mother and father good-bye said, "Had I not been blessed of my father into the leadership, the Chief of the tribe, I would remain and be as loyal as my lovely wife."

On the following day the great tent was struck, folded away, and, with its contents, laid in one of the market boats, together with other belongings of the tribe. They all then assembled in a circle around the grave of the old Chief, and with soft tread they marched several times round, moaning and bewailing the death of their centenarian Chief. They turned in their march to the landing, where the boats were tied along the river banks, some softly murmuring as they marched on, "he died of old age," others saying, "he died of fatigue in finding us a new hunting ground," while others cried in mournful song, "not of these, not of these, he died of a broken heart," all joining in this sad plaintive lay until they reached their boats.

Those who were to march over land were passed over the river, while those who were to go by water entered their boats, and as they were loosed from the banks and floated down the stream, they said "our eyes shall behold his grave no more, neither shall we lie down in the shades of these trees, nor shall our hearts be made glad any more by these little feathered songsters in these deep tangled wildwoods, that make merry music all the day long and soften the nights with their little notes." As they moved down on the swift current of the stream, with muffled oars, they looked back and said, "no more shall the twang of our bowstring be heard in these wildwoods. No more shall the keels of our swift canoes cleave these silver waters." They passed rapidly down the Choctawhatchie River and Bay, going South and Westward, out at East Pass into the great Gulf, turned Eastward, and sailed along Florida's southern shores in constant touch with the marchers on the land. They were seen as they passed Old St. Marks, marching and sailing on slowly, and there they passed out of view, to be heard of no more as a tribe, but not out of memory's sweet recollections.

The writer, ever on the alert to find some vestige of this lost tribe, has reason to believe that they settled along the Everglades and are there yet, not as a tribe, but merged into the lingering tribe of the Seminoles. In 1874, while in Tallahassee as a representative in the legislature, when Lieutenant Governor Gleason wanted to go to the United States Senate, and had himself elected Senator to the State legislature from Dade County by a majority of six votes, all the votes cast at that election, and a native Indian elected as the representative, he brought this tall, stout young Indian as representative to the legislature from down there and tried to seat him, that he might vote for him to go to the United States Senate, but failed. It was in carpet-bag days and they already had more pliable tools than he in the negro. It was in those days when the negroes had the majority in the legislature. I noticed that this Indian was very quiet and had nothing to say or do with the negroes, but kept close after the Governor all the time he stopped in Tallahassee, holding implicit confidence in all he told him. I sought an interview with each of them separately and then both together, and feel satisfied that this young Indian was a grand son of Sam Story. He said his father's name was "Sleeping Fire" and was killed when he was young. The third oldest son of Sam Story was named "Sleeping Fire". He said his parents came from the South and West years before he was born, so his age suits. They tell us down there that this remnant of Indians that were left in the Everglades are very pacific and chaste, and depend in the main for their living on fishing and hunting. Everything goes to prove that the Euchee tribe predominates in that remnant who are the wards of our State and are protected in their inheritance in the Everglades. "Blessed are the meek: for they shall inherit the earth."

Lovey Potter

This is the grand-daughter of Jim Crow and his wife Harriet, the daughter of their daughter Eliza, who married Jim Harris, a yellow boy at Freeport, Florida, just before the war. She is the great-grand-daughter of the Great Chief, Sam Story. Lovey married a yellow boy, Walton Potter, 35 years ago, and they have raised a large family of boys and girls. The girls are handsome, with long straight black hair and prominent cheek bones, showing more of the Sam Story race than the mother. Hon. Henry Bush, who has ever been a close neighbor to them, says they behave nicely and are very chaste.

The old Chief is not left without a representative in the land he loved so well. "Thy seed shall live in the land after thee."

Chapter Ten - Neill McLendon Getting Ready to Leave

About the time Neill McLendon was getting his craft ready for launching, he had many set-backs. He failed to get oakum and pitch from Pensacola and had to cork his vessel with the fiber barks of the cypress, mixed with the woven shreds of the swamp palmetto, and had to run his own tar from the split fat lightwood and boil it down, to pitch the seams. When these troubles were overcome, there came another. His ship-carpenter. Captain Dodd, split his foot open with the ax, rendering him helpless, so far as physical work was concerned. One hindrance after another came in their turn, but the old Scotchman kept surmounting them with his indomitable energy and stickativeness, until he was able to launch his boat, and rigged her for the sea. She was rudely but strongly built with the help and material he had to use. He gave her the name of "Euchee" in honor of the old Chief. The vessel now ready, he gave orders to his clan to make ready for the sea.

McLendon Leaves for Texas

His brother Lochlin, himself, and three others, with their families, together with the crippled Captain Dodd, and we think, John Folk, got ready on short notice to sail. It is said that he thought it a waste of time for his wife to go and tell her brother, Daniel D. Campbell, and other friends at Euchee Anna, good bye, when they were bothered so long in getting off. It was in November 1833, after the Euchees left in November before, that the "Schooner Euchee" turned loose from the same landing, sailing under the direction of Captain Dodd down the same river and bay, but instead of turning to the east, when they reached East Pass, as the Euchee tribe did, they sailed right on to the westward through that beautiful poor-man's inland channel, along Santa Rosa Island, to Pensacola, and cast anchor there for enrollment and to take on shipping stores. They were detained there several days on account of threatening weather. In the meantime, his many friends, the merchant-men and others, seeing his rude craft, and the precious freight of women and children, and a cripple that was to be both Captain and Pilot, who had never been to sea only along the coast, and without chart or compass, save McLendon's pocket compass, that he used to help him through the woods, these friends said to him, "It will never do for you to go to sea with such a craft and such a crew; if you were driven out to sea there is no telling where you would land without a navigator, even if you were fortunate enough to ride out the storm." He said with great emphasis, "I know it will do. I have a pocket compass along that always points toward the North, whether there is a North star to be seen or not, and any fool ought to be able to follow its pointing." They told him that the town authorities would not allow him to do such a reckless thing. He said, "I did not stop here to be dictated to by the town authorities." When they looked out on the bay the next morning with no change in the weather, they saw that the Euchee had weighed anchor, in the darkness of that hour, just before the dawning, and was out on the bosom of the briny deep, sailing along the southern coast to the westward under a stiff land breeze and under the threatening clouds and muttering thunders. The "Spanish Gazette" came out that day with a heart stirring editorial, written both in English and Spanish, under this heading, "A Most Daring, Reckless Deed for Man."

"Neill McLendon, from up the Choctawhatchie Country, in a two mast schooner called the "Euchee", built up there under the direction of an unskilled ship-carpenter, with tools and material unsuitable for ship building, a vessel wholly insufficient, both in model and material for sea-going, freighted with the precious souls of families of men with women and children, sailed out of this port this stormy weather, leaving under the cover of darkness, and when daylight opened up to view the little Euchee, we saw her sails spread to the winds, skimming along swiftly on the bosom of the deep like a flying sea bird to the westward, under a stiff land breeze, her objective point the great Lone Star State, Texas. On board of that little schooner, with the exception of a crippled sailor who had sailed a few times along the coast, there was not a man with nautical skill enough to pilot a skiff boat up the smooth waters of the Choctawhatchie. Had he waited until daylight to sail, the town authorities would have restrained him from such a perilous and reckless undertaking. His many friends here expostulated with him in all the kind words they were able to summons not to go upon the boisterous sea with such a frail bark, and it so poorly equipped; but to no purpose. We have heard of men taking their own lives in hand, and brook danger when destruction seemed inevitable; but never did we hear of a sane man, under such circumstances, taking his own, and the precious lives of families that we know were dear to him, and launch out upon a treacherous sea in the very face of threatening storms. We doubt very much if they will ever be heard of again"

Days and months rolled by and they bring no intelligence of the Schooner Euchee and the precious souls that went out into the gloom with her. Finally, when many months had passed, Colonel McKinnon received the letter below:

A Letter from McLendon

Galveston, Texas, Feb. 6th, 1834.

Dear John:

We were three months on the way. Stormy weather forced us to take shelter in every inlet and port between here and Pensacola. We were cast upon many reefs and shoals. We went through all the inland ways we could find to protect us from the savage waves. On several occasions we thought the little

Euchee was going to be lashed to pieces. The angry sea waves were stronger than I thought to find them. But after a long, perilous trip, we all rolled into this port safely. I left my family here and went through much of Texas. It is a fine, rich, grazing country, rich soil for farming purposes, plenty of room in every direction. We selected homes on South Boskey Creek, well up, and near the Brazos River. I sold the Euchee here today for more than she cost me. We go now with our families to our new homes. I thought of writing you from New Orleans, where we stopped for a time to make repairs, had to cork the "Euchee" anew from stem to stern. We like to have worn out ourselves pumping before we reached there. I made again to write you when we landed in this port, but thought I would wait until I had something worth writing; and we were so disappointed with this part of Texas, and so unsettled, I concluded I would wait until we would see more and get homes. Captain Dodd stayed with the Euchee and has a bad foot yet. Don't write until you hear from me again. We want to be remembered by yon all. We remember you Valley people with much love.

Your cousin,
Neill McLendon

Chapter Eleven - Settles Near Waco

It was a long time before they heard from him again. The Colonel received a short letter after so long a time, stating that they were well and pleased with the country, but that the natives were not such Indians as the Euchees; they were treacherous and revengeful, with no respecters of persons, when they sought revenge. Then in a short time the Colonel received a sad, sad, letter, stating that the Indians had burned the homes and massacred his brother and wife and mother and all the children except a five year old son, John, named for Colonel McKinnon, him they took off with them. This certainly was sad news to their many relatives and friends in the Valley, who loved them so much. Their homes were in McClellon County near the town of Waco. This county was called for Neill McClellon, as the Texans called him. After this there was a regular correspondence kept up between the two, with long intervals at times, until the Civil War came.

When that country was being settled up so fast, letters would come urging the Colonel to move out there at once, if he wanted to become rich, that one, understanding so much about law, writing deeds, and surveying lands as he did, could make an average of from $25.00 to $50.00 per day. Each letter was fraught with intelligence or rumors about the lost boy, that they kept him painted with the red man's colors, "that they were exceedingly kind to him. Sometimes they would hear of him being in the farthest West, in the Indian Territory, and as far up as Missouri, and when he became sixteen they made him Chief of a tribe, doing all their planning and tradings, and that he was exceedingly popular with them all, and was honored and well cared for." In

1850 my brother, Dr. A. D. McKinnon, went on a prospecting tour through Texas and when he came to Neill McLendon's he learned that there had been a treaty between the whites and Indians that brought about friendly feelings between them. This good feeling was brought about by the lad's uncle Neill, who made it one of the terms of the treaty that the young man they had stolen must be returned to his people, and this agreement was fully carried out. So my brother found the stolen boy, after so many years, with bloody savages, back with his uncle, his Scotch kin, where he was becoming day by day more satisfied with his rescue. Instead of the little helpless boy of five years, as he was held in mind, there stood before him a tall, straight, stout young man, weighing 185 pounds, a perfect athlete in bodily activities, with a mind well stowed with knowledge of the natural world, especially the savage part of it. His eyes, voice, and manners bespoke leadership. His uncle was fearful that the leading Indians would induce him to return to them, as they would never come to town without hunting him up. They made no trade without wanting him to pass upon it.

When Dr. McKinnon was ready to return to Florida, his uncle Neill thought it best for the young man to come to Florida, so as to wean him from his old associates. He loved the Indian apparel out of skins, so both of them had suits made out of dressed deer skins, bound with black braid, to wear home. His uncle bought him a fine horse and a Mexican saddle and they rode horseback from Waco, Texas, to Euchee Anna, Florida. I remember well the oddity of their suits. He was given a jolly welcome when he went among his kin in the Valley. He favored us with many interesting and startling stories about his wild life while roaming in the wild country with the savages. I remember him telling that they were once on a forced march and were nearly starved when they came to a pen that held two fat Texas steers that weighed 700 lbs. each, and they jumped over, slew them, and in a little while they ate every bit of them raw, save the hide and bones. He said the first big trade he made for them that brought him into favor with them as a trader, was when they had captured a splendid young negro fellow that was worth then twelve or fifteen hundred dollars. They sent him into a little town to trade him off, and he got five gallons of whiskey for him. A war dance was given him for the good trade he made. This Boskey John, as he was called, returned to Texas. Three years after the Civil War he fell from the third story of a house in Waco, breaking his neck.

Another younger brother, Captain C. L. McKinnon, went out to Texas in 1859 and returned in 1860. He found Neill McLendon, that same old negligible quantity he always was, with his leather girdle around his waist and his shirt collar thrown open, living like a king. His sons and daughters were all settled around him in good circumstances. Their homes were not disturbed by the Civil War and his generations there are among "the blessed who inherit the earth."

We leave this very remarkable character in the hands of his Texas friends who understand him, to tell of his worth. We shall ever remember him as a wonderful man, plain, outspoken, daring, and who loved his fellow man and exercised implicit trust in his God.

Chapter Twelve Walton's First Sensation, or Sam Story's and McLendon's Exodus

The peaceable exodus of Chief Story and McLendon with their families to the East and West, may be said to be the first real sensation that stirred the little Scotch Colonists from center to circumference. It was the topic of conversation at home and abroad, in church meetings and state gatherings, some sad, others glad. One would declare it meant a free license to destroy and waste. Another would say it meant unrestrained liberty and peace. Surely these quiet exits Stood for much in any way you look at them. Just what they meant to Walton no one may ever know. Had these men made up their minds to remain here and contend for what they honestly believed was the public rights of every individual in nature's domain, at this time, when there was no law, or none to execute them, no force could have been brought against them that they would not have been able to withstand; for with all their pacific actions, there never walked this great globe two braver men, more determined when they got their heads set. They could have commanded not only their own forces, but a very great majority of the pioneers were in full sympathy with their views and would have come readily to their help to be guided by their wise counsels, and they might have established here, in these infant days, a protection of the utilities and beauties of nature that would have found a hearty response one and a half decades later in that great literary teacher at Old Knox Hill. This too, with the friends they could have called around them, would have been invincible to any home force that could have been brought against them. And this combination would have given us moral force and culture along life's ways that would have been an example to the world, and would have given us today green pastures, rich fruits, more abundant granaries, game in plenty, denser forests, and a more healthful clime. We would have more abundant swinging gardens of grapes and flowers along our streams, gardens as rich in the production of fruits and flowers as were the gardens of Hesperides. This is no wild Utopian idea. It is reasonable, practical.

Now let us look at the pessimistic side a moment. Had they stayed and provoked a conflict of any duration, that would have caused a weakening of the forces. That Argus eyed, bloody Creek nation in our sister state, always on the alert, would have pounced down on these founders and annihilated them, and there would be no Scotch pioneers to write about today. Neither is this any wild pessimistic idea. It is a reasonable view to take, as the sequel will show after a while. These events came in parts of the years 1832-33.

Times Just After the Exodus

The aborigines and founders are gone and discussed, and the colonists appear to move on as though they had never lived here, or moved away. The moving on of the world doesn't depend upon any man, be he humble or exalted. We are very light when properly weighed. These early pioneers were wonderfully blessed in the years that were passing. No marked disasters had fallen to them or their efforts, common to colonies. They are blessed with health. Their labors are crowned with success; their fields are yielding plentifully, their cattle multiplying as the seasons come and go; and their homes are made more and more comfortable. Their work is not hard. They can live so easy in this beautiful land.

The women, as is always the case in pioneered homes, have the hardest time. It is they who go to the cry of the children, who look after the garden, and prepare the meals, who see to the milking of cows, and the feeding of the chickens, to the spinning and weaving of the cloth, and the cutting and making of the garments, to the gathering of the clothes and the washing, to the keeping in order of the home, and a hundred other things did these pioneer women have to do, yet, they too, are being content.

These people were so neighborly. They commenced socially with each other. If one or two from a neighborhood went to market, they took in their wagons the gourd of eggs, the coop of chickens, the bees-wax, the tallow, and the fat pig, for all the rest in the neighborhood and brought back merchandise for same. They were neighborly in the fullest sense. These people living the simple life here never thought of charging a stranger or traveller for a night's lodging. I do not suppose any one ever paid for a meal or for lodging in Walton until after the Civil War.

Second Epoch

Chapter Thirteen - The Indian War

This third epoch does not break upon them like a thunder storm, but they are lead up to it through sad paths, while they are not dreading or thinking of it. Would the reader be lead up to this epoch by this sad path, in an interesting and impressive way, then let him go, as I did at the last, in person to a point on the Western banks of Gum Creek, eight miles North of DeFuniak Springs, tell Jake Bell or Joe Stafford, who live nearby that memorable spot, that you want to see the mounds that tell the story of the first real trouble that led to the third epoch of Walton's pioneer settlers. They will take you to a little spot, stained with blood, near the banks of Gum Creek. Then they will lead you just a little ways off to a water oak hammock. In the midst of this they will point you to three little mounds of earth and say to you, these tell the tales of woe, the sad story that led up to the lifting of the curtain that let in the black darkness, the Indian War in Walton, that pressed so heavily on the good people in this happy land for nearly two years. If you cannot visit this historic spot in person, then come and go with me in imagination, as I really often did at the first, when a boy, and sit at the feet of one around the camp-fires on a cowhunt, and hear him tell the tragic story, as none but he could tell it, for he knew more about it than any other man. His mind, his heart, and his tongue were alive with it, as he talked about it. This man was Sill Caswell, then a sprightly young man in the prime of life, of short, stout build, short feet, having had his toes frozen off when a boy. He raised a large family of sons and daughters. His last son died at Euchee Anna last year. He died twenty seven years ago at his home at Alaqua, southwest of DeFuniak Springs. Listen now to him as he sat at night around the campfires on a cow hunt, telling us boys the thrilling story.

"In the fall of 1835, Big John Anderson, William Nelson, John Porter, Thomas Broxton, and myself went out on a cow hunt, in the range up and down Shoal River and its tributaries, looking after our cattle that fed in this range. When we were out there several days and had gone up Shoal River as high as the Cawthon ford, we learned that a short time before a marauding party of Creek Indians had swooped down through the lower edge of Alabama and into Walton, and fell upon Joseph Hart's families, who lived across Pea River and massacred him and all his large family in the morning while they were tending their cattle at the cow-pens, except one daughter, whom they stabbed and left for dead, but she recovered (and is the mother of George Marlow, now living at Lime Stone.) The next morning they came to the home of his brother Robert and attacked his home, but he was better prepared, was barricaded in his home, and he and all his family were armed with guns and drove them away, killing and wounding seven, and none of his family were hurt, except one daughter, Chacie, who was shot through the arm and who was the mother of our Henry Wilkerson with us to-day, and owner of the "Smith Mill." Henry Wilkerson had an uncle killed a few days afterwards by the same raid.

We learned that these plunderers were moving down the heads of Shoal River. This information turned us to the South East in the direction of our homes. In the early evening of that day, as we hunted up and down the creeks that we had crossed, as we bore homeward, along the banks of Big Swamp Creek, we found some large tracks, not very many. We knew they were the tracks of hunters, and persuaded ourselves, from what we had heard, that they must be the tracks of Indian hunters, and very probably a party from that band that did up the Hart families so badly. We hastened on our way. In the late evening time we were nearing the place on Gum Creek where we proposed to camp and take rest for ourselves and horses for the night, when we came upon an old mother bear with a bunch of good big size cubs. We shot and killed one of them, took it on to the camp, dressed it, built a little oak fire, and barbecued it before we went to sleep, leaving it near the live coals to brown and keep warm for our morning meal. It was fat, tender and sweet, just such a treat as you know we cow-hunters get on our trips, out of the deer and the turkeys that fall in our way. We had gathered in turns of lightwood before it was cleverly dark, so as to have a light to see how to get off in the early morning before it was light. We were careful enough not to build a fire that night, lest the blaze looming up might guide the hunting or straggling Indians to our camp. We all lay down early and slept sweetly, for we and our horses were very tired, having ridden fast all the day long. I got up very early in the morning. I was always, as I am now, an early riser, and tell my children that while I came very near losing my life by being an early bird (just the snap of a gun preventing), yet I owe my life today to being an early riser. As was my custom in camp always, I got up long before the rest, built a good lightwood fire, and fed the horses. I was riding a young mare not used to the woods life, and she refused her morning meal, so I took her by the halter led her a little ways from the camp, and down the creek, to let her graze on the fresh grass there. Thomas Broxton was the next to get up, and went down to the ford of the creek for water. The rest were up, or in the act of getting up. It was a dark, damp, murky morning, as I stood holding my mare to graze. Below me, on the creek, I saw a flash and heard the snap of a gun, I knew that it was the old fashioned flint and steel gun that always makes such fuss when it snaps, especially in a dark, quiet, still morning, when a fellow was on the alert. No sooner seen and heard, than I cried with all the force of my voice, 'Snap, snap! gun snap!' Before these words were well out of my mouth, the men in camp were on their feet rushing for their guns, which had all been carefully stacked around a tree at their heads and well protected from the dampness of the night. Broxton from the ford came rushing down between me and the creek in the very direction of the flash and snap, when I grabbed him from the dangers he was rushing into. There was snapping and flashing and firing and advancing all around the camp, and we could tell that some of our men in the camps were firing from the report of the guns. Unarmed as we were, we saw that if we went to the camp to their help, it would but be going straight to our death, so we sought shelter in the bed of the creek, that had a thick ti-ti growth along its banks. By the time we struck the stream, we heard a loud report from a gun that we knew to be Big John Anderson's, and I whispered to Broxton, "that is Big John's gun, and if it is in his hand, there is one dead Indian sure, for he never fails of his game when he pulls the trigger." The last gun fired; then came the rush, the tramp of hasty footsteps a struggle, the sound of mighty blows being struck, then the loud Indian war-hoop is sounded again and again; the horses all tore loose from their hitchings, and went in a mad rush, one after the other, across the ford of the creek near where we were, in its stream, on their way home. We knew there was no safety for us where we were, and I was no walker, and for me to try to hobble through the woods in the condition my feet were in, would be sure capture and death; Broxton said he would not leave me, and our only place of safety was to move up the stream. While we were discussing this matter, two Indians came following the tracks of the horses with torchlights crossing the ford near were we were, and when they passed on, we moved at once up the stream in the darkness, which was slow travelling; sometimes the water would be up to our waists and then not more than knee deep. The unwelcome morning began to send its gray streaks around us; we shuddered with cold and with suspense and fear and sorrow. And when the morning shed its light all around, and notwithstanding we had struggled hard against the current and quicksands, around the bends and crooks, we were but a little way from the ford and camp on a direct line; heard every word spoken but could not understand their dialect. We ensconced ourselves beneath the thick ti-ti that overhung the banks and were as quiet as a brace of doves. When daylight fully lighted up all things around, the two Indians that went in pursuit of the horses came back, passed up to the camp, jabbered there a little, and we longed to know what they were saying, but could not understand a word. In a little while there came other little bands who went up and down on either side of the creek a little ways, passing us, and then returned to the camp and made their report in a loud clear voice, but we could not understand their jargon. They ate their breakfast, faring sumptuously, we knew, for we had in our saddle-bags nearly a week's rations, besides the big fat cub of a bear we barbecued brown for their ravenous appetites. Breakfast through, they sent up another shout of victory, which was followed by their savage hum of sorrow, bemoaning their dead braves. As they hummed the death song, they silently stole away, and we could hear their footsteps tramp, tramp, tramp, growing less and less distinct, until the tramp and dirge song was lost to our ears, and all as silent as death, not even the chirp of a bird in the thickly woven branches above our heads, nor the flutter of a fish about our feet were heard. Silence reigned supreme around that sad gory camp.

We reasoned together a little, and we were both of the opinion that when they failed to find our tracks, they came to the reasonable conclusion that I, who had my horse in hand when they first flashed and snapped, mounted there, and the other missing one, had mounted his, and we were gone off with the stampede, as there were no traces to be seen around the crossing or banks of the creek; and that we might return in a short time with an avenging party of pale-faces. And this was what hurried them off so soon after they had breakfasted. So we moved up just a little ways where we could get out easily on to the east bank and with quiet steps and bated breath, we took a bee line course, through the woods, for our homes, never daring to look back until we had reached the top of the long hill we had to climb. There on its summit we stopped and looked back, and took one long searching view of all things in every direction. We neither saw nor heard anything out of the ordinary in nature, save the pale blue smoke as it slowly moved up that damp calm morning, above the pines into the skies, like unto the smoke of incense of old, to tell the story of that morning's sorrow to heaven; and as it passed up, the tears of the clouds rolled down in sympathy upon the shimmering cheeks of the morning. As we stood there in silence, we imagined we could hear the blood of our comrades ringing in our ears, crying from the ground to high heaven for vengeance. We followed on as rapidly as we could, which was slowly, only on account of my crippled condition. Finally we struck the road leading to our homes, saw that all the horses had passed on in uncurbed haste. We had gone but a little way in the road when we met ten men mounted with guns. We told the sad story as it was, and they turned for home with us, and when our homes were reached, and the sorrowful story told to their loved ones and friends, there was a rapid running to and fro among the homes of the early settlers. A company of thirty-five brave men were formed, equipped and provisioned, led by Arch Justice as Captain, — a well-known brave throughout the settlements, — a strong, quick, but deliberate man, who could see danger and knew how to meet it. Under the leadership of this man, we went on the war path to overtake the bloodthirsty Creek band. We came first to the fatal camp. There lies the dead bodies of our three friends near each other, and two Indian braves near them. A little way from the camp we find another Indian dead from a gunshot, and not far from this one lay another Indian with a hole through his head, made by the big bullet of Big John Anderson's gun. Sure enough, as we hoped, that gun was in the hand of Big John when it fired that early morn, and he had his Indian. Nelson and Porter had gunshot wounds, but neither were dangerous, — they were flesh wounds and not disabling, no bullet had touched Big John. The mighty Scotchman lay there on his back with a great lightwood club in his right hand, beaten to death with clubs and guns; by his side lay a great Indian, brained by the blows of that bludgeon clinched in Big John's hand. We were satisfied that our men reached their guns and fired every gun from behind trees that stood around the camp and drove back the first charge, and while they were loading, the Indians rushed on them and they lost their lives in the club fight. While our men had the advantage of the trees, the Indians had the advantage of the fire light of the camp. The damp night must have put the Indians' guns in bad fix for firing, from the snapping they did. We took these brave bodies and gave them as decent a burial as we could in an oak grove not far from the place where they fought so bravely, around which the modest violets are blooming there in the wild woods, and the moan of the tall pines through the music of their straws, together with the soft murmuring of the gentle flowing Gum Creek, make their dirge song.

And then we hasten close on the tracks of the retreating Indians. We overtook, surrounded and gave battle to them on a little creek not far from where it emptied into Shoal River, below the Cawthon ford, called ever after that "Battle Creek," on account of the battle we had that day with the Indians. We killed, or wounded and captured, all these braves and some women and children they had along with them. We sent them with the wounded and squaws with their children to Pensacola. We never lost a man. Trye Adkinson, father of our Jeff Adkinson on Alaqua, was a lieutenant in this Justis company."

1. William Cawthon.   2. W. J. D. Cawthon.   3. J. B. Cawthon

Now this is the story of this massacre, the opening wedge that brought on the Indian War in Walton, which made that sad epoch in the lives of the pioneers of Walton, as told by one who knew it better than any other living man at that day. Broxton lived to i ripe old age in that part of Walton which went to make Holmes County, and raised a large interesting family who are with us today.

Third Epoch

Chapter Fourteen - The Creek War in Walton

The Indian War of 1836-37 in Florida, and known as the Seminole War, ought to be called the Creek War of West Florida, where Walton was the great battle ground, for it was brought on and fought in the main by the Creek Indians in this section, and we believe if it had not been for them, the Seminole would never have suffered the war to have extended into West Florida. When the Seminole War progressed in the East and Middle Florida, the Creeks commenced their raids down in South Alabama and the West Florida counties, and it was close on the heels of these massacres mentioned above that the war in Walton began.

Colonel John L. McKinnon was the tanking military officer in this part of the State. Colonel George Hawkins of Marianna, Colonel of a regiment that fought in Walton, and was wounded in a battle at the block house near the mouth of Big Alaqua. Captain Lochlin McKinnon of Walton commanded a company of Scolch State troops in this war, and Captain Donald McLeod, afterwards appointed Colonel of militia, commanded another company of Scotch pioneers. There were several small battles fought here. The biggest battle fought in Walton was just a little South of the "Cow-pens," now known as Antioch, in and around Battle Bay. The Indians had collected there in numbers. The whites surrounded them and tried to drive them out or force them to surrender. They were repulsed several times.

The white troops knew that the Indians were short of provisions, as they were themselves. On the evening of the second day's siege, some of the white troops entered the Northern part of the bay and gave battle, while others kept guard around. A severe battle ensued, several killed and wounded on both sides. The Indians were routed and captured and sent to Pensacola. At the close of the battle it was found that Enos Evans, a brave young man, was shot down in the charge in the bay and left for dead. Colonel McKinnon, with a guard of men, went into the bay, found him alive, but severely wounded and in great pain. There was no infirmary corps in those days, following up the battles with litters and ambulances to take off the dead and wounded. So Colonel McKinnon had this wounded soldier, weighing 175 pounds, placed on his shoulders and he brought him out of the swamp to the open piney woods, where his horse stood. Colonel McKinnon was 6 feet, 6 inches high, his weight hardly every varying from 185 pounds, large bones and sinews, no surplus flesh whatever on him. In his prime he was considered the strongest Scotchman of the clan, not excepting Neill and Lochlin McLendon. His greatest strength lay in his arms and the grip of his big hands. Men are living today, Captain A. B. McLeod for one, who saw him wring the legs off of a five year old beef steer without a knife touching the joints. This Colonel took the wounded Evans before him on his big horse and carried him eight miles that night to his (the Colonel's) home, changing from his to Angus McDonald's big horse as they seemed to grow tired under their heavy load of human flesh. When they reached his home they laid him on a bed and he was in great pain. No doctor in the country, he probed for the bullet, found it lodged against his spinal column, and cut through his flesh, making an incision three inches deep with his sharp pocket knife, and took it out, and Evans got easy and well in a little while, and always spoke of the Colonel as his doctor and the best surgeon in the land.

There were not a great many lives lost in this war in Walton. It was a war of raids and destruction of property. It was a war of dreadful suspense, especially with the dear women. For the better part of two years they did not know when the Indians would be upon them to kill and burn. I often heard my dear mother say that she never lived in such suspense as she did during these two years, not even in the Civil War, which was very much like this Indian War in the last raiding years. The Indians would send raiding bands into the settlement, the women would flee from their homes with their children, all collecting at some one home. My dear mother's home was the city of refuge for those living South of Bruce Creek, and "Corn" Campbell's for those on the North side of the valley. On one occasion when they came, she. my mother, had two little Indian boys about ten years old whom my father had taken in battle. Walton's army was cut off from Pensacola by the Indians on the bay, and they could not send the prisoners down as the government required, so these boys were kept in our home for a number of months. They were exceedingly friendly and helpful around the home, especially in tending the cows with the milk-maids night and morning. They learned to talk English and became interesting pets in the family and hated to leave when the time came to

On one occasion, when the families came in for protection, there was an old Scotch lady that could speak no English, who was very much wrought up on account of being driven from her home by the Indians coming on them. She vented her spleen in abusing my father for bringing the Indian boys home, said, "it was their being there that caused them to come up into the settlements and that he ought to have killed them and left them in the woods." She said further, "that we ought to take them now and put them to death." My mother listened as long as she was willing, to hear the abuse of her husband without saying anything, and she too her guest, seeking the protection of her home, guarded well by her negro men against any ordinary raid of Indians. Then she turned to her and asked "Could you kill such innocent little boys as these?" The old Scotch lady replied "Yes I can." My mother knew that the old lady had a better heart in her than that, and put her to the test. She handed her my father's old sword and told her to do the work. Although the little Indian boys did not understand the Gaelic language they spoke in, they knew what the unsheathed sword meant, and they ran to my mother for their lives and clung to her as dear children. This scene scared the old Scotch lady and that put an end to the abuse.

Sometimes false alarms would drive them from their homes to this place of refuge, but the scare was as severe as if it had been real, the suspense as great in one case as in the other.

Just before the commencement of this war there moved a family of Pippins from Georgia into Mossy Bend, and when the war was practically over there came another family by the name of Coopers from the same neighborhood in Georgia, who were friends of the Pippins, and became their close neighbors. The mother Pippin, old Aunt Lavicey, and her girls, were very much amused at the old Scotchmen and women talking the Gaelic language, and they amused themselves often in the evenings by trying to imitate them, and they were very loud mouthed. One evening when they were in one of their biggest glees, the Coopers heard them trying to mimic the Scotch, and thought it was the Indians murdering the Pippins, and fled from their homes, told the neighbors as they went that the Pippins were being murdered by the Indians, that they heard the Indians talking, laughing and rejoicing over their killing them. Homes were all abandoned, women and children all fleeing to the place of safety, men gathering and preparing to fight the Indians anew. Quite a large company of ready men organized and moved to drive the savages from the settlements, and when they reached the Pippin home, found them all safe and in good humor, wondering what had become of so many of their neighbors. This was the greatest panic of the war, it gave severe imaginary trouble to the settlers.

Their Coming and Going

When these blood-thirsty warriors came into Walton to war, they marched down west of DeFuniak Springs by way of the Sandy Mountains, and took possession of the bay country and controlled the great inland water-way that connected Story's Landing with Pensacola. They had allies in Pensacola among the Spanish and Seminole non-combatants, through whom they were able to get supplies of ammunition and provisions. The Walton troops were able to keep the body of them confined to that bay country, but had to stay on the grounds all the time. And they, towards the end, succeeded in breaking up their line of communication with Pensacola and cutting off their supplies, which was the main cause of their withdrawal. Soon after they left here there was an increase in the Indian army in the Middle and East Floridas, and it is thought that when the body of them withdrew, they joined the army east of Walton. Governor R. K. Call sent orders to Colonel McKinnon to equip and mount a company of his best men and have them report to him on a certain day for service, that the Indians had reinforcement from some source. The order was promptly obeyed. Years afterwards, in the fifties, when I was a lad of twelve years, I went with my father to Tallahassee. We were invited, with other gentlemen, to Governor Call's home. As old soldiers ever did and ever will, they commenced talking about old times, war times. Governor Call told the story of calling on Colonel McKinnon for the mounted troops and the day came and he had heard nothing from him, but still expressed a belief that they would come. And on the early morning of the next day they reported to him at his home. He said "I went out and greeted a fine looking company of men, gave them quarters in the grove in rear of the home, ordered feed for their horses, and provisions for themselves, and told them that as soon as they got through with their breakfast to make ready to join the command in waiting. In a little while the orderly of the company reported to me that one of their horses, belonging to Pool, had broken his neck. I went out (he showed us the tree and how he was tied) and found the fine horse with neck broken in the simplest way I ever saw, tripped with a small tie-rein. I saw the tears running down the young man's cheeks; I spoke to him and told him I would make that all right. I went to the sale stable and bought him a better horse and they joined the command, and there was no delay by the accident."

Angus Douglass, my uncle, and Giles and Jim Bowers, James McLean and Kenneth McCaskill. John and Angus Campbell, and a great many who lived and died in Walton, belonged in that company. Though a boy then, I remember how proud I was when that great, good man, complimented my father and his other guests on the valiant work of the Walton boys, and I resolved then if I ever were a soldier boy I would try and be as valiant.

The Residue of Indians

Long after the war proper closed in Walton, there remained several small bands of Indians along the bay coast that gave much trouble to persons and property, robbing homes and killing stock and driving them away. They claimed that they were friendly and only remained for the wood's game.

The United States Government established a mail route from Tallahassee to Town Point, across the bay from Pensacola, along the old Jackson military road that ran parallel with the inland water way along the island and bay. No one lived along this way, so the contractor, Big Daniel Anderson, had to build station houses for the postman to lodge in for the night and places to feed their horses in passing. These were often robbed of their scanty furnishings by these Indian hunters. One of these houses stood just back of Mary Esther. Daniel M. McLean was carrier at one time and he stopped at this station for the night. It was a bright moon-light night, when he awoke just before day, looked out on the porch of the shanty, and there lay two great warrior Indians sound asleep, with their accoutrements buckled around them. He quietly slipped out at the back door with his mail bags, saddled his horse, mounted and got away from there in quick time. This broke up the mail carrying on that line for a while.

Old Joe

There was quite a noted band called the "Old Joe's Band" that roamed from St. Josephs to East Pass. They were the terror of this country for years, and were hard to come up with. They were quick, sharp, and fierce. They did nothing in the open. There were never more than three or four of them on a raid. The territory that they roamed through was full of game. Bread was the only food they raided for, and they used but very little of that. They were so very savage that the whites tried to exterminate them or drive them to their nation. In 1849 there lived on the Valley in Mossy Bend a man by the name of Kage King, a low stout built man, weighing 175 pounds, mighty in strength, a great wrestler and jumper of that day. It was this man King who struck the blow that drove from Walton the last vestige of Indians, and we have been free from them ever since. My younger brother, A. D. McKinnon, and I were going to school in Mossy Bend, when news came in that part of the Valley, that Kage King had killed Old Joe. The people were all astir at this report, and it was all the talk. The evening after the news reached the Bend, we boys were passing on from school, and as we were passing our Aunt's, Mrs. McRae, our cousin Christian called to us to come in and hear Kage King tell the story of killing Old Joe. Of course we boys went in and we all sat in that big open gallery in the big new house, and were as still as mice, while he told this thrilling story.

"I went over to St. Josephs to do some trading, returning with my pack on my back. On entering a swamp out from and opposite to St. Andrews Bay, at the crack of a rifle, the pack strapped to my back was struck. Looking back I saw a giant of an Indian running for me, loading his gun as he came. I thought, at sight, it was Old Joe, and so it was. I ran on the trail way for dear life, — he was gaining on me, — I dodged him at a crook in the trail, and secreted myself, and he passed me a little ways. I tried to shoot, but my gun failed me. I dropped it and my pack, ran into a pond of water full of cypress knees on its edge, which was nearby. I went in waist deep, sank down on the opposite side of a cypress knee from the trail in the midst of "alligator bonnets on water lilies," with nothing but my mouth and nose above the water, and remained as still as I could. In a little while he found that I had dodged him, and he came back. I could hear his footsteps tramping among the leaves and going around the pond. When he was on the opposite side of the pond he discovered my face above water and fired at me, missing me just a little. I knew this was no place for me. I at once jumped up, made for the trail, and ran with all the might that was in me. He, having used his last load, threw down his gun and came in hot pursuit after me. I kept my distance pretty well at the first, but could not hold out as he. I could feel that he was gaining on me, so I stopped at a turn of the trail behind a large tree just on the trail that I might rest and blow and be ready for him when he came up. He hardly passed me before he saw I had stopped. He turned, saw me, made for me with nothing in his hands. I struck him in the forehead with my belt knife and broke it. We hitched. I threw him easily but could not hold him down. He would get up and I would down him again. He seemed to be as much, or more worried than I was. We had it up and down that way for a long time. Finally I threw him, tried to hold him down while I would get my big jackknife from my pocket to use it on him, but found that I needed all the hands I had to handle him. Instead of getting up as before on his feet, when he rolled me off, he rolled on top of me to keep me down, while he rested and panted. While I feigned an effort to roll him off of me, I pulled my big jack-knife from my pocket, opened it with my teeth, made a desperate struggle, drove my knife into his side, and disemboweled him. He rose to his feet, uttered a loud war-cry, and sank to the ground. This war-cry was answered in the distance. He sat a few feet from me looking at me, but not able to move. I sat panting and resting in quiet too, when his distress cry was more fully answered by the coming of a tall slender brave, one of his sons, running up to us. I had my knife opened for him, but when the old hero saw him coming he cried in his Indian language, — and I shall never forget the words, (he repeats them) and I have learned since I came home that they meant in our language, "Flee for your life, pale face is too much for you." In an instant he turned and did run for his life, and I was glad, yes, I was glad when he turned. I gathered up my pack and gun and came on my way thankfully.

"It was deep dark when I reached Story's Landing. I came over and was glad I was at home again. On examining my pack we found one hundred and twenty holes through the bolt of calico. I knew I left the old giant breathing his last. I know he is dead. I don't know what will become of his body. I told the story as I passed on homeward. Men went to protecting their homes from his sons."

The writer spent the night not long ago with a man that lived near the ground of this deed, and who helped to bury Old Joe the day after the fight. David Tervin, uncle of our F. Q. Tervin, was among those that placed him under the ground, and was one of those who drove the remaining ones from the country, which was easily done after the death of their leader. His story of removing them is very interesting. They say he had three of his sons with him on that occasion, but they happened to be scattered at that time.

Chapter Fifteen - Intervening Times Between the Two Wars

After the close of this Indian War it took but little time to build up the waste places and for prosperity to crown the efforts of honest labor. I say without fear of contradiction that from 1840 to 1860, there was no country of Walton's area whose people were more happy and contented, more healthy and strong, more advanced in the tenets of true religion and culture, that comes more abundantly through advanced religious education, that there were no better livers and helpers of others, and a no more prosperous, in material wealth, in proportion to the money currency used in carrying on the great commerce of the country, than the people of this little bit of territory, — no, not even in this strenuous age of "get rich quick." Mind, I say, taking into consideration the common circulating medium in carrying on commerce. No one here in these times was trying to get rich, but everybody ever growing richer year by year. There were no strenuous efforts being put forth after the goods of the world, but everybody moving on in an industrious, simple, way, were gathering the world's goods about them. The resources of the country, the wealth that came so readily to the call of labor in those days, did not make drones or idlers of the people, but made them respondent to duty's call. Sometimes when I look backward to those old days, I find myself hungering after them, and the good, honest simple people that lived in them. They are not all gone. The seed is not all wasted; now and then you come up with a "chip off of the old block."

The scarcity of money was seldom thought of or discussed in those days. The people had learned how to do a great deal of work and carry on considerable commerce with but little money. There was a little bank in Pensacola, and one in Tallahassee, and not more than one third of the people knew of these banks of deposits and never sought any benefits from them. Think for a moment how the banks are scattered around us now, and hear the cry of hard times and no money.

We think we need more money to live well and happily than we really do, and these founders of Walton County have fully demonstrated this truth, for they were thrifty and happy when they handled but little money. But, of course, they did not live in this great accommodating age, "this age of paper sacks and free delivery, of free lunch and cold drinks — in those days of leaving the farms in the hands of tenants and flocking to the towns." We will learn after a while that these free luxuries are the most expensive and call for the most of our money, that we claim is so scarce.

For a long time there was not a store of merchandise in all Walton. After Euchee Anna was started, several stores were started up there, but it was a long time before there was a store kept there regularly. Giles Bowers, in partnership with Ramsey, opened up a little store on the bay, or on Four Mile Creek, and not far from its mouth, and called the place "Genoa." They ran business there but a little while when some one entered the land on which their store was built, and this broke up their business. Colonel McKinnon, father-in-law of Bowers, went to Tallahassee and bought forty acres just below Genoa, on the same creek, which offered a much better place for a town than Genoa did. He took his negro hands cleared off the banks of the creek, trimmed up the place for the town, and named it "Freeport", and then cut a broad straight road from Freeport through the "Three Mile Branches," causewaying them good, on into the Euchee Anna and Mossy Bend roads, making a direct route to this new place.

Giles Bowers was the first to build a store and start up a mercantile business there. Jesse McCullough built a store between these two places and for a long time these two stores, with the one at Euchee Anna, were the only trading places in the County. This was in the late '40's. Before this time, and long afterwards, the farmers and stock men would go regularly twice a year to Pensacola on the slow sailing boats and buy a supply of groceries that they could not grow, sacks of salt and coffee, barrels of flour, kegs of nails, and tobacco, spices and ginger. The small families that could not go would send by these and have their wants attended to. They would exchange their produce for these, often getting a bushel of coffee for a bushel of white lady peas. And these things were about all they needed, the rest was made at home.

Our children of today ask in astonishment, how in the world did they live well, where did they get any luxuries, or find any pleasure, how did they accumulate any property at all? They made a living at home and did not have to worry after money for everything. Their tables were always spread with the most palatable, wholesome and luxurious viands. These of themselves were accumulations of pleasure, that paved the way to accumulations in material property. And I do know that these people in their intercourse, especially the younger people, had the most innocent, joyous, health-giving pleasures of any people of this age. Their easy manner of accumulating wealth, the abundance of their tables, and unspeakable pleasures, are something to be coveted, to be sought after by this generation.

Mr. John McCullough is somewhat of an old timer in letting his mind go back in remembrance of the "good old days." It may do some one good to hear him do a little plain talking and illustrating. His talk did me good, gave me better ideas why things are like they are. I was waiting on him some time ago in the store, it was the end of the month and he was laying in quite a supply of family groceries and camp equipage, I laying them out in order at one end of the counter as he made the purchases. When he was through and was making ready to place his goods on the wagon, I, knowing what he was getting per day for his two teams, said to him, "John, you must be making good money now with your teams, you pay out nothing for drivers, you drive one yourself and your son the other?" He said "It does look so. I get $6.00 each day for running my teams for Beach and Rogers and can get the money every Saturday night." I said "That is $36.00 per week, and four times that is $144.00 per month, and twelve times that is $1,728.00 per year. You can't help but be making good money." "But I am not," he said, "I am not doing near so well as when I ran a little farm before the war and had my little bunch of cattle, my hogs, sheep, and goats around me on the rich range grass the year round. When I made everything I needed at home, or got it out of the woods; nor as much as I made running my little schooner down the bay with loads of wood or Lumber to Pensacola. See this axe handle? (Picking up each article that he had just bought as he spoke of them) I paid 15 cents for it, — this pair of ox-bows I paid 50 cents for those, — this box of axle grease 10 cents for this, — these six bars of soap 25 cents, — this box of baking powders 10 cents, this plug of tobacco, with this pretty tag on it, 15 cents, — these shoes in this pretty box $2.25 for these (and he went on to the end of his purchase.) Now, before the war, when I was on the farm, I don't consider these things cost me a cent, save the tobacco and shoes, and that was not much. On rainy days I would slip into the hammocks and get timber and make handles and bows that were worth two of these. When on a hunt, would take ax and tubs and cut on the oak ridges wood, and pile in heaps and put fire to it and when the hunt was over would have enough of oak ashes to make lye soap enough to last a year, and it would make the dirt slip, and not eat up your cloth like this lye and soap of today. When hauling up our winter lightwood, I would pick out the fattest pieces and run lubricating tar that would preserve the hubs of my wagons, and better in every way than axle grease. But these didn't come on the railroad and in pretty round boxes, neither did the shoes come in pretty boxes, nor the tobacco in caddies with pretty tags on every plug. My father, when he sold goods got all his shoes, men's women's, boy's and children's, in one big white pine box and they were better and cheaper than these. He got his tobacco in big boxes, long thick plugs, but no pretty tags. I heard Jim Driggers (a negro) tell you the other day if he was to carry a pair of shoes home without a box, his wife would run him off the place. That is the way with us all now, men and women, we want everything tagged up, flashy labels, well varnished, round and square boxed, paper sacked, and it must come on the railroad; so we have to work and pay all these fellows for these fancy cuts before we make anything for ourselves. And we are fools enough to think we are getting our paper sacks, free delivery, and pretty things for nothing.

"Pent up like I am here, I get no benefits from nature's bounties. There is nothing growing for me while I sleep. All I get now comes from my own exertions, and so much of it goes to others that there is but little left for me. I am longing for the country home, the farm life, as it used to be, where I can sleep in and breathe God's pure uncontaminated air, and work in his sunshine, where I can eat my fresh cornbread, potatoes and vegetables of all varieties that grow while I am sleeping, the juicy peach, the sugar fig, and the plump plum, fresh from the limbs, and the luscious grapes from the vine, and eat our fresh butter, sweet milk and home made cheese, which is far better than any bought cheese ever made, eat our own fresh uncooped chickens and eggs, biscuits made up with buttermilk and salaratus, without any of these concoctions in pretty round boxes called baking powders, to burn out our stomachs. How I long for the hot grated potato-pone, spiced up and baked just as my good old mother used to make and serve it with fresh home-made butter, this best of breads that we never see now-a-days. And there is the hog's head cheese or souse, sausages, opossum and potatoes, "crackling bread" and sassafras tea for supper, and ever so many other good things we had in the good old times that we never see now in town. O, how I do long for the old bread and butter days of long ago, the old unforgettable days before the war, the farm life, the old home, the living we used to have there, the country pleasure life. Give me these and you may have the canned goods, cold drinks, moldy vegetables and fruits, paper sacks and free delivery, and the strenuous city life and wear out yourselves working for others, while I'll plod along in that simple, independent way on the farm, taking my cold drinks from the old oaken bucket that hangs in the well." We must admit that there is lots of truth in the above statement, coming as it does from one who has served in both ages.

There is no doubt but that the years between the two sad epochs of Walton's history were her best, and the most accumulative in material, as well as in the higher order of life, — the mind and soul. And these riches were not acquired by the handling of an abundance of the currency of the country, but by using and conserving nature's offerings in a way, — they grew on these while they slept.

In those days there were owners of large and small stocks of cattle and sheep. Some of these stock men marked from 25. to 50 head of calves each spring, others from 300 to 500 head. These all fed together over the same range. They were hunted, driven up to mark and gentle at the same time, which was the biggest attention they got. These cattle had thousands of acres, that were not scorched to death by fires, to feed over.

These men tried to protect the range all they could from the ravages of fire, and kept good blood in their stock. Colonel McKinnon sent to Scotland and had shipped to him by way of Pensacola a young short horned Durham of the finest stock in Scotland; he weighed 1,000 pounds dressed when grown. This brought the grade of his stock up very much, especially the beef part of it, that was the most profitable in those days.

At first these cattle men lost much by the ferocious beast that claimed the woods, the bear, the wolf, and the panther. These got at first some of their calves, but they got in dogs and hunted and killed a great many of them out. Every family had their faithful yard dog, their vermin and deer dog; and every stockman had, in addition, his cow dog, his bear dog, his wolf dog, and his cur, these numbering from five to ten in each family, and even with all these, it took a long time to stop the increase of these animals.

After the cattle were breeded up and got the run of the good range for a while, weighing from 500 pounds to 700 pounds, it is strange to say there were hardly any losses of calves from these savage carnivorous animals. With their growth in better blood and larger limbs, they seemed to come to a better instinct, or a kind of reasoning, or understanding among themselves for the protection of their young and helpless. The mother cows would hide their calves together in the midst of the scrub palmetto beds that grew around the heads of branches and range bottoms, or they would hide them, when it suited them, in the long grass in the dimple of the hills; and the mother with the great steers and Durhams would feed around these places, keeping watch all the days and nights, and at first sound of distress, there would be a ready united rush of these watchers, with their great spear like horns, to drive away the intruder. These wild animals become as much frightened at these cattle as they were of the men with their guns and dogs; so it was almost sure that they would raise a calf from every cow every year or two. They lost none then as they do now. in the boggy branches, for they were thatched over with cane roots and turf that made it impossible for a cow to break through. So the man that had a good big stock of cattle had a bank that multiplied and doubled in interest, with but little expense. How these cattle men did hate the straggling fire fiend that went through their range with matches, dropping a live one here and there just to see a big fire in the woods.

I remember the first box of matches I ever saw, — it cost 25 cents. I thought they were the greatest thing in the world, and how I was astonished one day when a boy in the woods with my father, when we came up on an indifferent straggling hunter as he dropped a lighted match along his trail, just to see the woods burn. My father explained to him the damage he had done for the little bit of passing pleasure he claimed it was to him. And when, as we passed on, he turned to me and said, "I wish there was not a match in the world, they are a curse in our land, they are too handy in the hands of evil doers." It was this speech of his that astonished me. I would think how the neighbors in the settlement would have to run from house to house before daylight to get fire, when the covered coals on their hearth had burned out, — how the smokers would have to carry their tinder in their little horns, and with their flint and steel would have to strike fire to light their pipes from the bits of lighted tinder; and how in damp weather it was almost impossible to get fire in this way.

Many destructive fires are kindled by these plentiful matches of today in the mouths of the mischievous rat, and many kindled to his credit of which he is guiltless.

These cattle men would turn their beef into money every fall. They would not think of selling beeves under 400 or 500 pounds. There was no local demand for them, for every one raised his own meat. There would come in buyers, and some would sell at home and get good prices. Those that had large stocks would drive them in bunches of from 150 to 200 head to the markets. My father always drove his to market in great bunches, to Pensacola, Mobile, Montgomery, Eufaula, and Columbus, Georgia, and got the highest market prices for them, having them engaged by the pound before driving them, at 3 1-2 and 4 cents.

He raised a colt from a Spanish mare, Dolly, that he bought in Pensacola, the colt's sire was his big black stallion that he drove out when he came first to Walton, and as he was the son of Jack, he called him Jack-son. The colt took after its mother, — he was a beautiful pied family horse, worked anywhere, was better under the saddle than anywhere else. He was my father's "wood's horse," and none could excel him after cows. He lived to be 26 years old and was never sick. My father rode him in the woods regularly for 20 years. My sisters rode or drove him regularly when he was not on the cow hunt. He was a great pacer, a good walker. He in his color of white and brown was as familiar to the cattle in the woods as he was to the children in the home. Everybody in the country knew old Jackson as far as they could see him, knew his pace, knew his walk, knew his color.

In driving these bunches of beef cattle, my father always went in the lead of them and they would follow old Jackson wherever he went, coming to a stream that had to be swum, my father took Jackson by the bridle, got in the hinder part of a skiff, had some one to pull the boat across in the direction he wanted to go, Jackson would swim right after the boat, and the cattle right after Jackson, without fuss or trouble, until all were safely across.

Chapter Sixteen - Ferocious Animals

In the scores of years between the two sad epochs, there was a wonderful increase in stock in Walton, especially in cattle. Allen Hart, Colonel McKinnon, the Cawthons, Bowers, Caswells, Evans, Campbells, McDonalds, were among the biggest stock raisers. Other stock did not increase so fast. They had more fearless enemies, and were more defenseless. The wolf came twice and took sheep from the pen in the night time, when we were keeping ever so many dogs. I remember when the wolves would gather on the hills, just beyond our home, and howl there, and our dogs would answer them with their howls.

There was a branch between our home and the sheep range, and one Saturday evening there came a big rain and the branch was swollen so we could not get the sheep over, and next morning we found 16 of them dead beyond the branch, close together on the road. The wolves cut their throats, sucked their blood, and left them there.

Had it not been for such enemies as these, the sheep and hogs would have increased as rapidly as the cattle. The hogs that kept out of the paws of the bear and wolves were always fat in the woods, off of the abundance of mast and berries. They would often come running home in the day, from these beasts, and lie around the house for a day or two before venturing out. The families raised all they needed for home use around their homes, weighing out of the woods 300 to 400 pounds. But they could not dare go out in the big range to get food that was wasting there.

The writer was in Choctawhatchie swamp not long ago and saw a bunch of big red fat hogs that would have weighed 400 pounds, feeding on overcup-acorns that a recent flood in the river had piled up in great heaps against fallen timber. There is no trouble now for the farmer, along that water way to raise all the pork he wants, if he will give them attention enough to keep them gentle. It is better now than it was in the early days on account of the destruction of the wild beasts, especially the alligator. I don't suppose there was ever a country in which they were as plentiful and as large as they were in this Choctawhatchie country. I went down the river once to Point Washington. They had every 100 yards or so what we call "gator slides", and as we oared along these great gators would roll down these slides into the water like the launching of some large boat. Mr. Wm. McCullough killed one at Bay View, dried his carcass with its great mouth open, and I often placed my foot on his lower jaw and ran my knee under his upper jaw. I was sitting in the hinder part of a big sized skiff boat steering, while a negro boy was pulling me through Lagrange Bayou on a dark night, when we ran upon a large gator that struck the bow of the boat a heavy blow, which came near turning us out into that muddy water to take common lot with his alligatorship. When he struck, he blowed and filled the air with his musk and sickened me.

Dickson Jones, the father of our Mrs. Calvin Johnson of DeFuniak Springs, was wading across the mouth of a bayou near Freeport when a large gator lunged upon him, catching him by the calf of the leg, jerking and pulling him into deeper water, while he struggled and hollowed for life, trying to get loose. When he had pulled him in until nothing but his head was above water, he cried out, "O God save me!" and the gator let him go. The flesh he left on his leg perished away and he was a cripple the balance of his life. I heard him tell his experience in that trying hour, and it was interesting. The savage beasts seemed to grow more daring and aggressive as civilization pressed upon them. I remember on one occasion when we school children, seven of us, large and small, were going to school one morning from the "Old Place" to Hickory Spring School, the little ones on horseback, the larger ones walking, we came to the head of a branch that made close up to the road, and about half way between home and the school house on the Mossy Bend and Freeport road. Around this head was a broad bed of scrub palmettoes; in the midst of this bed were two large mother bears, six large cubs about as large as the common dog of today. They were pulling up palmetto roots with their paws and would sit on their haunches eating off the tender parts of them, while they looked at us, as indifferent as though we were some of themselves. The larger boys took the horses, one going back home with the news, the other onward for the hunters and their dogs. And those of us walking went on to the school, leaving these fearless bears to finish their breakfast of palmetto buds undisturbed. The hunters were soon on the ground on horseback with guns, dogs, and blowing horns. The dogs were turned loose on their fresh tracks at the head of the branch described, on the right hand side of the road as you go to Mossy Bend. The hunters went down on either side of the branch, keeping up with the dogs as they went on the tracks. making the welkin ring with such music as you never hear in these days. Before they reached the mouth of the branch where it emptied into the Seven Runs Creek in the thickets of the swamp, they came up with the savage creatures recruited by three papa bears, and right there the battle of the day was fought. At times it was doubtful which side would win. Victory came at last to the hunters towards evening, with heavy losses on both sides. It was both difficult and dangerous for the hunters to help the dogs with their guns. The ti-ti bushes were so thick they would have to use their hands in parting the way and take chances of seeing and shooting the bears before they would see them, lest they would see them first and rush upon them before they got ready for shooting, or their guns failed to fire. Several dogs kept a great bear at bay for several hours in a very thick place. At last they heard a dog squall and smothering as though his breath was being squeezed out of him. All knew that was our old Nathan's bark and squeal, the best bear dog in the pack. The bear had taken him in his fore-paws, drawn him into his great arms, and was squeezing his life out of him. My brothers could stand this no longer. Neill, the oldest, with the old flint and steel musket, given to much snapping, followed by Charles, the lesser, opened the way with caution, came in sight of the big bear close by, standing on his hind legs slapping the dogs away as they would come in front of him, when he looked over his shoulder and saw the boys coming up on him from behind, turned round and rushed on them in his madness, when they fired on him, and the old musket didn't fail them in that crucial moment, for at the crack of the gun the old bear fell at their feet, for the gun was powerfully loaded for the occasion. Had she failed fire, there would have been a mixture of boys, bears and dogs, that would have been serious sure enough.

Sure enough there lay old Nathan with his life hugged out of him by that cruel bear. This was the first and the biggest kill of the day. One after another of these bears were killed in pretty much the same way, until three of these large bears were killed, the dogs having killed four of the cubs without help. Night gave an end to the day's battle. The hunters' horns blew off the dogs, five of the best dogs were missing, among this number was long-eared speckled Nimrod, next to the best. The hunters went every man to his home, not bragging, but looking on the hunt as a drawn battle.

The wolf seemed to be more cunning and stealthy in his work than any of the ferocious animals, and the most numerous. My father built a pen on the heads of his mill creek and one on the heads of the Black Branch, close to his home. These traps or pens were made of small round pine logs taken from the forest around. They were 6' by 6' and 4' high, the logs were notched down and pinned together. It was floored. The top or trap was made solid and in the same way, with logs for binders, pinned across the top to hold it together. The back binder extended over and served as a journal to rest in bearings made in the top log of the pen, so that the top could move up and down easily. A trigger held up this top. A beef's head or the like, in fresh meat, was well tied to this trigger that was a steady support, but easily tripped. It was the business of one of the servant men, Anthony, to look after these traps every morning and keep them set and bated. Sometimes he would catch a buzzard, but there was hardly a week passed at first that he did not get a wolf or two. There was a powerful big young wolf that grew up in the range, larger by half than any of his fellows. He made an awful big track and was often seen. They hoped from year to year to entrap him, but he seemed to grow up in cunning as he grew in size, without being caught. My father promised that if he ever caught him in his trap he would mark and bell him and let him go and the bell might be the means of leading hunters to him in company with other wolves and be the cause of killing some of them. He went to Pensacola, had a good long sounding bell made to order, with a good well fastened clapper and staple, large enough to take two plies of sole leather. He brought these home, soaked the leather in tar and tallow, making it pliant and impervious to water, with a well-prepared deer skin whang to sew it around the neck of the wolf. This bell and strap hung in the hallway for a long time in waiting and advertising what it was for, until every one knew and were promised to be informed when the fun would take place, that they might come. This big wolf would come around the pen, but would never go in until all began to think he would never be fooled in. But finally, one morning soon, Anthony came to the bed room of my father, before he was out of bed, and cried with joy, "Old master, we've got the big wolf." He sprang out of bed, sent this boy across Bruce Creek to tell the Campbells and McLeans, this one to tell the McDonalds, and another to tell the McIvers and Andersons, telling them all to bring their guns and dogs. They all came, some bringing their children. All things were made ready and all met at the pen. They had two long chains with loops in the ends of them that they worked on the ends of poles through the cracks on either side of the pen, and got the chains from either side of the pen over his head and on his neck. The crowd stood back and around the pen. I, a boy of six years, sat in the lap of my older brother in the fork of a large oak tree close by the pen, where we could be safe and see it all. Men had great poles to lay on him and hold him to the ground until others could get hold on him, strong men hold to each chain. All things ready, the trap door was lifted, the big wolf bounded out, jumped up six feet high, and as he came to the ground the poles fell upon him and men laid hold on him with their hands. The bell was strapped securely around his neck and he was marked. All stood back a little, men held ready guns and clubs, and some held dogs, the chains were slipped from his neck, men let loose with their hands, the poles were lifted from his body, he lay a moment as if in a sulk, then, realizing that he was free, he jumped, shook himself, and ran in the way left open for him to the westward. When fifty yards away, the anxious dogs were turned loose and unbuckling their lungs in madness, they went in hot pursuit, their tongues answering back to the outburst of applause that went up from those standing near the pen. The ringing of the bell, the barking of the dogs, and the cheering of the people, put a move on the big wolf that he never experienced before, and this cunning wolf, realizing that the dogs were nearing him, turned at right angles to the South, across open hills and made good a swamp that was not far away, and was safe from the pursuing dogs. The dogs were blown off, all returned home well pleased with the best sport of the season. This wolf was seen regularly for ten years afterwards. Hunters killed several wolves in his company, led by his bell. He swam the Choctawhatchie several times back and forth. The last time he was seen was in

Washington County by a man on a cold rainy evening, while hunting his sheep. He was led by the sound of a bell to an old deserted house, thinking to find his sheep in the house. As he neared the door the old belled wolf, followed by two others, jumped out of the door and ran off before him, he having no gun to shoot them.

The following wolf story is taken from that very popular address given by Mrs. Ellen Call Long, daughter of Governor Call, in the early years of the Florida Chautauqua. At the close of her address, there was an unanimous request made, asking for her address on Western Florida for publication. She said in her address that she gave the story as given to her by one of the actors in the scene, Judge John L. Campbell. This is the story as she tells it, and he was present when she delivered it at the Chautauqua.

"My father and Colonel McKinnon owned large herds of cattle that grazed and roamed the hills and around the lakes about DeFuniak Springs. My father sent me often with the Colonel and one of his boys to look after his stock in this range. One summer afternoon when we were at the head of the branch that makes up to the road, west of DeFuniak Springs, and not far from the Double Ponds (now Lake Stanley), there came up a shower and we took shelter under the pine trees around that head. The rain over, the Colonel told me to take Frank, one of his negro boys who was with him that day, about my age and size, and go to the right of the ponds and see and take note of all we saw, and he would go to the left and meet us at the north side of the ponds. We had gone but a little ways on our route when we came to a large wolf den near the lake and saw that the old wolf and several young ones had gone in after the rain and were still in the den, as the tracks showed. We hastened back to the Colonel to tell him what we -had seen. When we told him all, he turned quickly, saying we must go and do away with them, it will never do to let them pass. When we got in sight of the mound showing the den, we dismounted and hitched. The Colonel took his long handled tomahawk from his saddle-bags, cut a long pole to run down the den to force the wolf out, got two splendid lightwood clubs with knots on the end about four feet long, handed one to me, the other to Frank. We went up quietly to the den. Sure enough they were still in the den, for there were their tracks only going in after the rain. The Colonel took me gently by the arm, placed me on one side of the opening, and just a little back, showing me how to hold my club in a striking position, and placed Frank on the opposite side in the same position, telling us that when he forced them out with the pole he would give the first blows with his tomahawk and if he failed to stop them, he would step back and for us to let in on the leader with all our might with our clubs. Then the Colonel took his position in front of the den, his faithful cow dog just behind him, while he held his tomahawk in his right hand drawn to strike, with his left he sent his long pole down the den for the wolves. I never heard such rumbling. Instead of one or two great wolves, it seemed to me there must be fifty down there. The ground began to tremble under my feet, my hair to stand up on my head. I was so mad (?) my legs felt curious, I could hear noth-

1. A. D. Campbell. 2. Judge John L. Campbell. 3. Alexander D. Campbell. Jr.

ing but great wolves rushing out. At last the Colonel dropped the pole in disgust, straightened up and said, "Pshaw, pshaw! I forgot that the wolf always comes out of his den backwards. They are gone. Throw down your clubs, mount your horses, we may overtake them yet and get the young ones with the dog." As we went for our horses, Frank said to me, 'If we find another wolf's den, we sure will not tell Old Master. I declare to de Lord, I nebber had such feelings in all my life. My legs got to shaking so I thought I was going to fall. If dat old wolf had come out of dat den and Old Master had failed to stop him, I nebber would have hit him. I done forgot all 'bout the structions he gib us. I forgot I had a club 'til he told us to throw dem down. Dis nigger just hisn't going to find no more wolf dens, dat's sure." We went only a little ways around the lake before we came upon the old mother wolf nurturing her little ones in a palmetto bed. They ran off when we approached. The Colonel tried to make Tyler go for them, but not a bit would he go. He was about as much awestricken with the scene at the den as Frank and I were. He as much as said, "I am your faithful cow dog, and it is not my business to chase wolves," and not a bit would he go, with all the urging. And we were glad, we had about come to the same conclusion as Tyler."

This is a true story, as near as it can be told. John L. Campbell tells another joke on the Colonel about his watch. "The Colonel had a large English movement, double case, silver watch that he bought when he was twenty one years old, gave $125.00 for it, which he carried in his pocket for sixty years and slept with it under his head every night. It has now the same very heavy crystal that was in it when he bought it. (His son, John L. McKinnon, has the watch now and it keeps pretty correct time, and it is near 100 years old.) It seldom got out of fix, and when it did, he carried it in his pants pocket the same as he did when running until he went to Pensacola or Tallahassee himself and had it cleaned and repaired. He was going to Tallahassee on horseback in the early days of this country and left his watch hanging in the room he slept in on his way, and went five miles before he missed it. He had his saddlebags key tied to his watch chain and had to go back for it, or cut the strap that fastened his "saddle-bags. After this he adopted the plan of loosening his suspenders from his pants, wrapping them around his watch, and putting them together under his head, so that he could nevermore forget his watch, and kept this up until his death. He claimed that his watch always carried the correct time, and didn't like for any one to doubt it, kept it proved up with a sun dial that he always carried in his pocket. We were going down Choctawhatchie Bay together on one occasion on a sail boat, we drifted along all night with light winds. There were several other passengers on board besides myself and the Colonel. Next morning we all got up and were out on the deck of the schooner except the Colonel, he was always slow to go to bed, and not early to rise in the morning. He was in the boat's cabin dressing when some one on deck said, 'the sun is up." The Colonel looked at his watch and said, "No, it lacks three minutes of being up." They all cried out on deck and said, -'Your watch is wrong this time, put your head out of the cabin door and you can see the sun up good." The Colonel came out and said it was the water of the bay lifting or reflecting the sun before it was clearly up. Several said "the water cannot lift or reflect the sun so that we can see it as clearly as we see it. Your watch is surely three minutes behind time." The Colonel said, "Let me demonstrate." He took an empty basin put it in the bow of the boat, had us all stand in a line at the stern of the schooner, and then placed a silver dollar in the bottom of the basin and asked if we could see the dollar. None of us could see it. He said for all of us to stand steady and keep our eyes on the same line of vision we had while he had some one to pour water in the basin, when we all, without moving our heads or changing the line of our eyes, saw the silver dollar come up plain to view, while it actually lay on the bottom of the basin out of our sight before the water was poured into the basin; so we were not so sure then that the Colonel's watch was three minutes slow."

The catamount and panther were terrors in the land and gave great trouble to stock men. Mrs. Howell, a very small woman, the mother of Alex and Charlie Howell at Euchee Anna, was going through Choctawhatchie swamp near the Cow-ford on a trail, her little son Willie, about six or eight years old, was following close behind her on the trail, when a large catamount from the bushes jumped upon the boy, catching him by the back of the neck, threw him to the ground, and would have torn him to pieces had it not been for the brave little woman, his mother, who turned at the squall of her boy, found just such a club as she could use effectively with the super-human strength of a loving mother, fighting for her child, and gave just such blows as only a mother can give under such circumstances, and drove the monster off her boy, following him with blows that finished him on the spot. This son, with the marks of the catamount on his neck, lives in Washington County, having raised there a large family.

When I was a boy of eleven years, I was at Freeport in the store of my brother-in-law. Giles Bowers, there came over from Point Washington a man by the name of Smith, who had with him a son eight years old. He was a great hunter, had a long Buchanan rifle, and before he took his gun from his shoulder. Bowers said to him, "Smith, a panther killed a calf of one of my milk cows up on Four Mile Creek, above my home, last night. I know he is up on the creek now, and you can kill him in a little while if you will. If you go and kill him, I will give you one dollar's worth of ammunition for your old rifle." "I will go," said Smith. He tried to persuade his boy to stay at the store until he came back, but like all boys away from home, he would go with papa. They had to go farther up the creek than they thought. The boy was very tired. They were on one of the heads that made up pretty close to the Euchee Anna and Freeport road. The father told his son that he wanted to go down the fork of the branch and come up the other branch and that walk would be too much for him, and put him on a plain cow trail that led to the big Euchee Anna and Freeport road, which was but a little ways off, and on across that road to Lafayette Creek, and told him to stop when he came to the big road until he would come down it in a little while to him. It was a drizzly evening and the trail was very plain where it crossed the big road, and the pine straw had fallen thick about the crossing, so the boy passed on over the big road without noticing it, and when the father came, he saw by the tracks what his boy had done, and hurried on after him. He had gone but a little ways when he found the panther's tracks following on top of his boy's tracks. Excited to the highest pitch, he rushed on, fearing the ferocious beast might overtake and destroy his boy. As he hurried off in the very agony of suspense, not a great ways from Lafayette Creek, he came to a cross trail leading from up Lafayette on to Freeport, and to his joy, he found his boy's track on top of his first tracks and that of the panther's. He is filled with joy, "my boy is safe, I am between him and the panther. I see now my boy followed the trail on to Lafayette, turned up the creek, crossed a little branch and struck this cow trail leading to Freeport, and has gone on there. Shall I lay in wait and kill the panther as he comes on the track? No, I shall go and know that my boy is safe." Following on in easy haste, as he neared Freeport the path began to branch off and grow dimmer and dimmer until there was no path at all, and no tracks could be found of his boy in any direction among the long grass and branch heads near Freeport, and about where the bridge is now on Lafayette. He becomes troubled again and says to himself, "Is it possible that my boy has wandered back up the Lafayette, to be destroyed by the panther?" He ran round and round, crossing and recrossing the little branch heads, but no tracks of his boy could be found. The evening was fast passing away, again he cries out, "What shall I do? I will go to Freeport and get help to hunt for my boy for I don't know what to do of myself." And he went in haste. It was only a little ways off. As he neared the store he saw Bowers standing in front of the store and cried to him as he came, "my boy is lost, come and help me find him." Bowers gladly replied, "Your boy is safe, he is here." And there was gladness in the father's heart and joy in the boy's when they met. He told Bowers the story and he took his big dog "Lock," and they went together, put him on the fresh track, and he soon put him up a white bay tree between Freeport and Lafayette bridge near where D. McLean and Blackman now live. The old hunter threw up his old long rifle to his face and brought him down, a dead panther, to the ground. He got his ammunition, went back over the bay that night with his boy, a happy man, and always loved to tell the story of how happy he was when he knew that his boy was safe. That was the last real big panther I ever saw in Walton. But saw and hunted its cousins often afterwards. Is there not a lesson in this story for us all? Reminding us that we should ever keep a Great One between us and our enemy that is ever on our tracks to destroy us?

Chapter Seventeen - The Great American Bald Eagle

This bird, symbolical of American liberty, is a great bird, and develops a faculty, or instinct, very near akin to reasoning. They give much trouble in the range to sheepmen. Since I have lived in DeFuniak, J. Love McLean, Bazey Andrews (a colored man) and myself were on a cow hunt in the southern range. We were on horseback, each had a dog, but no gun. As we passed up east of the scrub and near the "scrub pond," we heard a great noise in the air. We looked to our right and there was one of these great bald eagles, swooping down on a fleet-footed doe, striking her at one time on the head, and then on the rump, tearing the flesh each time with his great beak and talons, repeating these blows. On nearing us, the scared doe saw us on the slant of the hill, ran to us, stopped in our very midst, looked up to us with her soft, dreamy eyes, as much as to say, "will you not protect me from this terrible bird of prey?" The eagle poised in mid-air for a moment just above us, then flew away across the pond and lighted on the lowest limb of a very low pine, under which were ewes and lambs feeding. When our dogs came up they chased the panting doe from our midst into the "scrub" that was close at hand, where she was safe from all. We passed through the pond, rode immediately under the bird, hollowed and squalled at him until we found that there was no use wasting our breath, and could never make it fly away. It would move sideways back and forth along the limb looking at us, as much as to say, "you kept me, through your dogs and the "scrub" from dining on venison. I will see to it that you will not keep me from dining on tender lamb. I am the great bald eagle, symbol of American liberty. This is my country, where in the mischief are you from?"

We had to go on and leave him there, knowing well that he would soon dine on lamb meat. We reported that evening to the sheep men and they went in quest of the saucy rascal. Are we not reminded here that there is a Refuge for us when we are pursued by the evil one, that is more secure than the "scrub" was to that stricken, soft-eyed doe?

Years ago I built a saw mill at the conjunction of Lafayette and Four Mile Creeks where there had been for years eagle nests. When we began to clear away for the mill and to fell the big timber around, the eagles began to move their nests farther up Lafayette, flying away with the great sticks and lining in their talons that it took to build their nests, as much as to say, "we want more elbow room, the world is too big for a fuss, let us have peace." Captain John Watson and myself were drifting along slowly in the Narrows on the island side, just before crossing over to Mary Esther on the main land, and were very much interested in a fish hawk's fishing in the clear shoals as we drifted on, — he would ascend high up in the air, sail around until his eagle eye would catch a shoal of mullet in the shallows, then he would bundle himself into a ball and come down with a force that would send up the splash of water several feet in the air. He repeated this several times and got nothing. Finally he swooped down and came up with a big mullet and flew off down and across the Narrows towards his home on the main land; but there was an eagle secreted on the island watching him, and as he mounted up with his catch, the eagle came on swift wings from his hiding when the hawk was opposite, and made for him to get his fish. He found that he was not swift enough for the hawk, and when near the old eagle nest on the point of land not far from Mary Esther, and projecting from the island and separated from it by the little bayou, he poised in the air, fluttered his wings and made a loud call that brought a swifter flying eagle that sailed straight on a bee line after the swift flying hawk, gaining ever}' moment on it, and when up and underneath the hawk, the eagle struck up for the game and failed to get it. The hawk clung to it and flew on for its home. Then the eagle rose in the sky and followed on. When over and some distance above the hawk, the eagle gathered himself up into a ball, as the hawk did when fishing, and came down with a force that knocked the fish from the grasp of the hawk, and caught it before it reached the water and flew away with it to the old eagle nest, while the hawk sought a better place for fishing, away from the eagle nests. While we were interested in this battle in the air above the waters, we thought of this fable and its lesson, namely, "That a long time ago when birds and animals could talk, the fish hawk borrowed the eagle's fishing net and forgot to carry it back to him and ever since then the eagle has made the hawk fish for him."

Snake Stories

We want everything in this book to be true, just as it is stated here, and it is with some diffidence that we venture on a snake story, as there are so few who believe a snake or fish story; I will venture a short one that I know is true. The man lives now that told it first to me and says he will swear to it. When so many of us Scotch people lived at Freeport several years ago, Dr. John Wesley McKinnon, father of our Mrs. S. K. Gillis, lived there too; one of the Infingers on Alaqua was sick and Jesse Evans, now living at Rock Hill, came after the Doctor; they went on the way together. They had a little dog along and it bayed something off the road a little ways. They rode out to it and found that it was a large rattler. Dr. J. W. McKinnon dismounted, went up behind the snake that was watching the dog, and placed his riding switch in his right hand about his head grabbed him by the neck, held him up and out by his left hand at arms length, run his right hand into his pocket pulled out his knife, opened it with his teeth, and while he was making his graceful curves in the air, cut off his head, threw his body down on the ground, saying, "go now, you bloody bones." When Evans told me this story as above, I asked the Doctor if it was true. He said it was just as Evans had told it, and said that if you would come up on them from behind and be quick, there was never any danger.

I will venture just one more. I know this one is true, "because I saw the man that told me of it." When the peninsula west of Point Washington extending to East Pass belonged to Walton, and was claimed by Washington County, there was a general election in Washington. The tax assessor's and tax collector's offices went together as one office. The incumbent did his duty as officer so well that it was thought no one would come out against him. Finally a man by the name of Melvin announced himself for the office, claiming that the present incumbent failed to do his duty in not going over all the territory, not as far down as East Pass, to assess and collect taxes on property there, amounting to $150.00 or $200.00, from which the county and State would realize about $3.30 each year, a distance of about sixty miles from Vernon. He claimed in his canvas, if the "dear people" would elect him, he would see this matter properly attended to. This was the only issue between them. The race was made, and he won. Unlike the most of officials of today, when the time came he mounted his mustang, with books in saddle bags, and goes out to this work. When night was creeping on him he found himself on a dim trail, the grass up to his knees, and he on his pony. He felt sad and lonely, everything around looked so snaky and foreboding he wished in his heaft he was back home with his wife. Finally he saw through the dim twilight a log cabin in the distance on his way. This cabin stood just where Santa Rosa City now stands. He rode up, asked the lady if he could have lodging with them through the night. She said her husband was not at home, but was expecting him every moment; that it would be a bad chance to stay with them as they had neither meat nor bread nor corn to feed his horse. This was some distance west of Point Washington and twenty eight miles from East Pass. In a little while the husband came up, repeated what the wife had said, and agreed, as the only chance, to do the best thing they could for him through the night. They put his horse up and gave him all the peas in the hull that he would have and plenty of hay. They had for supper plenty of good coffee, peas, sweet potatoes and fresh fish. This was so much better than he expected, he was cheered. After supper they sat and talked a while and they were social and communicative, and this is what they talked about: "I saw something suspended by a string from the rafters that were low, that I took to be ears of pop corn. When I inquired about it, they kindly took it down and showed me that it was rattle snake rattles and I had never seen so many and such large ones before. The wife with the assistance of the husband and children commenced at the bottom, counted them and gave a little history of each, as she went through them. This one was killed in the field, this at the spring, this one out at the cow pen; the children gathered some oak limbs in a pile out yonder, for cooking, I went out in a day or two, picked up the pile of wood, and this one ran out of the wood when it was in my arms, and I killed it. I killed this one out there in the corner of the chimney yesterday, they go in twos and I think I saw the slide of his mate near the gate this morning. This was all awful to me. I thought I would not try to sleep that night; but when they said it is time to go to bed, I was so tired and worn out with the long ride, I was ready to go. They put me in a little shed room in a little short bedstead made of boards set up in the corner, next to the main building. I had no light to help me to bed, but I dropped off to sleep in a little while to dream of snakes. Some time in the night, in one of my restless moods, half awake and half asleep, I straightened my foot out over the bedstead and something struck my right ankle with force. I knew that it was a rattler, jumped out of bed, ran into the house, told them what had happened, and they soon had a fire kindled, examined my ankle, and saw enough to know it was the strike of a rattler, for there was the rake of his cruel fangs. They bound my leg tight above the ankle to keep the poison from spreading, hurried to make tobacco tea. I called for my writing material and wrote my dear wife a few parting words. I drank and drank profusely of the tea, and threw up the black poison, growing weaker and weaker all the time. After a while the old man said, 'he has stood it so long I have a hope for him,' but I was so weak and sick I thought I must die. Again I heard him say, 'don't give him any more of the tea, I believe he has thrown up every particle of the poison,' this gave me cheer. Then in a little while he said 'He is doing so well let's take off the bandage.' The bandage was removed, my blood went bounding through my veins unrestrained, and I began to be myself again, and in less than half an hour, I could sit up and walk about. All of them rejoiced with me in my narrow escape, and the efficiency of the remedies used. The old man said 'they were the best he had ever seen and never knew them to fail if commenced in time, and that my case was a severe one, for the rattler had given me a long and deep rake.' The old man further said, 'there must be no sleeping on this place until that snake is killed, and told the boys to go to the wood pile and split some fat splinters to make torches for the hunt'; the boys with sticks and lightwood torches were placed on the outside of the house, the girls with sticks were to watch by the fire on the hearth inside of that room, and the old man and wife with torch and stick went cautiously into my bed room, while I stood near the door watching. When they had entered a little ways into the room, they stopped and pointed towards the foot of the bed I slept upon and spoke to each other in a low tone that I could not catch, but I shivered. The old man called to me. 'stranger?' I answered, but did not go in, 'were you sleeping on the back side of the bed next to the wall when you put your foot over the bed and was bitten?' "Yes sir, I was." "Come in here." "I hesitated — I trembled"; "there is not one bit of danger now, I want to show you." "I went in trembling, and he pointed to a flour barrel full of wool, on the top of the wool was an old setting hen. He said, 'now stranger, me and my old woman are of the opinion that it was that old hen that bit you on the ankle and not a rattler. She is mighty crabbed, but a mighty good brood hen, and my old woman always sets her, she is such a fighter for her biddies. I tell you stranger she is one of the "Old Blue Hen's Chickens,' said the wife. "See here stranger," and he ran his stick out over the bed as though it was my leg and she struck it with a vim. 'Now, I am of the opinion that she is the critter that bit you," and I was of the same opinion too, now. "My old woman says she is due to hatch out today, and she don't want to disturb her, so if you think you can lay on the front side of the bed and not stick your foot over the old hen, you can lay here and sleep in perfect safety. All of us need sleep, you especially, for it was mighty early in the night when the old hen bit you. I know you must be weak and sleepy and you have a long ways to ride tomorrow and through big grass and ponds before you get to East Pass, and there is no house between here and there where you can stop and rest." Surely I was weak and sleepy. I lay down on "my" side of the bed and let the old hen have "her" side undisturbed, and slept sweetly until after sunrise, with my feet drawn close up to my body. When I got my breakfast and horse fed, I thanked them all for their kindness, and tried to pay them, but they would not have a cent. Then I left, but not for East Pass, no, I went straight back to Vernon. At the next election there was no issue between us; the plank in my platform that I got in on, I had kicked out, and I was left."

The Deer Hunt

In the early days deer were so plentiful in Walton County that there was nothing interesting in the hunt save the shooting down and eating them. I heard my mother say my father was starting for a month in the woods for a beef; he would go but a little ways from home when he would kill a deer or two and come back and stay until the meat was about out, and go again, and so on until a month had gone. It was not until they became scarce in the woods that the chase became interesting, when the blooded deer hounds were in pursuit, men on the drive and on the stands of their regular runs, firing as they came by, their guns keeping time with the music of the hounds in the chase. I will not attempt to give one of these interesting deer hunting scenes, for Walton has today one of the most interesting and successful hunters she has ever had. I would say here to those who are fond of romantic hunting stories, that are true, to go as I did not long ago for a few weeks with Mr. Charlie Meigs over his hunting ground among the prongs of Shoal and Titi Rivers, and have him show you the places and tell you the stories of the sure enough real chase and adventure in hunting, and I'll guarantee you will have all in romance and pleasure along that line you want.

The Fox

Neither will I say anything here of the fox chase of the early days, for Walton gives you here in DeFuniak a scientific sportsman after that game in Dr. G. P.

Morris, who far excels any of the fox hunters in those early days. If you want to have a real booming, gushing day around DeFuniak, come on horseback, before the dawn, as many ladies and gentlemen do, and follow the Doctor out on the hills with his woods pony and pack of trained fox hounds, be there in the rush of the morning, when he turns these anxious big pups free on the trail of the cunning fox, follow him in the chase, sometimes at full speed, turning the fox from his haunts in bay on this side and then from a titi branch on the other side, keeping him out in the open on the hills and ridges, to give sport in a long chase; what new-born music in that early morn, will greet your ears on these open hills, coming from the kettle and 'bass drum beats of horses' hoofs, striking the hollow earth in perfect unison, with the

1. JOHN B. MEIGS. 2. C. D. MEIGS.

varied tuned chin music from the pack: and to be there when the cunning rascal is forced to take a tree, and see him lie across the limb of a tree, look down complacently on the scene below, as if saying, "my cunning has saved me," while the angry dogs howl and bark in fury and jump up the tree several feet, trying to reach him. The dogs are often called off, and he is left there in safety, feeling no doubt "my cunning has saved me." The Doctor never takes them except for specimens in taxidermic work as done in Palmer College.

Chapter Eighteen - The Negro in Walton

In the outset I will say without fear of contradiction that the negroes of Walton, as a whole, were the happiest and best contented people in our country; and why not? They all had good masters, were not put away off in quarters with a heartless overseer to manage them. They were never overworked, they had plenty to eat and wear, they were clothed and fed from the same well filled store house that their masters fed from; they had opportunities to procure luxuries and conveniences if they wished them, in sickness their mistress looked after them and saw that they were well cared for; her physician was theirs; their spiritual interest in the congregations were provided for. They were all Presbyterians; they held their regular weekly prayer meetings in the quarters; they never fell into the clutches of the law; they were looked after and punished by their masters for their wrong doings as they corrected their own children; and it was seldom they had to receive corporal punishment. The young white boys and girls were taught to treat the old ones with marked respect; it was always "uncle George, Aunt Millie, Uncle Sam and Aunt Harriet." And this respect was kept up by older ones, even by white people who owned no slaves. They had no burden of taxes or doctor bills to meet, or politics to discuss. The Christian spirit that prompted their owners to see that they were protected and treated right, was strengthened by a commercial interest in them.

We can't remember of the hundreds of negroes in Walton of more than two or three that ever ran away from their owners, and these cases were only for a short time, when they returned. When they took wives outside of the quarters, they were permitted to go see their wives regularly, especially every Saturday evening and stay until Monday morning; and when a swap could be made to bring them together, it was made, if the parties desired it.

My father had a young negro boy who took a wife belonging to Mr. James Evans and Evans had a boy that took a wife belonging to my father; as they lived 15 miles apart a proposition was made to make a swap and bring the men together with their wives. But neither our boy or girl would begin to consent to the swap, yet they knew that Mr. Evans was a good master. It was seldom that these changes were accepted by the parties when proposed. There was a wonderful attachment existing between master and servant in Walton, that can't be satisfactorily explained to some. They were always jealous for one another's good name and standing. No master or mistress wanted their servants talked about as trifling or worthless, neither did the servant want to hear hard things said about their masters or mistress without objecting, and they were ever ready to report against such a one. All things were claimed in common; it was our horses and cattle, our white children and black children.

Their Holidays

In the days of slavery there were only two holidays, the fourth of July and Christmas; they had these days and always a week at Christmas time. They enjoyed themselves in innocent amusements pretty much as the whites did, singing plays, the old-fashioned dances, and some borderline amusements. The men loved to trap fish and hunt. They seemed to enjoy the log rollings and corn shuckings very much; and they looked forward to these times with great interest and pleasure, and talked of the good times long after they were gone. Around the log heaps they could show their strength that they were so proud of. Around the corn piles in front of the big crib doors they could sound to their liking their great voices in the soft moonlight nights, as one of them stood on the corn heap, leading in the song, while the rest, with their great voices would follow in antiphonal choruses. When the corn was shucked two of them would take the master or overseer on their shoulders, march around the house with him, all following singing their best yodel song; then he would bring out the "little brown jug" and give them a drink, and they would sit down to a good well prepared supper, this over, they would have some sports, then go to their several quarters and have something to talk about, until the next corn shucking. So it ever went with these happy people.

The Boyds

Several years after the war. Rev. J. B. Boyd, a Presbyterian preacher and president of a female college in Monroe, Michigan, on the recommendations of Dr. Dabney, came with his family, wife and two grown daughters, and preached four months in our Presbyterian Church at Freeport. They stopped in our homes, and while with us he and his family went up and down the bay with us to Pensacola often on the mail steamer, "C. Fischer." One morning while laying at the wharf in Pensacola, we were sitting in the cabin, when the porter announced to me that there were four colored women out there that wanted to see me. I told him to bring them in, and in came the four colored women, with nice bandana handkerchiefs neatly tied around their heads, as in the old days. They all four rushed to me at once to shake my hand, or tell me "howdy," they were so really glad to see me, and I was glad to see them, it had been ten years since I had seen them. They were taken from our home when the Ashboth raid passed through Walton on to Marianna. They asked me all about the old home, the horses, cows, sheep, about old master and

1. Dr. C. B. McKinnon.   2. Chas. B. McKinnon, Jr.   3. Col. N. J. McKinnon.

mistress, and the boys and girls. They all wanted to know a lot about "Sis," if she had grown large or married, if we had gotten any of the oxen or horses or mules back. One of them said to me "I saw Mr. S. C. Cobb riding one of 'our horses' down here and I sent word to old master that she was here." I told her he got the word and got the horse too. Three of these were sisters, Caroline, the cook, Black Flora, assistant cook, Dorcas and Sindy were both field hands. I went several times to see them in their homes, found them at times in plenty, and again scant and in distress. Caroline said to me on one occasion when I went with the doctor, C. B. McKinnon, my nephew, who was doing charity practice for them, when her husband "Uncle Joe" was going out slowly with a loathsome cancer and when the larder was scant, "The war didn't do much for me in giving me freedom, you know old master always promised me when I would have as many children as old mistress had, he was going to set me free and take care of me as long as I would live. I done had that many before I was down here two months and one more since and he is a great big boy now, that makes 14 for me, and I am not free yet, and don't expect to be 'til I die." She is still alive in Pensacola.

When they had gone, Rev. Boyd and family, who sat there and observed all that was said, turned to me with a look of astonishment and said, well my dear sir, if what we have seen and heard today is a shadow of slavery in the South, we of the North have had it represented to us in a very unjust light. I have learned today and in the few months I have been in Walton more than I had learned from books in all my life. I have never seen such unfeigned attachment expressed in words and acts. Mrs. Boyd asked if one of their sisters still remained with us, the "Sis" that they were asking so much about. When I told her that that was my own baby sister, Kate, that they knew, they were the more astonished, and said with added surprise, "Well, well, did I ever dream of such wonderful attachment. It is now that I understand the story of 'old mammy love' and care for the white children, that I thought once was a myth, a dream for orators to spout on."

Aunt Caroline visited us once since we have lived at DeFuniak, her children come often. Uncle Joe, her husband, was a preacher and his last pastoral work was serving churches in Mossy Bend. The first time he came up there to his work, which was after he had been gone twenty-five years, he stopped at the old homestead with Bazy Andrews, who married one of his nieces, a young yellow negro man that had been on the place for fifteen years running my farm, and made me more clear money than any one made before or since, and when Uncle Joe saw me in the afterwards, he said to me, "I stayed at the old home with Bazy Andrews and his family from Friday night until Monday morning, and what a change there was in the 'old place,' all our cottages in the quarters done gone, the most of the stables and cribs falling in, no big cow pens full of cows, just Bazy's little one and a little bunch of cows, where there use to be several hundred to milk, — the nice peach and plum and apple orchard all gone, just the pomegranate orchard, with its yellow, brown and purple fruit, was all that looked natural, and it seemed to me farther from the 'Big House' than it use to be; the deep brick curbed well that we thought would last forever, it was tumbling in; and too, that big two story white house with its wide hallway through it, that we could see from the distant hills on that high 'Pleasant Hill' among the pines and cedar, was shut out by the scrub oaks on my way coming; and when I reached it, what a change in it, the white paint had worn off, the window panes were broken out, the most of the blinds had slammed to pieces, the long broad steps were becoming rickety; and then, there was none of you white folks in the 'Big House,' just Bazy and his family, and so many of my white people that used to be so happy in that 'Big House' were gone, gone away to Heaven; and so many of my colored people gone like our cottages that stood in the groves in the rear of the 'Big House' so many of them gone too, I hope, like my good white people, to the better land.

"Bazy and my niece Kate, and the children were just as kind to me as they could be; but Sunday, there, was the lonesomest, the saddest day I ever spent on this earth: In the evening as the sun was going down (you know in the days when you are sad the evenings are always the saddest part of the day) I went out and sat on the cow pen fence to watch them drive in the cows to be milked; I looked around me and saw the great changes on every hand, and thought of the many, many happy days I had around there, when there were so many of us living at that old home of plenty and contentment, before I had learned anything about care and want; and how they were scattered now, like sheep without a shepherd; I became so sad that I hung my head and could not keep from crying to save my life. I don't know whether I shall ever want to go back there again or not. Bazy and Kate love to stay there; they weren't old enough to remember away back like me."

Out of the many negroes on our plantation there were but three who used profane language; and they had been often reproved and were very particular when or where, they used it. Very few of them used tobacco, and my father always furnished these with it. All the farm hands had their little private crops and were allowed to sell and do what they pleased with it; they had time on Saturdays to cultivate them. Each family had their little chicken house and lot in the grove back of their cottage and marked their chickens by cutting off certain toes. My mother saw that they got plenty of milk and butter, bread, meat, potatoes and syrup, they had gardens in the plantation for vegetables. Some of the owners of slaves weighed out their rations in accordance with the United States Army regulations. Ours always wanted old missus to see it dished out to them. My father tried hiring two or three overseers and they were so unsatisfactory that he quit bothering with them; he managed them himself with a negro foreman until his son, Neill L. McKinnon, was large enough to take charge of them, and he managed them all the time until they were freed; and they thought more of him than they did of any of us.

During all these days of slavery in Walton, there was never an overt, or an attempt, to "the nameless" act committed by one of Walton's negroes. But just after the war, a young buck negro following close after the example set just before the close of the war by negro soldiers in their hellish nameless act, committed North of Euchee Anna, while passing through there on the Ashboth raid, entered, in a state of nudity, on a bright moonlight night, the home of one of the best families at Knox Hill, prompted and led on, we know, by the Euchee Anna negro soldier shame.

At that time a number of us boys who had been spared and had just returned home from the war, trying to start life anew, were holding a literary social in the academy near that home. The news soon reached us, we went in a body in hot haste, heard the horrid story, got the tracks where he leaped out of the door on his all fours, followed them to his home where he lay, feigning to be asleep, and had to drag him from his bed before we got him out of that pretense. He was identified by the lady, his feet and hands fitted exactly in the tracks made where he leaped from the door. A faithful negro boy testified that he saw him near that home just before the act, so we were satisfied beyond a doubt that he was the fiend. We went to the old men, and his former owner, while they lay in their beds asleep in the quiet night, and counseled with them. They all agreed with us that it would never do to turn the incarnate fiend at large. There were no officers or law in force in our land. These old men told us that with these conditions they could see no way but to swing him up; but they said too, "It is our opinion that General Ashboth will have every one of you in Fort Pickens in less than 48 hours"; we thought so too, but we said with one voice and with one heart, shame be to us if we let this brute go, better far we had fallen and our bones were bleaching on some battle field rather than let such fear drive us from the proper protection of our mothers and sisters and the dear ladies of Walton, who had worked so faithfully and cheered us so heartily while at the front, and were now honoring us in defeat. We left him swinging from a limb in the forks of the public road North of "Old Knox Hill." This put a stop to any more such work in Walton unto this day. The sequel will follow.

Negroes in General

Now the truths that we have stated in reference to Walton's negro slaves, can be said in a measure to be true in general of slavery in the South. We don't pretend to claim that all slaves here had as good, considerate masters, who looked after their general interest as these, neither do we deny the charge that there were cruel, neglectful masters, who treated their slaves shamefully; but these were the rare exceptions, and not the rule. They were not treated as the Northern abolition fanatics of that day would have you believe — as "Uncle Tom's Cabin" — that book in its highly exaggerated panicy paintings, that had more to do with the flow of fratricidal blood that drenched our Southland for four years, than any other one act. In the very nature of things, these wild statements could never have been true. We ever had good wholesome state laws for the protection of slaves and these were executed about as well as any of our laws are. The commercial interest in his slaves would have held the heartless master from the treatment alleged.

Where They Settled

The most of our slaves when taken away settled in and around Pensacola and New Orleans. I have seen them in those places at work and in their homes; and say without any mental reservation. I never found that cheer and happy looking faces that I always found in their little cabin homes and in their work on the plantation. It is better with those who did not go to the cities. This, too, can be said in a measure to be true of freedom today in the South. But you say, they have now that long coveted independence and liberty that is so dear to every human creature. Yes, and the Scottish Bard makes his aged hero hunting work say,

"If I'm designed yon lordling's slave.
   By nature's law designed,
Why was an independent wish
   E'er planted in my mind."

Now, from my close observations, there was very little, if any, of this "independent wish" planted in the minds of these simple, happy people. We, and I speak in general terms, would not, if we could, have them back in slavery. We would be a happy, prosperous people today if we were freed from them, from the responsibility that rests upon us towards them, as they lie. Lazarus like. at our doors, tampered with by designing, unprincipled politicians, who care nothing for their welfare, and by soft eyed women, who know nothing whatever about their wants or how they must be treated to be happy. The world must acknowledge today that they ought to have been made wards of the government, placed to themselves like the Indians were, and looked after, rather than turned loose on us, clothed with the garments of citizenship, with the ballot unrestrained in their hands, to hold offices and make laws to govern us, a far more superior race in every respect than they, led and tampered with by a low grade of unprincipled carpet-bag officials. Wise men knew that this could never stand. It failed under the very point of the bayonet; when the fanatical abolition spirit was at its highest. And the negro ought to know by now that these moves in Congress just before every general election, by designing politicians, to give them more political power, are not for their good, but for their hurt, that it is awakening a feeling against them that has made the negro problem national, and has stirred up a race feeling against them up North, that is more bitter than any experienced in the South. For the Southern people understand them better and feel more kindly towards them. This political move with them was never in the plan of Mr. Lincoln, the shame lies with the revengeful, fanatical politicians that lived after him, and it rests as a dark ominous cloud, pressing down upon them, making them twist and wince under its reflex influence.

Would that the monumental statue of Mr. Lincoln, standing in Springfield, Illinois, today, had his mortal mind and eyes with a vision to look upon the situation of the negroes there, just as it is at this writing, and run over the country to and fro, North and South, see the negro freedman in his home, at his work, in his squalor, in his prison, and had a tongue that would tell us just what he thinks now of the situation, his condition, and of chattel slavery in the South, after nearly a half century's experience in freedom, — if his condition, physically, mentally, morally and religiously are very much bettered. This would be interesting reading, and I have no doubt but many would be astonished at his report.

We believe that the freedmen in Walton are in many respects above the average in morals and home comforts, all from early training and knowing to remain in their proper spheres. One of the colored elders of the Presbyterian Church, in his report to the Presbytery, said, "While many of my race had to go to jail, I want you white people to know that none of them were of the "old time family negroes, but are from the young, brought-in turpentine negroes."

It has been and is today, the wonder of the world, how it was that these slaves remained so loyal and true to their masters in their Southern homes on the farm, all during the four years of Civil War, that was claimed to be waged for their freedom, when they were being tampered with in so many ways, tempting them to incendiarism, to desert and go on the war path. And it will ever be to the glory of the South, through all time, that her people have gotten along so well as they have through such ordeals as have existed. The negro had as much contempt for the deserter as their masters had. We long to see them in their place and under conditions where they may enjoy this freedom and liberty in its fullest measure, without disturbing us in ours. We really think that the government ought to have divided them out in the several States of the Union. This would come nearer solving the negro problem than anything yet proposed. Time is the great arbiter of all things, the revealer of all truth. What we don't know now, we shall know hereafter.

Chapter Nineteen - Physical Improvements

In the more than two decades that intervened between the two sad epochs — 1837-1860, in Walton's history, there were wonderful advancements on every line; great thoroughfares were opened up through this territory, East and West, North and South; the roads leading from Pensacola to Tallahassee and from Freeport by Euchee Anna on to Geneva, Alabama, were established as public thoroughfares; and ferries were established on the rivers along these roads, and the travel through the country increased very much. The unwieldy flat bottom boat, built by the old Scotchman at the Scotch Landing on the Choctawhatchie, that had to have a fair wind to make time, was supplanted by the round knuckled sailor, with sideboards and then center boards, that held them to the wind, so that they could be sailed right into the winds eye. The "Richmond" was replaced by the "Henry Etta," the "Dodo" by the "Lady of the Lake." Instead of being three or four weeks on a trip to Pensacola and back, it could be made easily in one week. The barges on the Choctawhatchie River were followed by the steam boats that found watery graves in that river. The "Julian" — the 8th of January — the "Mary Clifton" and the "New Boston" that old Captain Berry and John B. Croft brought out here. When they entered this river it was as nature left it, and there was a ready snag for every boat to hang on that tried to navigate its waters. Freeport was established, and regular weekly trips were made from there to Pensacola by sail boats. And the Valley Scotchmen found it much easier to haul their products to Freeport and get their merchandise in return, than to pole their boats up the river to the Stories and Scotch Landings: so commerce was being increased.

Some may ask where did the trade come from that kept a boat running on this line once a week? There was a plenty of it, and it increased as the years went by. There was the abundant product of the farm through the fall and winter months. There were the chickens and eggs in abundance all the time, dried venison, the fatted lamb, the pig, the goat, tallow, raw hides, beeswax, salt fish, honey, deer skins, bear's and panther's skins, furs, and the gopher.

The large framed Valley Church took the place of the age-old hewn log church; and they have now a stationed minister and the word preached to from three to four hundred people regularly on the 1st and 3rd Sabbath in every month. The other Sabbaths were given to mission work, — and this order has followed unto this day. The Knox Hill Academy with its advanced education, takes the place of the little log school houses that dotted our country, and it is doing its finest work. Young men and young ladies are being launched out on life's sea for a higher and a better work.

What a prosperous, blessed country! What a happy appreciative people! The marvel of the passer-by. Happy in their homes, in their families; their slaves contented in their homes and multiplying. — up to this time only four of our negroes had died; three of them died of senility. — Uncles George and Sam and Aunt Milley, and Esther, a young girl that died of a burn. Their granaries were overflowing, and their cattle feeding on a thousand hills. A bright blue sky is above their heads, and a carpet of green pastures at their feet. The stately oak, the nutting trees, the lofty pines with their sharp needle foliage standing in their easy natural places all about. How readily these could have joined in with the Psalmist in his song of the harvest home, that issued later in the song of the reapers, "Thou crownest the years with thy goodness. Thy paths drop fatness; they drop upon the pastures of the wilderness and the little hills rejoice on every side. The pastures are clothed with flocks, the valleys also are covered over with corn; they shout for joy, they also sing!"

The Earliest Schools

These pioneers knew the value of an education. They sought strenuously from the beginning to procure good, available teachers. They dotted the valley with little round log school houses, with floors and seats made of puncheons, and a heavy puncheon or huge slabs resting on pegs in the side of the house for a writing table, with half of the log in front of this table cut out, the full length of the table, to serve as a window to let the light in for the scribes. The cracks between the logs were never ceiled, all left open. There was a stick and clay chimney in one end for the winter fires. There were no such things as steel pens in those early days. The goose quill was used altogether, and in selecting a teacher one of the prerequisites was to see that he had a good pen knife, and that he could make a good pen and set a good copy. If he passed in these, he generally passed in all. The ink used was home-made and was generally pressed from the poke berries. There was a school at the Ridge, at Knox Hill, Valley Church, Euchee Anna, Mossy Bend, Hickory Springs and at Colonel McKinnon's "Old Place," — he kept a school there for a while for his and his neighbors' children. Mark A. Cook taught this school and it was under his pedagogical skill that the writer learned his "A, B, C's." He wrote a beautiful hand and could make a good pen.

Professor Henry taught at Knox Hill, Rev. Robinson at Valley Church. Henry taught too, at Euchee Anna and several other places. Major J. M. Landrum, father of our Dr. Landrum, taught at Euchee Anna. Dr. A. D. McKinnon at Mossy Bend. These were considered pretty fair teachers for those times, but these soon found better places, in the ministry, at the forum and in medicine. Then there came a class of "board-arounds-with-the-children-teachers." These got poor pay, and gave poor "teach." They were pretty much after the order of Ichabod Crane of Sleepy Hollow. The most of the pupils had to walk three and four miles to these schools. What a stir now if there is a mile to tramp to our better schools.

Chapter Twenty - John Newton, the Teacher

Now, there was a better day coming in education for these anxious people. Honest seeking after knowledge will be rewarded. "We must educate — we must educate or we must perish," was their motto. Six years before McLendon and his party made their way on the Indian trail to "Sam Story's" camp at the "Old Place," there was a boy born, — April 33, 1814, near Pittsburgh, Pennsylvania, to educate their generations. His parents died when he was quite small. He commenced working about from place to place where he could get schools to go to, when he was only large enough to carry drinking water to the laborers in the fields. Schools were quite scarce in that 'far West' country at that time; but he worked and went to school when he could; and worked himself into Amherst College, Massachusetts, when he was quite a young man. When he was through there, he came down into North Carolina among the old Scotch people and taught his first school for them. Then he, like most young men of that day, goes farther West, to Arkansas and then leaves Arkansas for Florida, intending to go to Tampa,— "Man proposes, but God disposes." He drifted into Pensacola and took in the town, and in a little while, in a quiet way, without obtrusion, as none but he could do, learned all about that city, its people and surroundings. This was in the fall of 1848. He learned through old Dr. Brosnaham and other Spanish merchants there, of the Choctawhatchie Country and the Scotch settlers in the Euchee Valley, and their efforts to educate, getting his information of this country and its people from the same source that McLendon got his from, nearly three decades before, but to find a different people or nation. And these merchantmen cited him for further or fuller information, as they did McLendon, to those in charge of a produce market boat, that made regular weekly trips up the bay. But when they introduced him, on arrival of the schooner, to the men in charge, instead of their being tall, stout, red faced men that they introduced McLendon to, they were two pale faced young men. Dr. A. D. McKinnon and Captain C. L. McKinnon, in charge of the schooner. These merchantmen gave the valley people a good sendoff in introducing this young prospector to these young boatmen. This is in substance what they said, — "Mr. John Newton, these are young McKinnons, sons of one of our up the bay customers for many years. Mr. Newton is an educated man, has taught school some, we would like to retain him in our town, but there is no college or high school here, in fact there is such little interest taken here among our heterogeneous peoples, we didn't feel that we, like we are, could encourage him to stop with us. We told him of our many Scotch friends in the Valley and that these people were very much interested in education, that they are always inquiring after better teachers, and that we did not believe he could go among a better or a more intelligent people. — a people who would take good care of him and know how to appreciate worth." and they asked them to take charge of him and give him such information about the country and peoples as he would like to know. They had him go on board the schooner "Henrietta" with them. He soon took in the situation there, asked several intelligent and pointed questions about the way, the people and the country, and arranged to sail with them early the next morning. On good time they loosed from the wharf and with a fair wind they were soon across Pensacola Bay, doubled Town Point, and headed up Santa Rosa Sound with a

Rev. John Newton

good stifif wind, and as they glided through the beautiful clear waters of the Sound and Narrows, with the mainland on the left, with its green grass and stately pines, and Santa Rosa's Island on the right, with its white sands protecting them from the surging waters of the gulf, the young Newton, like all lovers of nature's works that are fresh from His hands, untarnished by man, was much pleased, yes, more than pleased, he was charmed with its beauties on every hand, as they sailed by. And it was then he had a desire for a home by the sea shore along these clear protected waters, where his eyes could feast upon these beautiful green-thatched mounds, and hear the murmur of the great waters as they were checked up by these white sands; that was never satisfied until in years afterwards, when he built him a home, a lovely home in a grove on the mainland along the quiet waters of the Narrows, nearly opposite the Ladies' Walk on the island, and called this home "Mary Esther" for his wife and daughters.

They left these friendly waters and entered the more turbulent Choctawhatchie Bay, passed through this and up the Four Mile Creek, a little ways to the commercial town of Free Port, On the next evening my brothers carried him up with them to our father's, Colonel McKinnon, ten miles away on the valley at the "Old Place" and left him in his charge.

Chapter Twenty-One - Medley in their Physique and in Attaining Aims

It is well to note here the medley of similarities and dissimilarities in the making up, the aims, and the information gained, that led McLendon and Newton to the same country to carry out their purposes in life. The one was a stout, brawny, middle aged man of Scotch extraction, from the heart of the South, — the other a slender, fragile young man of Puritan extraction, from the heart of the North, — one has a common school education, the other a collegiate, — in faith they are both Presbyterians, and are pioneers, the one in the physical realm of nature, the other in the domain of the mental, the intellectual. They both come to the same place, the Land of Flowers, Pensacola, and receive information from the same source, the Spanish merchants and market boats that led them to the same locality, the "Old Place," — the first coming 28 years before the latter, on a trail way over land — the latter on God's long prepared road, a water way; the information from the market boat, that led the first directly on his trail way to the "Old Place" was received from red faces, aborigines. That received from the market boat by the second that led him directly on his water way to the "Old Place" came through the pale faces, sons of a pioneer.

When they finish up their work here, and feel that they are not appreciated, and want more "elbow room," the first turns his face to the West and goes by water never to return again: the second, like him, turns his face towards the farther West, but goes over land; and at the call of many friends, returns to finish up his work, and now sleeps in a grave overshadowed by his great work. Quite a mixture of times and of ways and of means and of purposes to the same end — education, in the physical cultivating in the mental, in the moral.

The young Newton remained with the Colonel from Friday night until the Sunday morning next. The Col. was much pleased with his conversation, his learning and his manners. He was 5 feet, 6 inches high, and weighed 110 pounds — was straight and slender, had large round head, covered with a heavy coat of dark hair, that never thinned; he had very large deep grayish blue eyes, — remarkable admixture in colors — marvellous eyes, shaded with heavy eyebrows, and protected by long eyelashes; these flashy, piercing eyes, rolled searchingly beneath a prominent forehead, and lit up a dark sallow complected face. You could but be impressed in his presence; he was very prepossessing in his quiet way; away from him, you could hardly point out the striking features that impressed you. On Sabbath morning the Col. took him to the Valley Church, I will let Mr. Newton tell of his introduction there; I heard him tell it often with delight. "It was a bright sunshiny day, but pretty cold. There were quite a number of old Scotch elders and others in their substantial home-spun jeans, suits of blue and dark brown; some sitting on the long door-steps basking in the sunshine, while others stood around them under and leaning against the great oaks that stood in front of the church. The Col. introduced me to all of them, telling them where I was from and how I came. I received a handshake welcome that I rarely met with in any other country. I met there Archibald McCallum, Daniel McLean, Daniel Campbell, John Gillis, several McDonalds, and a host of other Macks. After the hand-shake, some of them resumed their seats on the steps, among them was Archibald McCallum, whose fingers were drawn with the rheumatism, and he sat resting his hands on his knees, and talked to me. In a little while there walked up a stout, chunky, jolly looking man, his florid face covered with smiles and contentment. The Colonel introduced him to me as Elder Daniel S. McLean, who gave me the same hearty greeting and hand-shake, accompanied with words of welcome. He then went around and shook hands with all the rest and inquired after their welfare. When he came to McCallum sitting on the steps, he said, 'And how do you feel today, Archie?' 'O, I feel badly, badly.' Donald S. replied in his broad Scotch brogue, saying, 'Pshaw! there is nothing the matter with you, Archie; Arch, you have just got the hypo.' Archie straightened himself up a little and said, 'You are a liar, you are a liar, "Chunky;" you are a liar, sir!' All understood the joke and seemed to appreciate it, laughing heartily, especially "Chunky;" and I thought the good old soul would split his sides laughing." "Chunky" no doubt felt that he had made a ten strike in taking that joke on his friend and neighbor, Archie." It no doubt seemed strange to the young Presbyterian collegiate to see old Elders taking such rough jokes on each other in front of the church on the Sabbath day, but he soon learned to understand them, and that their quaint way of expressing themselves was with no irreverent meaning. This little episode calls to mind a clipping that came to my hands a few days ago, and I give it here with due deference and reverence to all to bring out further the true Scotch-Irish characteristics of their kin that went up into the mountains, when they came to the valley.

"KENTUCKY, FAIR LAND, famed for heroic men, lovely women, horses, whiskey and lavish hospitality, from whence came the McDowells, the Aliens and Harrisons, men who have fertilized the Nation with their genius, culture and blood. Col. E. C. McDowell, in describing the traits of the less favored citizens of Kentucky, the mountaineers, (diamonds in the rough) mentions a characteristic mountaineer from his State, Jim Mullens, a Corporal in Col. McDowell's command during the Civil War. Jim, like his kin, always used strong expressive language. After the war, Jim got religion and returned to his mountain home to preach and exhort. In one of his addresses to a Sunday School class he urged the boys to live right and tote fair. In closing his appeal to the class he said:

So live each day.
That you can look every damned man
In the face and say,
Go to Hell.

Poor Jim died last year. His Sunday School Class buried him and placed a Stone over his tomb with the following epitaph:

HERE LIES JIM MULLENS, AGED 66 YEARS,
He did his damdest,
He could do no more.
"For of such is the Kingdom of Heaven."

An honest tribute from friendly souls who expressed their appreciation for the departed as best they could."

Chapter Twenty-Two - Newton the Knox Hill Teacher

After the sermon was preached that day they held a conference and it was agreed that they would meet the next day at the Henry School house, that stood near a spring N. E. of the Morrison place at Old Knoxhill, and several hundred yards N. W. of where the Academy was built. The Campbells, McLeans, Gunns, Morrisons, Gillises, McCaskills, McPhersons, and McDonalds, were well represented in that meeting, and they arranged then and there for John Newton to be their teacher and for him to commence in the little Henry school house with the understanding that a better house would be built out of the best material at hand. The school commenced right away. And a good sized split log house was built on the top of the hill, well-proportioned and far ahead of any building of its kind in the country; and it was furnished with single desks and black boards. The school was moved in a little while into this building. In a year or two the school improved so that the building would not accommodate the school, and a large two-story frame building was put up in front of the log building. One could stand in the upper story of this building and see the smoke of the steamers as they moved up and down the winding stream of the Choctawhatchie, — could see the contour of Oak and Orange Hills over the river thirty miles away in Washington County, like two little twin mountains asleep in each other's embrace.

Chapter Twenty-Three - School in Center of Valley

This old Knoxhill in the center of the Valley is one of the most beautiful elevated places in the county, commanding a splendid view in every direction, that took in the beauties of nature in the Valley. The very ideal of a natural place for a school or college. This new building was nicely painted and ceiled, with black-boards set in the walls. Great maps of both hemispheres, seven feet square, hung upon the walls in the back of the building, and on either side of the teacher's rostrum; on the wall was all sizes of recitation maps. The two rooms were well furnished. This building presented quite an imposing appearance to the passers-by from the public road, as they went to and fro from Pensacola to Tallahassee. Completed and furnished, the school was moved in and went on without a jar, until there was from 85 to 100 regular pupils matriculated. The larger students were put upstairs on their trusted good behavior; the little people were kept below under the watchful eye of the teacher. When there was trouble above, those giving it were brought down and given seats in the front of the lower room, which often happened when they got ofT of their dignity. The steady rapid growth and the results in education became the wonder of West Florida and South Alabama. Many would come to see the Knox Hill Academy and the wonderful teacher. The other schools mentioned that dotted the Valley melted away under its shining light. Those that lived too far away to send their children from home and were able to board, sent them, and those not able, moved nearer by. But a great many of the pupils, especially the larger ones, were transient boarders, from Pensacola, Vernon, Marianna, Quincy, and Geneva, Alabama, and some from Georgia and from the wealthy farmers around these towns. It was a well advertised school by its work, and had many ardent friends outside of Walton, — Judge Wright of Pensacola, Dr. Philips and Tom White of Marianna, Wm. J. Keyser and Col. George W. Walker of Milton. Walker spent a great deal of his time in Walton and would often visit the school and hear the recitations and published its praise where he went, as the best school he had ever entered. He was, at his own volition, a live traveling, working agent for the school as long as he lived; and knew more of its worth than any outside man. The people from a distance learning of the strict discipline in the school, and the wholesome management of bad boys, and that the teacher would keep them in their places at all hazards, would bring their boys and girls from other schools, where they were giving trouble and put them in this school. These pupils made teaching burdensome and hard on the teacher and the other pupils, until they were broken in, and the trustees often protested against taking them, but he invariably felt that it was his duty to take them; and we don't know of his having to expel a single pupil during all the years that he taught here. His motto was, "You must learn and obey." This motto was carried out strictly to the letter and spirit, for his was an advanced education from the start, lessons from and outside of books — lessons from nature — how to protect dumb brutes, and the little birds and growing trees.

The school was a Presbyterian Synodical, religious, educational institution. He opened his school every morning by the school reading the scriptures, singing a hymn, and prayers. He had recitations every Wednesday evening, lessons in the Shorter Catechism and every one had to recite these lessons as promptly as they did their other lessons. There were Methodist, Baptist and Catholic, as well as Presbyterians, in this school. Some of the Catholic boys protested, saying "their church didn't believe in the teachings of this Presbyterian book, and their parents did not want them to study it." He said the book was not made by Presbyterians, but by men wisely chosen in the most cultured age in all our history, and from the different faiths, and it was only called Presbyterian because they believed it was right; and it made no difference whether they believed in it or not, it would do them no harm, but good, to know it, and they "must" know it; and most of their parents rather than take them out of the school had them to remain and learn.

Laboratory

He had fitted up a laboratory that would have done credit to many of our colleges today. The split log house was used as the laboratory building for experiments in chemistry and physics, giving the school illustrative lessons once a week, which were looked forward to with much interest for enjoyment. He got up a good big, well assorted library with many readable uplifting books. He segregated the old blue back speller, and kept none but the popular text-books of the day. He had, once a week, declamations, compositions and oral and written discussions on subjects that he would name. He had oral critics from the school on the exercises of that day, and one selected to have a written one to be read at the following week's exercises. In these exercises he took great pains to instill patriotism into the young minds and hearts of the pupils. He had the big American speaker, and would have the larger pupils to learn and deliver with feeling, the stirring speeches of Patrick Henry, Clay, Calhoun, Webster and others, on love of country.

Chapter Twenty-Four Fourth - July

On the 4th of July he had the older boys — the graduating class, to get up a big barbecue and had them to prepare and deliver original patriotic speeches under his correction, and had one of them read the Declaration of Independence. He procured Washington Polk, an old noted drummer, to beat the drum for the school to march by, and one to blow the fife, which made up the instrumental music for the occasion. Pretty much all Walton were seated under or about that great brush arbor, and the school seated on the platform, orators in front. The vocal music was led by Dr. Kirkpatrick, who led the school in ringing tones, opening with "America." Then the Declaration of Independence was read in a loud, distinct voice. Then Young America — the Academic orators, one after another, stepped to the front of the stage in their order and made the woods ring with their patriotic orations. After the speaking, a sumptuous well-cooked barbecue dinner was served after the regular 4th of July style, — but in decency and in order, for there was a "manager" there. This was a grand enjoyable occasion in front of the old Academy, and under the auspices of the graduating Academics, overlooked by their teacher. This was the first 4th of July celebration of the kind in Walton, and we may say even the best. Mr. Newton was very fond of music, but had no voice of melody to make it. He would always raise the morning hymns in opening his school, until he had gotten some of the boys trained for it, — but the boys said he raised them all to the same tune, "There is a Happy Land." He understood the rudiments of music and taught sight-reading to the school. He was the first to introduce the blind notes in Walton.

He was very anxious to procure a good music teacher for his school. Finally there came this Dr. Kirkpatrick, who was a master in vocal and stringed instrumental music; and he secured him to give his school lessons in reading and vocal exercises once a week in the evenings; he had no instrument save the violin, and he used this in assisting in the pitch: we all enjoyed this very much, especially when he would give us some lively music at the close.

In the course of time there was a piano introduced in the settlement, then another and another. Then he sent off and procured the services of a young lady graduate to teach the young lassies in this school and arranged for the use of a piano.

He taught nine months in the year, in terms of three months, commencing the first of January, giving a month vacation between each term. At the end of each term he had a public examination in all the studies; and a public exhibition in declamations, essays, debating and dialogues; all had to take some part in these. On one of these occasions he had his music teacher to drill the music class in some familiar short pieces or easy exercise, to play on the stage on exhibition day. She protested strenuously, saying that they had only been taking lessons five months and weren't proficient enough in music to play in public. But he insisted, said there would not be much expected of them and that they would be that much farther on at the close of the next term. The lassies went to him and plead with him, telling him that they knew so little that it was too embarrassing for them to expose their ignorance in public. He told them there would be no one there able to criticize them except their teacher, and that they must practice and do their best, and that was all that was asked of them. So teacher and pupils realized whom they were dealing with, and there was no use in trying to turn down his will; and so they went to work practicing with all the skill they could summons. The piano was put in place the day before the entertainment, and they had several rehearsals in his presence and he was much pleased with their little pieces.

Early in the evening of the day before the entertainment, it was learned that a lady professional from Milton was up to enjoy the musical feast of the next day — a Mrs. John G. McLean. This, of course, cast a gloom over the musical department of the day. The thought of being criticized by a professional, and she a lady critic. In the early next morning to add to the gloom, the word came that their young music teacher was sick and could not be there, — of course she was, enough to make her sick. So the young music pupils felt relieved and went to the principal and told him the news and asked him if they would not have to abandon the musical part, as they had no one to direct them. He very emphatically said, "No, I'll direct you, you all know your pieces and must play them," and when the time came, they did play them, and the professional said they all did well for the short time they had been taking lessons. Yet the most of them declared they were so embarrassed when they sat at the piano they were not able to separate for a moment one key on the board from another, that to them it was a streak of black and a streak of white, that it was through the force of habit or practice that they struck the right keys. The old hero carried his point and the people were pleased as never before, so you can get at an idea of what kind of a teacher he was from this little incident. The lady professional was gallanted to the piano by Mr. Newton, and her white fingers galloped over the keys, touching the white and the black here and there, rolling out such stirring music as was never heard in Walton before. It was then and there that we knew what a piano was, and how much music there was in one. This was another crowning day in Knox Hill Academy work, and it introduced many another piano into Walton.

Mr. Newton advanced pupils in his Academic course, high enough to enter, on a rigid examination, the regular sophomore class at Oglethorpe College, in its best days and highest curriculum. He advanced young men that went direct from his school to the study of law at home. He prepared a class of brilliant young men for the law school at Lebanon, Tennessee, who graduated with honors and bid fair to be ornaments to the profession, and was an honor to Walton and our State; but that cruel war claimed the most of them. One of them had attained the rank of Colonel, others Majors and Captains, before they fell on the bloody field.

Mr. Newton was a natural pedagogue, he knew just how to get to his pupils' minds and hearts. It took him but a little while to size up a boy or girl and know what was in them. He was a wonderful judge of human nature. He taught eight hours regularly every school day, and did a great deal of extra teaching in the mornings and evenings and at noons. He commenced each quarter's term on Wednesday morning, so that the pupils from a distance would not have to travel on the Sabbath to be present at the beginning. He held Sabbath school every Sabbath evening in the Academy, he was superintendent and required all the pupils to be present, unless they had a good excuse. It was a very interesting school. He went in the morning to church at the Valley and sat in the gallery in the midst of the boys. No boy was allowed to fight, swear or chew tobacco. You would never see a girl or boy sitting in the school room with dirty hands and faces or finger nails in mourning. If their clothes were coarse or common, they had to be worn right. He not only kept close to his pupils through the day, but he made regular rounds after supper to see if they were preparing their early morning lessons. If any or all of the class failed at the regular recitation, he stayed in with them at noon or in the evening until the lessons were properly recited. I have known him to stay in with pupils until he had to light the candles for them to study by; and would often have to go with the smaller ones a mile or two. who were afraid to go home in the dark. When he exhausted all other means to make them "learn and obey." he never failed to use the rod freely. Many complained at his whipping too severely, but it amounted to nothing. I never knew of one taking his child from school or of a pupil resisting his chastisement, and it came often and severe, irrespective of size, age. sex or previous conditions. In his last years of teaching he used the rod sparingly, learned a better way. when he had fewer and better scholars. If you sent your child to school to him three months, you 'knew he had learned. I know of dull boys, almost stupid, of whom he made first rate scholars, who would never have amounted to anything at the common schools. You would hear complaints at his severe discipline, but never at his "not teaching their children well." You hear the unrestraining parents of today and the unrestrained pupils of this generation saying, "If he had treated one of my children that way I would have gone for him without gloves," "I would run away from school and live in the woods before I would study and be treated that way,"— and all such talk, when we know they would have submitted as we did under similar conditions, knowing that he was making of them better sons and daughters. I heard lots of the boys swear that when they grew up they would whip him out of sight, and I have seen these same boys grow up into manhood in his presence, honoring him above all other men with their praise. See that those over whom you have control will do their whole duty and they will love and respect you.

He often laughed at little incidents that occurred in the school, and the boys were always ready to laugh out with him, they said it helped keep off the blues; but sometimes they missed and laughed at the wrong time, and got a thrashing.

One declamation evening he called on a bright little red headed, black eyed boy to read his composition. He jumped up and read aloud,— "The Rabbit.

The rabbit has long ears, big eyes and a white tail about one inch short. "Long, John," said Mr. Newton. "No, sir, it is short," and read right on. That short retort brought down the school, and brought no chastisement.

The boys used to say they had signs by which they could divine whether the day was going to be an easy or a hard day, — if he came whirling his walking cane in his right hand (he was left handed) or lifted his hat from his head and ran his fingers through his heavy head of hair, or if he used the Lord's prayer in opening the school, they knew to be on their "p' and q's." The better sign for a good day or a bad day would have been to ask ourselves, did we employ the evenings in preparing our morning lessons, or did we waste them.

Chapter Twenty-Five - Lessons Outside of Books

He had an aversion to eccentricity or oddity in manners. The roll being called, the pupils all answer "here," except a freshman from some little town who answers "present." "Sam, the roll is called to learn who are here, — "here" is a proper answer; you answer "present," after this you answer "here," like the rest, and don't be odd and conspicuous, and you stand in prayer with the rest." To the rich farmer's boy with his kids on in school, "Will, pull off those gloves. Cats with gloves never catch mice." To the boy or girl with a sheet of paper written on one side and thrown into the waste basket, he would lift it up and say "Willful waste makes woeful want."

You would never find the wolfish winds chasing waste paper around his grounds. This was before this wasteful "Tablet Age."

To the boy sticking his knife in one of the young trees on the grounds, "Why do you do this — how do you know but that this water that follows out the incision of your knife is not tears of the tree, as real as those that would flow from your eyes were I to lacerate your body with this cane? Do this no more lest I make you realize what tears are." "He that planteth a tree is a benefactor to the human race." The boy that threw a stone at the little bird was called in and given lessons on ornithology: "He that would ruthlessly place his foot upon a worm, I would strike his name from my list of friends."

He was a great friend to dumb brutes. He loved the singing birds, the lowing herds, the bleating sheep and gave wholesome lessons on their treatment. But he hated the "grunting hog" and would chase him from his grounds. He would not eat a bit of them and we thought he was a Jew on this account for a long time. He had no carnivorous appetite. He lived on coffee, butter, biscuit, eggs, and now and then chicken and a little beef and fish.

Let Every Tub Stand on its Own Bottom

The quarterly entertainment is coming around; two lassies of fourteen summers feel that they must have help, other than their own to do justice to their class and age. They seek this help from a young lawyer, a graduate of the Academy, they ask him to let the help he gave them be in as plain, simple language as he could express himself in. They received the promised help in due time; read, studied it over well, and met for consultation. One was very outspoken and said 'T can not use mine at all, I don't see where I could wedge in an idea that would pass as my own. When the teacher will see these well rounded up rhetorical flowery sentences and big words, he will know at once that it was not my production. What are you going to do about yours?" "Well," said the other in a more thoughtful mood, "I am thinking of getting some one to reduce it to its 'lowest terms,' and may be then I can work on it and get enough of my thoughts in it to make it pass." It is enough to say they fell back on their own resources and did not attempt to pass it on to their teacher, which was the better.

His Aesthetic Nature

He was exceedingly tasteful in his home, in his grounds and in his dress. Though they be ever plain, they had to be in decency and in order; and he impressed this virtue on his school. He was a great admirer of curbed fashion, or style in dress, especially with the ladies. He encouraged these tastes in his school: he wanted his lady pupils to have their Scotch plaid dresses in good style, in good taste, and their head wear in good shape. He was a subscriber for "The Ladies Bazaar," a ladies fashion journal with the latest Paris styles, and instructions for cutting, fitting and measuring, the first of its kind introduced in Walton. He took great pride in passing it around among his lady pupils and ladies of the Valley which brought about a neatness and style that was pleasing to him, a grace in fashion's beauty that made Walton's daughters more winsome.

His Ethical Nature

He never liked to discuss enigmatical points in bible history with the caviler who cared nothing about the "weightier matter of the law," who cared to know nothing about the salvation of his soul; but rather avoided such a discussion. He was passing down Choctawhatchie Bay with a Jew who was loaded with catchy questions and thought himself real smart. Mr. Newton turned him down several times, answering him according to his folly, and tried to avoid him. After a while he thought he had him cornered and said to him, "Mr. Newton, there is one thing about the bible that always bothered me, 'Cain went into the land of Nod, and there he knew his wife; now where did his wife come from?" Mr. Newton replied. "There is but one thing that bothers me about that marriage. Cain was a very, very wicked man, killed his own dear brother, and I am afraid he didn't make a very good husband." He boarded the steamer "C Fischer" at Mary Esther as a passenger for Pensacola. It was a very cold windy day, there were quite a lot of passengers on board, he entered the cabin and found them all seated around the heater, not a vacant chair. A young man from up the bay, on his way to a medical college bounced up out of his seat, called to him to take the seat he had vacated for him. Mr. Newton turned to the seated crowd and said, "I have traveled several times from the lakes to the Gulf and from ocean to ocean and this is the first time on the public thoroughfares of our country I ever saw a young man surrender his seat to an older man." Quite a compliment to that young man; and let me say here, that young man is being blessed bountifully in this world's goods.

When he lived at the Narrows he got on board of a schooner at Mary Esther to come up to Freeport; after they had sailed away up to the head of the Narrows, he looked down into the boat's cabin and saw several passengers sitting around a table with their jug, smoking, playing cards and using profane language; he quietly asked the Captain to drop his anchor and put him out and he would walk back home; that the night was too cold for him to stay on deck all night; and the fume was too much for him in the cabin. When the anchor was dropped the men came from the cabin; met him on deck while they were getting the skiff boat ready. They behaved very respectfully in his presence. When the Captain returned, these men still standing on deck, asked him why he had abandoned the ship? He told them who he was and why he had gone back home. They exclaimed, "We are ashamed of ourselves, can't you call him back, it will be away in the night before he reaches his home." "Yes," said the Captain, "for it is a six mile walk, but there is no use for us to try to stop him." These men told the writer afterwards that they were ashamed to go to his office in passing Mary Esther.

He was teaching, and we hope this pointed lesson did them good. A young man in no good condition entered his home puffing away at his pipe and said, "How are you all today?" "We are all very well, but we will not be so long if you keep on puffing that pipe." The young man's father told me of the insult and was very much incensed at it, said he had befriended him during the war at the Navy Yard when he was passing through the lines, and he was going for him when he met him for treating his son so badly and that his son was going to give him a piece of his mind the next time he met him. I told the father that that was no insult, that was his friendly way of correcting the young man, that he was just teaching. The young man passed there often, said nothing and smoked nothing, and that was the last of it.

Some of the Effects of His Teaching

In passing from Mary Esther to Euchee Anna, he stopped a while in Freeport. They had no preacher or church building there and they asked him if he would not stop on his return and preach for them in the school house. He kindly consented to preach for them on the coming Sabbath. They were glad, and published it. He came promptly, had a pretty good congregation, preached, and his congregation went to their own houses. "Rev. Newton went unto the mount of Olives." No one asked him home with them. There was no hotel in the place at that time. It was all business. He remained in the school house where he had preached, reading his bible until he got cold; and as there was no heater in the house, he went out and rolled some small logs together and gathered up chunks of lightwood, and soon had a good fire and warmed himself. Mr. Rossin, the poorest man in Freeport, but the Good Samaritan, saw the light of his fire when it was dark and went out and had him to come to his house and lodged him for the night. Some of his friends who would have been "sure" to have asked him home with them forgot about the preaching and were not there. Now, what a sore rebuke this was to those who forgot the assembling of themselves together on the Lord's day for worship, and they sorely felt it, too, and to those who cared not to entertain strangers, these will never entertain angels unawares. He was teaching by object lessons.

He was wanting a good milk cow and asked a friend of his in Freeport if he would purchase one for him. He said he thought he knew of one that would suit him. So he left the money with him to make the purchase. The cow was sent down by the friend's freight boat. In getting her on the wharf at Mary Esther, through carelessness and indifference, they broke her leg and injured her in other ways, rendering her worthless as a milker. Mr. Newton, of course, was much displeased at the wanton carelessness and indifference of the Captain and his men in handling the cow. He wrote a short spicy letter to his friend about her treatment and condition; in the main to have the Captain and men corrected. In answer his friend wrote, "I bought the cow, fed her a week here, put her on board of the boat, sent her down and put her out on the wharf for you, and now you don't seem to be satisfied." The following was the reply, "You boast you bought and fed the cow for me a week. I gave you the money to make the purchase, and if the milk did not pay for the feed it must have been a poor purchase. You boast that you put her on board of schooner, shipped her and delivered her on the wharf. I have always understood that it was the duty of a merchantman, owning a freight boat, to load and unload freight. I paid the freight as charged and you made the delivery, such as it was. Now you seem to think you have been a great benefactor to the old cow, come down and knock her in the head, get her out of her misery, and finish up the good work." This closed the correspondence; but there was a little feeling left. Some time afterwards his friend was passing down on his boat to Pensacola. It was in the night time when they passed Mary Esther, and knowing that Mr, Newton never liked for his friends to pass without calling, he said to this same Captain of his boat, as he left the schooner in skiff boat to go out to the office, "If you tell Mr. Newton I am aboard, say to him that I would have gone out to see him, but I was not feeling well." The message was delivered. When the Captain returned, Mr. Newton would go out to the schooner with him, notwithstanding it was a dark, cold, windy night, and the captain tried to hinder him on this account; but he would go, saying, "Shall I have a friend who is sick and sends me word that if he had not been sick he would have come to see me, and I, who am well, refuse to go to see him, and he so close by and so easily reached? I will go and see him." He went, and there was never more the least bit of hard feelings between them. This was the fruits of respect shown.

Conductor Discharged

The Presbyterian Church that he was pastor of at Mary Esther was under the government of the Northern General Assembly. When the Assembly met at Boston, Mr. Newton went as the representative of this church. He got a through ticket from Pensacola. Beyond Atlanta the conductor forgot to call out the station where the road branched off that he was to travel, and when the conductor found out that he was on the wrong road, he talked ugly to him and made him pay full rates to where he reached his road on which his ticket was good. On his return he stopped over a day in Atlanta, went to the official railroad headquarters in person, found ex-Governor and ex-United States Senator Brown of Georgia president. He laid his cause before him. And President Brown, without further inquiries, directed his secretary to write a discharge for that conductor and to refund Mr. Newton for all the money he was out. He said to President Brown: "It was not for the refunding of the money that I stopped, but I felt it my duty to see, as far as I am able, that public officials should be made to do their duty to the public." Public officials, for their own good, should be made to do their respective duties to the public."

Respect Shown

He commanded respect wherever he went, especially among those who knew him. I remember on one occasion when he was passing through Freeport on to Euchee Anna, and was about to be left by a friend that came for him, and had been in waiting for some time, the boat that was to bring him having been belated, his friend started off, but was stopped by a call that "Mr. Newton was coming up from the dock," and as he was passing hurriedly by a store in which there were several of his old pupils, they all ran out on the street to shake hands with him in passing. And when they leisurely returned to their places in the store, each one picked up his cigar that he had respectfully and intuitively laid aside when they went out to meet him, neither knowing that the others had laid theirs down until it was observed on returning to them. Live so as the mere mentioning of your name calls for respect. There was nothing conventional or prolix in his work. His prayers were short and soul-stirring. His sermons were never longer than twenty-five minutes, but to the point. He preached a sermon that I would call an "arithmetic" sermon, that had more in it for its length than any sermon I ever heard. His voice was low and soft, but very distinct. He was very modest. Rev. R. Q. Baker, pastor of Church at DeFuniak Springs, would have him preach for him one Sabbath. He used part of the sermon on the mount, and after service he modestly remarked to a friend, "Wasn't that the best sermon you ever heard?" and said to Mr. Baker, "The next time you make me preach I'll take for my sermon the shorter catechism."

Chapter Twenty-Six - A Man of Few Words

He placed this notice to his patrons on the bulletin board, when getting ready to go to California: "Notice. Let us settle up. John Newton."

He hired a man with a horse and buggy to send him to Marianna. The horse sickened and died. This is the letter he wrote to the owner, save heading and date:

"Mr. Calhoon: "Dear Sir, Your horse is dead. John Newton." This letter was criticized by some, saying that it was lacking in sympathy. He was never lacking in this. The driver came and could tell him more about the horse than he could.

At Florida Chautauqua

He visited the Florida Chautauqua in its earliest years and was very much pleased with the entertainments and management, and made there, many new friends and acquaintances, and they were equally as well pleased with him. And when some years passed and he was coming no more and they wanted him to come, Dr. A. H. Gillette, superintendent for the management and self, sent him a complimentary ticket and sufficient funds to pay all expenses from his home and return. This was his reply to that complimentary, save heading, "Dear Dr. Gillette, Thank you and management for tickets and money. Conditions are such that I feel I ought to return same; 2nd Samuel, 19th Ch, 35 ver. Yours truly, John Newton."

When post master at Mary Esther, the citizens near there wanted another post office. The regular form was presented to him for his approval or disapproval, with a blank of several lines for remarks, the spelling was laughably bad. All the statements were correct. These were his words for the blank. "Correct except the spelling. John Newton, P. M."

After he became a minister I addressed him as Reverend. He came to my desk with an envelope in one hand and a pencil in the other, and said to me, "That is your work?" I said "Yes, sir." He drew a pencil line across the "Rev." and said, "Just plain John." I knew after that to leave off the Rev. Don't presume on titles.

Burying Ground Proposed and Improved

While living at Mary Esther, feeling that he would spend all his days there, he selected and improved a burying place on Santa Rosa Island, across from his home, on the top of one of those beautiful green thatched mounds, leaning over towards the Narrows and overlooking the Mexican Gulf, among tall pine trees. My wife and I visited the spot and thought nature had embellished the mound with its highest art. Yet he had planted other varieties of ever greens there, that seemed to know they must grow too in that white sand. I said to him, soon after the war, I got on the U. S. mail Steamer at Acqua Creek for Washington City, and as we steamed up the Potomac and when nearing Mount Vernon, the U. S. Mail Steamer commenced tolling its great bell in honor of the Father of his Country and kept it up until we were well beyond the place — that I thought it a beautiful way of showing honor to the distinguished grave; and in the days to come I would see that the U. S. Mail Steamer "C. Fischer" would do his grave like honor. He thought I had reached high up for a pattern and was claiming some lease on life. Years after this pleasantry on so solemn a question, and not a great while before he took his departure, I asked him if he still wished to be buried on the Island. He answered me in the Latin tongue: "Tempora mutantur, et nos mutamur in illis." (The times are changed and we are changed with them). "I am Hke the old Scotchman I met while in California; he lived in a new town; there were two grave yards started, one on the hill, the other in the valley. The ladies in charge of the one in the valley thought they would be the 'early birds' and drum in time for their burying ground; so they approached the old Scotchman in their modest way, and after apologizing for their seeming previousness, they explained to him the advantages of their burying place over the one on the hill. Then they asked him if he would not agree with them to be buried in the valley when he died. The old gentleman thanked them very much for their interest in his last resting place and was pleased with the advantages they had named, and would go with them to the valley, but that he had promised the other ladies some time before to go up on the "hull" with them when he died. So I have promised the daughters to go to the Valley to be buried there." I told him that I was glad it was not his modesty that drove him from the Island, 'lest we should do his grave Mount Vernon homage.

A Great Worker

He was the greatest worker I ever met; find him when or where you would, he was at work — digging at the roots of some great tree to enrich it, or to take it down by the roots (he could never stand a stump on his grounds.) Or you would find him in his study digging at the roots of some great science. I called to see him in his home in Pensacola a few years after he moved there, was directed to his study where I found him all alone digging away at a problem involving a spheroid in calculus that he said "came up in my mind to bother me and I must solve it." "Work while it is called today."

Chapter Twenty-Seven - A Man of Prayer

He was pre-eminently a man of prayer and when that hour came it was never side tracked for anything. I was in his home on a festive occasion, at a marriage, when the family prayer hour came he summoned the little merry party together, where he stood by a lamp on the mantel with bible in hand; all quiet, and standing, he said, "God has been good to us through another day, let us worship Him." He read a few verses of scripture, led in a short prayer, and we were soon gone to our play. Going down Choctawhatchie Bay together in a small sailing market boat, crowded with passengers, the wind high, rolling up waves that seemed at times too much for the little craft, we sought a quiet resting place away from the crowd in the forecastle of the little ship, where we had a long quiet talk about the past and the promises of the future, such a talk as we never had together before or afterwards. When it was getting night and about the hour for his evening worship, we sailed out of the troubled waters of the Choctawhatchie Bay into the quiet waters of the Narrows that he loved so much, he said, "The Lord has brought us through the deep waters into a quiet haven of rest, we ought to worship Him, we have been lounging about here the most of the day. let us stand for prayer." And there, standing with heads and bodies bent in the shallow forecastle, we made our evening sacrifices.

The mail steamer often had as passengers his old friends and pupils from up the bay who would never pass without calling in his home. It would often be about the time of his evening prayer, sun-down — he always ate supper soon, said "late suppers always took from the housekeepers the sweetest hours of the day, when the family ought to be sitting together enjoying the evenings." Seats would be provided for his guests in the front sitting room and the services would commence by his repeating a passage of scripture followed by those on his left, until all had repeated a verse, then he led in a short prayer, and these friends knew to have a verse ready if it was about sun down.

I was in his home in Pensacola just before his death; I asked him if he could sit up. He said "No, only as my daughters help me and they help me so cheerfully I almost feel as though I was helping myself — love makes life's burdens light." When the hour of prayer came, we gathered around his bed, he said "If the heart is right in prayer, it makes but little difference about the position of the body, we are going to worship, so each can take that attitude in prayer that they like, but I must take the attitude of lying down." He repeated a passage of scripture and the rest of us followed and then he poured out his soul in prayer to his God that he knew he was soon to meet. "The prayer of the righteous availeth much." I have written many little things about this great life and left off many big things in it — "straws show which way the wind blows."

Storm Life

We must see by now that we are dealing with a great teacher, a teacher in the school, in the home, in the community, on the public highways of life. A teacher in literature, in society, and in morality, and of the soul, a teacher in nature, animate and inanimate, and a teacher of public officials; wherever he went, whatever he did, he taught by precept and by example. Such a life must of necessity have been aggressive.

He had his share of the jars of life. He passed triumphantly under many deep, dark shadows and after the clouds rolled away, goodness still issued from his life. The old Latin dictum runs: "Poeta nascitur, non fit." The same is true of the teacher of the mind and soul, "he is born, not made."

Symbolizing Springs

There are springs on either side of his Mary Esther home issuing from the mainland on the shores of the Narrows, mingling their sweet waters with the bitter salt waters of the Gulf — that symbolize his life — notably, "Camp Walton's" and "Wheeler's Springs." Out of these, issue pure, clear limpid water. It is here that the cattle and other beasts of the wild woods come in the hot noon time to slake their thirst. It is around these that the merry warblers gather in the early morn and dusky evenings for a dip in these cool flowing springs. It is here that the fresh water sailor boy fills his water barrel with refreshing fluid as it gushes from the white pebbly sands beneath the bending tree limbs, kneeling and drinking deep at these fountains of genuine flowing waters as the thirsty literary youth drinks deep from the Pierian Spring sacred to the Muses. There the angry Gulf rolls its turbid tide over these sparkling springs, covering them, for a while, with dark bitter waters. But soon the tide turns, they are rolled away, and there they are as pure and as refreshing as though they had never been submerged in bitter darkness. So it was with this teacher's useful life in Walton. Clouds and darkness rolled above and overshadowed it; but these would soon roll away, leaving it as pure and as unsullied as though it had never been overshadowed.

His Politics

He was a born, educated abolitionist — was bold and outspoken — but never obtrusive — strange anomaly of character in this our far Southland. "But he was a man for a' that and a' that!" At that day no other Northern man could have held and expressed his views on slavery as he did and be safe in this section.

So now, even the casual reader at a glance may realize readily and understand fully his great appreciated worth as a teacher by this tolerance on the part of trustees and patrons in those eager days. So too, they can more fully appreciate Walton's Scotch Presbyterian proverbialism for advanced education.

Chapter Twenty-Eight - Contraband Books

When Mr. Newton's name was a household word in the Scotch homes, — his faithful work at its very zenith — when scholars from a distance were clamoring for board and places in the Academy, a pestiferous cloud began to gather around the old Hill, resting just above the Academy. Some flashes of lightning played around and mutterings of thunder issued from it. This ideal teacher had placed in the school library eight or ten new volumes of books that the trustees feared militated against their economic institutions. So at once these old Scotch trustees examined the books and pronounced them not suitable books for the scholars to read — that they were slightly tainted with abolitionism and must be segregated from the other library books. He met and discussed the matter with them, said "there was nothing taught in those books but what the children and their parents ought to know," and in the end he said "if the books go, I go to return no more to this hill as a teacher." After the trustees discussed and meditated long over the matter, the books went and the teacher went.

These books were "Chambers' Miscellanies." They were very readable books for young people — not deep — a little trashy — there was a vein of abolitionism running through them but nothing at all after the order of "Uncle Tom's Cabin" — something for that day, nothing for this day. I read them all, was edified, amused and don't think I was any the worse for having read them, if no better.

This action of trustees and teacher spread a gloom over education in Walton for a while that was felt throughout all Western Florida and Southern Alabama. The teacher of course, had plenty of calls. And the Academy had plenty of offers from teachers such as they were. Mr. Newton went to California and stayed a while, returned and taught at Marianna and then at Orange Hill. In the mean time the trustees were being annoyed with teachers that were so different to their old teacher, until they became thoroughly disgusted. They advertised and got one direct from Ireland who proved to be the biggest mistake of all, Rev. Robert Bell, a Presbyterian preacher, who had sat long at the feet of old "Professor Gillum." He had drunk deep at the fountain of Irish wit. He preached stirring sermons in his Irish brogue. He took charge of the school and was liked by all the pupils, especially those who did not care to learn. When his Latin and Greek classes went to him for help to read a hard sentence, he pointed them to his translation on his desk with the Latin and Greek in their regular constructed order and the translation in small letters just beneath each word; it was the same way in the mathematics. He used these in hearing recitations and they were there for the classes to use when they wanted to use them. Of course the recitations were correct and fluent so far as rendering the English was concerned; but making a dull sluggish class so far as improving the mind in working, thinking or reasoning. When it came to analyzing or parsing the sentences, or scanning the verses, they soon learned to turn his mind to some of his anecdotes until the time was up.

There was no discipline, hardly an attempt at any. He kept the school in a running down condition for three or four terms. It was so very different to the splendid discipline of Mr. Newton's school, and different in every respect, that the trustees became perfectly disgusted with him and moved him out. They began to realize what they had lost in a teacher and to fear his like was not to be had. My father determined that he would not throw away his children's time any longer with such a teacher. He sent me to Orange Hill to see Mr. Newton and arrange for board, to go to him over there. J went and found him hard at work, teaching, not in the big academy building that Rev. Porter Everett was to build for him, but in the house he commenced in, and it did seem so strange to me to see him teaching in that little house full of children; he did seem to be out of his place. I told him what I came for and to my surprise he told me that it would hardly pay for me to come then, as he did not expect to teach there much longer, and that he thought I could have an opportunity to go to him nearer my home; but for me to say nothing until things materialized. I knew that the trustees were disgusted with their mistake and felt there and then that he saw the mistake of his hasty action. I said to myself, these conditions are bringing them together. Then I would ask myself how can they come together? The trustees will not reverse their action on the books and he said he would never come back to that Hill again as a teacher. Both parties I knew were very determined when they got their minds set in a way, and then I remembered the old proverb, "Where there is a will there is a way." And the cloud began to roll away.

In a little while the two school buildings were moved to New Knox Hill where it now stands, two miles to the north — ostensibly (it seemed to me) to be more in the center of the community. It could not have been in a more central place than where it stood, if they had considered the Mossy Bend settlement; but Bruce Creek intervened. The two-story frame building was cut down to a single story. Mr. Newton did not want again, any of his pupils above his head, and they all agreed that they did not want any more big schools as they had been having and the big log building was placed close by and in near reach of the Academy to be used for the little people and his assistants; and a small room was built onto the rear of the Academy for a laboratory.

While this locality with its inviting shades of oak and other nutting trees standing thick on the grounds was beautiful for situation, it is nothing to compare in picturesqueness with Old Knox Hill.

In Jan. A.D. 1859 the school was opened in the new place and dedicated anew to the work. This dedication had the reflex of the old, as did the dedication of Zerubbabel's temple. While the nearby ones and the young people rejoiced at the coming of the new, the older pupils who remembered the glories of the old sorrowed when they remembered its stateliness as it stood overlooking all on the dear old Hill.

More Scholars

Notwithstanding both trustees and teacher desired a small school, it is marvelous to tell that in just a little while the school was as full as it was when he left Old Knox Hill. The pupils from the towns and country that had attended the old would not be turned away from the new, knowing that they would have the same good teacher. So the school filled up to overflowing without a word of advertising.

The dark cloud that had overspread the Academy moved away or rather the Academy moved from under it. There is a bright sky above now, education has taken the lead again in Walton, and there is fair sailing ahead.

Chapter Twenty-Nine - His Home

Before the school commenced, at a short distance south of the old building and well back from the public road, in the midst of a grove of great spreading trees that extended to the road, there went up a modest little cottage to be the home of the teacher. When it was completed and about ready for occupancy, Henry Wright, an old pupil from Pensacola, and myself called in and went through the building and grounds. Henry said, "Mr. Newton, why didn't you build a large two-story dwelling in this pretty grove and paint it snow white, it would show off so elegantly from the public road?" Mr. Newton answered him thus, "Henry, when you take a book with pictures of homes in it, and leisurely and thoughtfully turn over the leaves to see the home pictures, on which page do you linger longest with delight, or fancy you see the most happiness, the pages with the palatial homes or the pages of the modest cottages in the grove?" "In the cottage homes," said Henry. "So do I," said Mr. Newton, "I prefer contentment, happiness in simplicity, rather than great show in splendor with discontent; thus it is that I live in a cottage, and I dare say 'filthy lucre' has something to do with it too. If that public road out there was a stream of running water, such as the Narrows along Santa Rosa Island, I would feel settled here for life." That cottage was occupied and there was happiness and contentment in it for a great while. Many were the conjectures about how the reconciliation between teacher and trustees was brought about. The old Scotch ladies would discuss it with their husbands alone and then they would meet and talk it over in conference with each other, but could never surmise how or who made the first advance. Those that knew kept it to themselves, and it has remained a mystery with some until this day. But we larger school boys had our ideas about the whole matter, just as big school boys will have, and we would whisper in the ears of our mothers and big sisters that there was something bigger than moving the Academy from the old hill that brought about the reconciliation between the two parties. We believed that there was a love story in it — we believed that Air. Newton loved all of his scholars here more than those he had in his school over the river, and that he loved one of his earliest pupils over here more than all the rest of us. — that there is a pretty bright blue-eyed lassie, with auburn hair, blond complexion, full of fun, the jolliest girl in school, more lively, by far, than any of her sisters, and we believed that this lovely maiden had more to do with bringing him back than anything else, and we believed there was a plighted faith of love between them — an undergrown requited love that kept burning and drawing all the time he was gone to California and across the river — that there was an old Elder and Trustee, the nearest neighbor, who was an admirer, and we believed a confidant of hers, and we further believed that it was through these two that the advance was made that brought him back. The old Scotch women hushed us to silence at such an unreasonable story — that we had no grounds for such ideas — that Mr. Newton would not like to hear it said that he thought more of one scholar than another — more of the scholars here than those he taught at Orange Hill and Marianna. We told them that an old lover had told us that when a fellow loved a girl in real earnest he loved everything around her home or in the settlement, loved the old folks, her sisters and brothers, her schoolmates, that to him even the chickens cackled nicer, the roosters crowed better, and the pigs squealed sweeter, the birds sang more joyfully and the sun shone more brightly around that home than any other home in the world. And we told them that he did not mind walking away up on the Ridge after supper to see if the pupils were studying their lessons up there and that we could see a leaning towards her people and home. They said we were on the old, old road of partiality in school, and that it was as unjust as it was threadbare, that it was a shame for us to be talking about a teacher loving, courting and marrying one of his pupils; and that we must stop it and not cause the girls to be skittish of their teacher and for us to say nothing more about it." And when we stopped talking they would ask us more about these things; and we just told them what we believed; that the old lover told us where there was true reciprocal love existing neither teasing nor anything else ever got in the way, when they got ready to marry. So we stopped talking only when we were asked about it, and that was pretty often, but kept on thinking and holding our opinions about things.

Chapter Thirty - He Marries

Just a little before the school opened in the moved Academy, the marriage bells were ringing. Then this announcement was made: This evening, December, A. D, 1858, at the home of the bride, a daughter of Mr. Angus and Mrs. Catherine Campbell, Mr. John Newton and Miss Margaret Campbell were united in marriage. Of course we boys said "We told you so" — boys do catch on to a thing or two now and then. They came into their cottage home and did not have to go far, far away to find it. In the course of time their home was blessed with the advent of a little son, Angus.

This was but a bubble of joy and beauty in that home — the sun shone brightly for a while and then came the shadow of a cloud and out of the cloud a voice calling to little Angus, "Come up higher, to your happy land far, far away." Then there was sorrow, heart wringing — a little vacant crib-chair. Then resignation. "The Lord doeth all things well." The night passeth away, and then cometh the morning. A daughter, Esther, comes to cheer the home — the express image of the mother — her prattling voice and clattering little feet make merry music in the home all the day long. And it is all well in the home, — it is all well in the school, moving on with the days — work, work, "learn and obey"; these were the watch words through sunshine and through shadows. So it went on in the new as well as the old, growing better and better from day to day, until the cruel war came with its grim visage to disturb all.

He taught through the first years of the war with success and pleasure, but toward the last years, the war became so cruel and sectional feeling so stirred up in Walton and in the South; and seeing so many of his brightest young pupils to whom he had looked forward with delight, hoping to see them representative men of the highest type, who would do honor in their homes and in high places in Church and State, cruelly cut down in the beginning of life, like grass before the mower, by an uncalled for war, he felt again that his life work was not appreciated, that it was a failure, that it was growing too bitter for him here, that he must get from under the foreboding cruel hanging cloud. So with short notice he got ready, and he, with his wife and little daughter passed out of the Confederate lines, by way of Pensacola Navy Yard, on by a circuitous route, to California on the Pacific Slope, where he remained until a little while after the war closed. And I may say safely, to a very great extent, the cloud followed him, "He changed the place but kept the pain."

In his stopover in Warrington at the Pensacola Navy Yard his own and his families lives were endangered by a band of robbers. His attention had been called to their movements in the early evening by a friend and this saved their lives, or at least their money. He lay awake all night with his ready pistol in one hand and his knife in the other; they made several approaches, but found that he was on the alert each time. The welcome day came and he had better protection as long as he had to stop over there. Another daughter was born to them in Illinois before they reached California, Christian, — she too bears the lineaments of her mother, — while she has the quiet graceful movements of her father, and something of the color or flash of his large piercing eyes. The curse of war had permeated our whole land and he found it in California as well as in Florida. His family had a severe attack of the loathsome scourge of small pox and his wife is in a poor state of health. So there was not much sunshine with him on the Pacific slope in those days; neither was there much over the work he left in the Land of Flowers. Some of his old pupils taught the Knox Hill school the last years of the war and a while after the war, but it was never brought up to the full standard of former days. He was gone this time to California a little more than two years. He left in 1863, returned Feb. 1866. This is the second time he is called back from across the continent to teach.

Marianna thought Knox Hill had had him long enough and secured his services for a while but Knox Hill got him back again in charge of the Academy and again he is doing splendid work in straightening out the crookedness that came in with the demoralization of the war. The school grew to the proportions that he would let it grow to; but not so large as his ante bellum schools. He had a great many things bearing upon him to make him sad and dissatisfied. He had been driven twice across the continent and from the lakes to the gulf hunting rest in peace. Now his dear wife is taken from him, September, 1866, to the home of her first born, and this is a wrench to his poor heart.

He sees the negroes turned loose and wandering "like sheep without a shepherd." He feels it is his duty to minister to them in things moral and spiritual, — and he dares to do his duty as he ever did all other duties. He had them to build a brush arbor and he would go every Sabbath in his quiet way, and give them wholesome instructions that tended to make them better Christians and better citizens. Some few passed some severe criticisms on his work and motives, that were the best and the purest, and they knew they were. And there were so many changes in these reconstruction, carpet-bag" days, that he bitterly condemned — and none for the better — the sadness and gloom would not be driven away. So he leaves the old Academy never to return again as teacher. The school has been taught, as a general thing, ever since, by some of his old pupils or by some of their children. So the changes in Walton brought about by the war and the projection of the R. R. through her territories, and the public school system, has brought this once great school down among the ordinary of today.

Goes to Missouri

Mr. Newton seeks relief now, not on the golden shores of the Pacific, but among the Bleak Hills of Missouri. He writes me from there that he has found the place up there for me, to sell out and come there at once, that with the rush and energy that I was using in Florida, I could get rich in a little while, and could do lots of good with money there — that one could make more stuff there on one acre than he could on five in Florida sand lands — that it was the best country he had ever lived in. He wrote me this in the spring of 1868, and in February of the next year, 1869, I was passing through Euchee Anna when I learned that he had returned and was then in the place, at his brother-in-law's, Rev. W. P. Harrison's. I went at once to see him, found him sitting alone by a good fire. After a hearty handshake, I said to him, "You didn't stay until I got there." He laughed heartily and said, "No, but every word I wrote you was the truth. but I didn't know half. Two-thirds of the work done there was expended in preparing for the severe winters, — every horse, cow, hog, chicken, — every living thing, had to be well housed. The man I boarded with had to haul his wood for the winter twelve miles over a muddy road, and had to pay six dollars per cord for it. This morning I got up here and found that there was a cold snap on, so I took my ax and ran out into yonder oak grove, cut some wood, picked up some lightwood knots, and I have had a comfortable fire to sit by all day. I tell you the country is nearer on an equality than people think it is, — there is more in the people than in the country." This is the judgment of a great scholar that traveled much with his eyes open. When the Irishman was asked if he didn't believe one country was as good as another, he said. "Sure, and a blamed sight better." Let us have a good country wherever we live.

Some of us boys who were thinking right strong about that time of marrying our sweethearts, speaking from experience now, — said we thought we could find something besides the cold North winds that brought him back to the Land of Flowers, we thought there was a warm young heart here that beat in unison with his warm heart, in a cold body that was the magnet that helped draw him back. There was a pretty fair complected, round faced young lady with large pensive blue eyes, dark auburn hair, low of stature, but stout in form, left behind; and we made up our minds that she had more to do with his coming back here than the cold rigors of the North or the warm sunshine of the Southland. We did not dare tell this to our mothers, nor the other old Scotch ladies, but we told this in confidence to our sweethearts, who said. no. no. this young lady is the very opposite in appearances to his first wife, and they would not believe us, notwithstanding we assured them that he was acting lots like we did in the presence of our sweethearts, and we told them that we had learned that opposites had nothing to do with marrying when the parties loved and got ready to marry.

So things moved along with all of us in a regular way for a little while and a change came. My sweetheart and I got ready to marry, and there was nothing in the way. He was a Presbyterian Preacher, living in the same town together with myself, and on account of the relation that had existed between him and me as teacher and pupil, I felt as though I would like to have him unite us in marriage, and I asked him if he would not officiate. He said that he would be more than glad to do so, but as Rev. Mr. Harrison was the pastor of the Valley Church, where my membership was, he thought it would be more appropriate to have Mr. Harrison as the leading minister and he would go and assist, which was as agreeable to me as it was to him. We were a little slower than he thought we would be, and we were about to run into his time. So, when we got ready, it was a very, very, cold day in the last days of December of 1870, and a long drive through the country which necessitated going on the way a day ahead. There was a double pressure upon him; the same that was upon me, but I was better prepared to bear it than he. We both would have to go in the cold, but he would have to talk and work in the back ground, I was working and talking in the open. He came to me and said, "It is so very cold that I fear I will have to decline the pleasure of the occasion, if you will excuse me," and I did reluctantly, but did it willingly under the circumstances. The cold is more severe when you have something on your mind and heart that you want to keep under cover. In short, when my wife and I got back off of a short trip this is what happened before we returned, "Rev. W. P. Harrison, on this day _____, united in marriage Rev. John Newton and Miss Mary Campbell (daughter of Angus and Catherine Campbell) both of Freeport, Fla." This lady was a younger sister of his first wife, and our wives were first cousins. They moved to his long desired home on the Narrows, to Mary Esther, — in the spring of A. D. 1871. There was born to them a son. The sequel is short and sad, — the mother — the wife — died. Oh, how ready are the feet of sorrow to follow in the steps of joy! He is left alone with his two little daughters, in his home by the sea, away from old friends and kindred. Sorrow is no respecter of persons.

The little babe is left with its aunt, Mrs. Christian Harrison, and she has been a faithful mother to him and he was named John Daniel. While he bears the image of his mother, he is very much like his father in manners and business, with eyes very much like his. especially in expression. He is now a grown up man with a wife and little son, and is a loving helpful son to his foster mother in her declining years of affliction. The Lord can turn our sadness into joy. Let us abide our time.

> "I know not where His islands lift
> Their fronded palms in air;
> I only know I can not drift
> Beyond His love and care."

Mr. Newton built a neat little school house at Mary Esther and opened up a school for the natives about him. Many of the patrons there could not read, and he opened up a night school and taught them. Some of his old patrons from Freeport, Marianna, Pensacola and Geneva, found out where he was and sent their children down there to him. He held Sabbath School and preached for them every Sabbath. He did missionary work up and down the water courses for five and six miles out from the bay.

In writing to me on one occasion this is what he says, "I went out into the back country on a missionary tour yesterday, I met father, mother and eight children, shook hands with them all; in a little while the oldest daughter, 14 years old, went out, washed her face and hands, and when she returned, I jumped up to shake hands with her. when her mother spoke up and said, "you have already told her howdy." Now, you want to know if I accomplished anything. Eight children got their hands and faces washed. 'Cleanliness is next to Godliness.' When I started home the father, through kindness, would have me take with me a half bushel of nice sweet potatoes; I was afraid to refuse, lest I should offend him, and spoil my missionary work. It was about all I could lift, so you know I had a time getting home with them. It was five miles to my home, had to put them down every few steps to rest. The daughters say he gave them to me for a joke, — I think better of him. He had promised me he would come and bring the children to Sabbath School and church. I called his attention to this promise; he said 'I have been so busy that I have not had time to go, but I will come day after tomorrow,' which would be Thursday. I told him what day that was and that we had Sabbath School and preaching only on Sundays. Then he said, 'I will wait and come some Sunday.'

Mr. Newton had many tempting offers to leave Mary Esther, He was called to Milton to teach and had $1,500 per year guaranteed to him there by Mr. Chaffin. He said to them, "If you have that much money to give for a teacher you can get a better one than I am." So he went back home (and as he would often say) to crawl up into his little shell. He showed me a letter from Mr. Moody asking him to send his daughters to him at North Field and they would educate them and pay all necessary expenses. He said that was good and kind in him, but that if he accepted the kind offer he would lose the pleasure of educating them himself, besides having to be without their company so long. He spent many quiet happy days with his little family in his gulf coast home. But by and by there came along a gallant, cultured, Scotch boy of a stately, manly form. He was from amongst those who "go down to the sea in ships" — Capt. Augustus E. Axelson, who made love to his oldest daughter. Miss Esther, and was accepted, and they married. This spoiled the nest on the Narrows, but made a better one in some ways, in the city of Pensacola, This was in A. D. 1889. So he spent his last years, that had many happy days in them in the home of his son-in-law, well cared for by him, and in the loving care of his daughters.

He often said to me, while teaching, after mentioning one after another distinguished school teachers, who had fared well in the close of life, "I wonder if there is anything good in store for me in the end." I mentioned this saying of his to him in his last days in Pensacola, and he said, "Things in these last days of mine are good enough, better, may be, than I deserve. I have a good home and I am well cared for, what more could I wish." His Mary Esther friends hated to lose him as a neighbor. They said he made a most excellent, generous neighbor.

Generosity

He had a barrel of good country syrup that was leaking and asked me to look out for a better barrel for him. Before I had gotten it, he said to me, "don't bother, we have learned how to stop the leak, — we draw a gallon and give it to our neighbors when it commences leaking, and it stops." It pays to remember your neighbors.

His Health

He was seldom ever sick, didn't eat enough to make himself sick. He understood hygiene and taught it by precept and example. He had a little book on psychology and physiology — "Know Thyself" — it was the best of its size I ever saw. His advanced classes had to know this book.

He was the first man person to milk a cow in Walton, and taught old Scotchmen that it was their duty to milk, and not their wives. He taught those who were careless about the Sabbath not to write, receive, or send off any mail matter on the Sabbath. Some of his best work was done outside of the regular school hours, and without a thought of its being appreciated.

Three young ladies in our public school here met to consult about needed helps for their pupils, that would require forty minutes of their time after school hours; one, the most efficient to lead in that work said, "no, the patrons will not appreciate the giving of our time to them." What would this great teacher think of such an idea? Some of the best work done in the world is unappreciated work.

The reader may wish to know something of his assistants. Daniel G. McLeod and Angus I Gillis, graduates from the Academy, were the only assistant teachers, outside of his scholars, in the school, that he ever had in all the years he taught here, and they only served but a few terms; they were taught by him and knew how he wanted them to teach, and followed strictly his directions. He did all the disciplining and was responsible alone for progress and behavior. Would hear their classes two or three times a week while they would hear his. Now, let me emphasize here, lest I forget, that co-operative sympathy between these old Scotch patrons and teacher had a great deal to do with the continuity and success of this great school. Patrons, be ever in sympathy with your teacher.

When the school had grown so large, the trustees offered to procure a regular assistant outside. He told them such teachers as they could get would be more in the way than good, and would have no assistants except from those he had trained. His tuition was $2.00 per month for all grades, and would never agree to have it changed; and if any failed to pay him, no one knew it, save himself. What splendid teaching! What poor pay! Well might the trustees and patrons be satisfied with results. What would our public school and collegiate professors of this day think of such pay, and such sacrifices for the moral and intellectual up-lift of this generation of youths. He fully exemplified in his personal life the greatest thought of all life — that we are in this world to serve — to serve others — to serve our God.

Teaches Half Century

For nearly half a century he was a most acceptable teacher, in the broadest field of education, to Southern Alabama and Western Florida — teaching through the most trying years. None but a genius, could have commenced, continued and ended triumphantly as he did. Coming into a new country, amongst strangers, unheralded, without friends, without money, with no personal magnetism in a commanding physique, but rather of a very fragile personnel, and with no deep toned sounds of command, but with a clear distinct clarion voice, as soft as a maiden's. Yet he was respected from the start — he asked and it was given — he commanded and it was done — he moved things all around him — there was no waiting with him for something to turn up, he turned things up himself.

The great power house from which he drew his inexhaustible resources lay deep down in a heart, resting in his fragile body, brim full of love for his fellow man, and his God, furnishing him too, with the courage of his conviction. We all soon learned that the channel that this power moved through lay in the glint of those marvelous eyes.

In Pensacola, November 25, A. D. 1893, in the home of his son-in-law, Capt. Augustus E. Axelson — these wonderful eyes of Rev. John Newton, the great teacher for years, at Old Knox Hill — were closed in death. His sleeping body was borne to the L. & N. R. R. and carried to DeFuniak Springs, where it was met, by ever so many, of his old pupils and friends, placed in a hearse and carried, not to the beautiful mound by the sea, near his Mary Esther cottage home, to be laid in the white sands thrown up by the ocean, and bleached white by the sun — fit emblem of his life — not to sleep there under the dirge of the murmuring waters — but it was taken to the more appropriate, if not the more beautiful spot, — Euchee Valley's city of the dead — where so many of his pupils and dear ones rest — under the very shadow of Old Knox Hill, where the grandest work of his life was done, over whose hills the morning sun, rising beyond the river in its glory, throws a flood of rich light about his grave, and the evening setting sun in its beauty, sends back gentle rays of soft purpling light, through the open branches of the great trees, to say, good night — rest in peace.

Here, in his narrow house, beneath the clods of the Valley — under the shades of the trees, and near by the many, many dear ones of his life, sleeps in silence and in solitude, beneath the shining stars, one of Walton's greatest men. We often wonder if Pennsylvania ever dreamed that she had such a son at work in the Land of Flowers. He was one of the "lonely mountain peaks" shining above the clouds in our moral world.

Chapter Thirty-One - Churches

With the Scotchmen, the school goes along together, hand in hand with the church to the end. No sooner had they gotten their families settled down in rude homes and their family altars established here, than they set about to build a house where they might meet together and worship the Lord in the congregations. They brought a minister along with them to blaze out the path to heaven for their generations. They met at a central point in the valley with ax, saw, mall and wedge, and felled great pine trees, cleaved them in twain, hewed them down smooth, brought them up out of the woods on their shoulders, and soon had erected a large commodious house, well proportioned where they might worship together.

Some time after the church was built, on May 26, 1828, they met and organized the Presbyterian Church of Euchee Valley, Rev. McQueen of North Carolina moderated the meeting and Rev. Witherspoon was among the very first to serve these early pioneers.

The first Elders were, Daniel S. McLean, John L. McKinnon, Donald McLean, Peter K. McDonald, and Archibald McCallum. No Deacons are named. Miss Sallie McLean of Euchee Anna, who was considered the very best authority on Euchee Valley Church history, gave me more information along this line than any other. She says for nearly a decade after the organization, on account of the raids on our Northern frontier by the Creek Indians, there was very little done and few changes in church affairs. She tells us that in this interim there came on horse-back from Tennessee through the zone made open by a treaty with the Creeks in A. D. 1829, Rev. ____ Bryson, who spent several weeks preaching for them. His son, Rev. ____ Bryson came a few years ago and preached for their sons and daughters.

The writer was moved to this work from an ardent desire to give a true and full history of this old church. The reader will have to imagine how very blank he felt when he found a gap for years and years in the early life of this church in which he could find no written records whatever, and that too, in the times when its history ought to have been the most interesting — and when he found out too, by searching, that so much that he had gathered through tradition was very conflicting. He sought faithfully and prayerfully from every probable source for reliable information, and got that which only muddled what he had already gathered.

The Lost Records Found

After all efforts of gaining any reliable incontrovertible information had been abandoned, a niece of mine. Miss Aramenta McKinnon, handed me a nice leather bound little volume saying, "When Uncle Daniel L. McKinnon was over from his home in Marianna last week, he gave me this book to look over, and told me to hand it to you, that it might be interesting to you and others of the old church." I opened it anxiously, found that it was our old church sessional records, kept regularly by my father from May 27, A.D. 1842, to February 27, A.D. 1852, just the very thing we had been searching after for months, and we were glad. Our brother hadn't the remotest idea that we were searching for it, and we never had a thought that such a record was in his possession all these years; it had the hall-marks of having gone all through the Civil War, — it had good blank pages in it that were so scarce in those days, and on some of these, in his handwriting, were places and dates of battles and hospitals where he had been. We acknowledge the hand of

Providence in bringing these precious records to us just at this time.

We copy in full below the very first sessional record, leaving off the names of the three members who were arraigned before the session, so that the church members of today may see that the early church did not wink at intemperance and Sabbath breaking as some would have us believe at this day, but were as ready to correct it as now.

"May 27, 1842.   Church Session.

Constituted by Rev. A. M. Mooney from Ala.

Donald McLean, Daniel S. McLean, Archibald McCallum, John L. McKinnon and Peter K. McDonald, Elders.

Opened with prayer by Rev. A. M. Mooney, moderator.

"A," "B" and "C," charged with intemperance and in violation of the Sabbath; were heard, and with humility and signs of true repentance made the necessary acknowledgement, were admonished from the chair and restored to their former fellowship. It was ordered that this decision be read from the pulpit on Sabbath morning.

John L. McKinnon, Clerk."

It is claimed that the Sabbath breaking mentioned in the above sessional records was going with and after their mail on the Sabbath.

These records run on regularly, giving accounts of sessional meetings with several ministers from different localities moderating the session and the receiving of new members and the baptizing of their infants, with nothing out of the ordinary until Nov. 26, A.D. 1848, when the new church building was dedicated. Pretty nearly from the day the Valley Church was organized, there was a continual growth, spiritually and numerically. For many years it was the only church organization in all this country. In A.D. 1847, the numerical growth and attendance increased so that there was a lively call for a larger building to worship in. It was then that the second church building went up, a large frame building, 50 feet by 100 feet, with large and commodious inside galleries on either side. This building would seat comfortably from four to five hundred people. The gallery on the east side was reserved exclusively for the colored people. It was not an unusual thing to see this building filled on preaching days from Sabbath to Sabbath.

Mr. John Gillis, who learned his trade at Pensacola Navy Yard was the architect that constructed this big new church building.

It had to be recovered in the late '60's. A little later it was reported that the shingles on the building were yet unpaid for. A congregational meeting was called to take steps to raise the money to pay the debt. Several speeches were made on the ways and means of raising the money to liquidate the debt, the most of the speeches were burdened with "hard times — scarcity of money" and the like, as is usual. There was a tall visiting Presbyterian preacher present who rose and straightened himself up and said, "Do as the Apostle James tells you to do, 'Go to the rich and howl for the money." Mr. Newton followed this speaker, saying, "We have no rich to howl to, we need none, the debt has already stood too long, let every man run his hand down in his pocket, or arrange now, for his part of the money and wipe out the debt today. It is my opinion that our prayers here will rise no higher than these shingles until they are paid for." The debt was paid then. And this building stood until it was torn down recently and replaced by the neater, smaller building that now stands on the same grounds.

Chapter Thirty-Two - The Ringing out of the Old and the Ringing in of the New

This is Judge John L. Campbell's remembrance of the big new frame building taking the place of the age-old hewn log building of long ago, and corroborated by the found records. This is what he says, "The new church was finished up and ready for occupancy some time before it was dedicated and used. Many were the questions and conjectures with both the young and the old, as to why the old church was not abandoned and the new dedicated and used in its stead. Rev. Samuel E. Robinson, a tall black eyed, curly dark haired handsome young man, was the pastor in charge and on hand; but he would give no satisfactory answers to these questions: neither would the old elders answer satisfactorily.. Finally in the course of time the elders gave out this information. We, the session, with Rev. Samuel E. Robinson moderator, in view of the fact that a very important church marriage is being arranged for solemnization here soon, deem it wise, appropriate and befitting, to ring out the grand old log church by solemnly uniting a fair bride to her bridegroom in the holy bonds of wedlock, on the Lord's Holy Day, and after the joyous union, take leave of the old building and proceed on the following Sabbath to dedicate, with appropriate ceremonies, the new church building for worship. While this announcement relieved the anxieties in one direction, it increased it in another, — who are the contracting parties, and when are they going to be ready? These were the all-absorbing questions for the colonists to discuss for a while, and many were the conjectures, for both the groom and bride were very bashful and reticent, keeping their own secrets. In a little while everything is understood through this card, namely, 'On Sabbath morning at 11 o'clock A. M. Nov. the 19th A. D. 1848, the Rev. Samuel E. Robinson and Miss Jane Williams, daughter of Mr. and Mrs. McCray Williams, both of Euchee Ahna, Fla., will be united in marriage in the old Euchee Valley Church, Elder John L. McKinnon, J. P. officiating. All are invited.'

This was a surprise to all, and every lady was there at the appointed hour to witness the occasion. The house would not begin to accommodate the comers, — hardly the lady attendance. — the large trees that stood around the old church gave shelter to those that stood outside, while their falling leaves on that November Sabbath reminded all of the passing away of the old for the coming of the new. Let it be remembered that Col. John L. McKinnon was the first Justice of the Peace and the only one for years in Walton, that all law matters were conducted through his courts and in the absence of a minister — which was often — he always solemnized the rite of matrimony between those seeking union, and in the solemn and impressive way in which he performed this duty with scriptural charges and prayer would impress one with the idea of ministerial work. As the only minister present was one of the contracting parties, the duty of uniting them fell upon the Justice of the Peace — Elder McKinnon. At the appointed hour, young manhood with blanched cheeks, ennobled in taking on new responsibilities and by his side young blushing womanhood, the beauty of the Valley, — stood before the Col. in the space reserved for them, in front of the old altar. In this presence the Col. was at his best, he commenced by asking, "if there is any one present who knew any good reasons why these parties should not be united in marriage let them speak or hereafter hold their peace." Then he had a short prayer — spoke of the marriage institution in the Garden of Eden, its responsibilities and blessings, its recognition and approval by our Savior; and having had them make public acknowledgements of their plighted love and obedience before that crowd of witnesses, he pronounced them man and wife, and said, in ringing tones, 'What God hath joined together let no man put asunder.' Then he closed with a short pathetic prayer, asking God's blessing on their united lives and on the occasion. Now. let me say here, that it was the universal custom in those days, on occasions like this, for the minister or officer officiating, at the close of the marriage ceremony, or prayer, to say to the bridegroom 'Salute (kiss) your bride.' The Colonel did not leave this out. but the young, timid, blushing groom held back, when the Col. said, 'if it is shamefacedness that holds you back, I will kiss her for you.' and kissed her ruby lips, while her cheeks flushed with beauty that made the bashful young husband proud of the smiling beauty, brought out by the substituted kiss of an old man. So all was done now in order. The joyous taking in of the new ministerial bride and the taking leave of the old primeval log church, made the day full of joy and gladness to all.

Chapter Thirty-Three - Dedication Day

"Sabbath, Nov. 26, A. D. 1848, at 11 o'clock A. M., as announced, these Presbyterians met to dedicate the new church building that stood just a few paces east of the old, — the young bridegroom of the Sunday before. Rev. Samuel E. Robinson preaches the dedicatory sermon, he too, was at his best on that occasion, — it was a solemn reverential occasion, that filled our souls with joy — a day so full of good things that it has been long remembered by many of us, together with the many days that have passed since — days making green, sweet recollection pages. The many fine gospel, orthodox sermons that have ever fallen from the lips of our 'old time religion' preachers hang around our memory still; and we are glad to know that we have this same old time preaching there today, when we are able to go to hear it, and there are ever and anon occasions that bring us together there. We all want to go by that way when we go up higher."

These found records show that Lochlin L. McKinnon had been added to the eldership and Alexander McLeod, John Gillis, Daniel G. McLean and Daniel G. Gunn were the deacons, when the church was dedicated. The minutes on that occasion, with Samuel E. Robinson pastor and moderator, show a full revised list of members with a roster of one hundred and fifty-three members.

These records show that Rev. A. M. Mooney was more regularly with these Scotch Presbyterians in their sessions and worship than any of the other visiting ministers, and there were long intervals in his coming. Rev. John Warnock of Alabama was with them December 17, A.D. 1842. Rev. M. A. Patterson in February 27, A.D. 1853, preaching and baptizing their children. When these ministers would come into the settlement, word was sent to every home for eight and ten miles round and all would come and stay during the meeting. They came for the word and remembered every text and fond word of the minister about the wisdom and goodness of God, long after they were gone. There was no whining about long sermons and prayers; they were seeking that better land where praises never end. When they had no one to preach for them the old elders would meet every first and third Sabbath mornings, read the scriptures and hold prayer meetings; some of these old elders would have to pray in the Gaelic language, their native tongue.

When I was quite a boy, I went to spend a night with a niece and nephew, younger, but very near my age, with their grandfather. They told me their grandfather, Daniel S. McLean, always held family worship by reading from his Scotch bible and prayed in Gaelic. I expressed some trouble lest I might not know when to get up, when the little nephew said. "I know when he says amen, and I'll tell you." So when the amen was pronounced in Gaelic, the little fellow bounced up in triumph, slapped me, and crying out, "He's done — that's amen!" The niece was a bright little lassie, learned every one of her grandfather's graces and prayers, and has never forgotten one of them; only a month ago at our table she was called on for a blessing, when she repeated the morning blessing of her grandfather in Gaelic that she had learned more than sixty years ago.

These old elders were very prolix in their services. They earnestly looked forward to that day of eternal praise and ever prepared for it. Judge Richard Campbell told this joke on Col. McKinnon that he loved to tell in an appreciative crowd. "In passing from Pensacola on to Tallahassee, I would often stop my nights in Walton with the Col. One cold winter night, after supper was over, as usual, the Col., with his good wife and his great family of sons and daughters, and the house-servants, gathered around the ingleside in a large circle. Before us on the hearth stood the ever present large, highly polished, brass andirons, or fire-dogs, loaded with a big back oak log and one smaller in front, and one on top of the two, with bits of split lightwood stuck about in them to make them go; making a good cracking fire to sit by on a cold winter's night. The Col. took down his big old family bible, held it before his eyes while he rested his trembling arms upon the old armed chair, and read a long chapter from Matthew, commenting a little as he read along. Then he took down his big Presbyterian hymn book and read a long hymn clear through, while the rest of us were being furnished with smaller ones from a platter in the hands of one of the house servants. We sang the whole hymn through, the Col. leading the music. Then we all bowed reverently on our knees around the family altar, the Col. leading in the evening prayer, confessing all sins and asking forgiveness, acknowledging all blessings and giving thanks, he prayed for a blessing on our country and those that rule over us, for the preservation of our "glorious union;" he plead for blessings concretely and abstractly on every family and everybody. When he was about half through with the prayer, the fire had died down and the room became a little cold, the Col. paused a moment in his prayer and said, 'why in the world don't some of you put on a stick of lightwood?' The boys seemed to be resting so well and I being near the wood box, got up quietly and laid a stick gently on top of the back log, where it did no good in the way of replenishing the fire; but the Col. went on to the finish of the prayer, regardless of the heat or the cold in the room. When he reached the end with that solemn Amen, that welled up from the heart, the lads, whom I thought were asleep, bounced up readily and seemed to be very much refreshed. The Col. got after them for the way they chunked the fire, when I had to tell him it was I who had put the chunk on. Then he said, 'Richard, there is a proverb that says, 'it takes either a philosopher or a fool to make a fire, it appears that you are neither.'

The morning worship was not altogether so long. The Col. was a late setter and not an early riser, yet he would be out quite early among his cattle.

The memory of these devout family services linger with me until this day, and my heart is made gladsome because of them. I am ever reminded of these, by that solemn, reverential family prayer in Burn's Cotter's Saturday Night — prayer that every family commencing life should read and study and put into earnest practice.

Their first regular stationed preacher was the young minister, Samuel E. Robinson, mentioned above, who boarded at the old McCaskill place with "White Findley McCaskill; taught school at first, and then preached for a long while. The next was Rev. Peter Donan from Pensacola, for a little while. Then came Rev. W. H. Crane from Quincy. Florida for one year. Next came an old Scotchman. Samuel Campbell, from Virginia, for one year. Rev. Robert Bell, the teacher from Ireland for a little while. Then came Rev. J. W. Butler, who was with us when the war came, and stayed one year. Then Rev. Bouldin, an old man from Tennessee, who came during the war and preached a few times and was laid at rest in the Valley Church yard. The next was Bellum and Post Bellum Minister Rev. Wm. P. Harrison, a Scotch Irishman from Georgia. He came in the dark days of the war, — married one of Walton's daughters, Miss Christian Campbell, daughter of Angus and Catherine Campbell, Rev. John Newton officiating. They lived at first at Knox Hill, then moved to Euchee Anna and built for themselves a comfortable little cottage in a grove of large trees near a bold, gushing, cool spring.

They had their rich vegetable and flower gardens, fruits, in the juicy peach and the luscious scuppernongs in great abundance — had their chickens, their pig, their cow, and their horse, all of their own thrifty earnings and good financial management, in spite of carking cares. They both saw better times in their ante bellum days for their parents were well to do in the goods and chattels that the war swept from our Southland. But I doubt very much if they were happier in these possessions than they were in their little cottage home by the public road or through street. In the first years there, their cottage was warmed up by a large heater. They never liked this arrangement, and as soon as they could, they had a chimney and an open fire place. There was no brick to be had in the country, so he had a stick and clay chimney built. I called the evening he built his first fire in it; found him sitting in front of a cracking fire, sending out its heat from a cheerful blaze — a perfect picture of contentment. I was seated and we discussed the change, the cheer of the live flames on the hearth over the smothered flames in the heater. For a moment he fell into one of his thoughtful moods and on a sudden he raised up his head, turned toward me with expression in his face that I shall never forget, and said, "never did I dream that I could be as happy and contented as I am right now, in a log house with a stick and dirt chimney to it." And he was happy and contented — those large beaming blue eyes rolling beneath that prominent brow, sparkling in that broad florid face, said so, more clearly than his lips expressed it. Then I said within myself, truly possessions have but little to do with our happiness in this world.

He served the church faithfully for many years until he became superannuated, and soon he led the way to that brighter world, that he had been so long, alluring his people to. His body was placed in that valley of silence that it might rest there for a while with others of Walton's fallen worth. The home in time was vacated, decay was doing its work, the Vandal's hand gave it a blow in passing. But it is occupied now by another and being renovated. I never passed this home in its decadence, and my business called me to pass often that way — but what I was reminded of Goldsmith's Village Preacher; and the appropriateness of applying his lines to our preacher and his wasting home. And I would find myself repeating, as I passed, the lines that I learned and had never forgotten when a little school boy at old Knox Hill.

> "Near yonder copse, where once the garden smiled.
> And still where many a garden flower grows wild;
> There, where a few torn shrubs the place disclose.
> The village preacher's modest mansion rose."

She Longs for the Valley Worship

I remember years ago visiting the home of one of his old parishioners, a sweet old Scotch soul, who had spent her earliest best days in Euchee Valley;

and then moved to a distant town. And the burden of her conversation was about the people of the valley, the church, its minister, its congregation. She said to me, "I long to hear some of those good old sermons from the mellow voice of Mr. Harrison, to hear again those dear old songs, — All Hail the Power — Jesus Lover — Nearer My God, and the like; sung by that great congregation, carrying all the parts with a sweetness and distinctness that we could hear every word of poetry as we came up from the old spring. The people down here have never heard dear Old Hundred sung aright. I believe if they just could hear it sung by the Valley congregation, they would drop their squalling solos and high church music and go to worshiping God aright in song."

True, there was a peculiar sweetness in the old valley music of those days that would make melody out of discord, — it was from the soul. It might not have had much of Chopin's nocturnes in it, but it smacked of the sweet rythm of harmony with God. It may have had nothing of "Wagner's Thunder," but it made the welkin ring about the "dear old spring" on Sabbath mornings with its unmuffled notes in harmony with nature's God.

The next was Rev. W. D. Humphries, who served the Valley Church for one year.

Next comes the present incumbent. Rev. R. Q. Baker, from Liberty county, Georgia, a graduate of Oglethorpe College, of Puritanical extraction, a wounded Confederate soldier, who served as a private all through the Civil War. He entered upon the practice of law after the war, but his conscience drove him into the ministry. He has a giant analytical mind, is a deep thinker, a profound reasoner, a ready debater, and shows his worth best as an impromptu speaker. He never writes a sermon or an address, yet his vocabulary is large and of the smoothest, choicest words that are expressive and impressive. He has served the Valley Church for thirty years and no one is tired of him. He wears better than any preacher I know. It is a notable fact that those who sit under his reasoning sermons for any length of time, are never afterwards satisfied with sensational preaching. He has a big place in the hearts of these Old Valley Scotch. He baptized and married off more of their children, and buried more of their dead, than all those who came before him. He has no stereotyped funeral sermons or prayers; his heart has been wrung and twisted so that it runs readily in sympathy with every condition of life, and it is an outpouring of the soul in real sympathy. He served Walton acceptably for twelve years as Superintendent of her Public Schools. In physique he is tall, straight, agile. His complexion is a dark sallow, yet he is as tough as whitleather. He has small, sharp, snapping blue eyes, in a round head covered with a heavy coat of dark, but now iron gray hair. He is exceedingly conscientious and set in his ideas of right; so much so, that some of his best friends say that his conscience in keeping him straight leans him just a little too> far back at times. This we do know of a truth, that the promptings of his conscience, as he interpreted it, and as his old pastor Dr. Axson, under whose ministry he had sat for many fruitful years interpreted it, after communing together in prayer with their God to guide them to interpret it, led him to make sacrifices at the call of their Lord, as they heard Him on that eventful occasion, that sends many sharp arrows we think, and gloom at times, to his perturbed, poor human heart and mind, but in the end we believe glory to his soul. Few are called upon in our days to make so great sacrifices, and none could have responded more heroically than he has. Other ministers of less courage and less theological research, may have taken a different view of his situation and may have fallen short of obedience to their God. Let nothing come between us and our call to duty from our God.

Chapter Thirty-Five - The City of Our Dead

The stranger in passing the Euchee Valley Cemetery, seeing that large enclosure filled with marked graves, reasonably comes to the conclusion that he is traveling through a very sickly region, while in fact he is passing through one of the most healthful sections. But when he learns that Walton's people have been burying their dead here for near a century, and for a long time this was the only burying ground in the country for both whites and negroes, then he will understand. There are so many people whom I have heard express a desire to be buried in this shady Valley of Silence, notwithstanding the oft misapplied statement, "As the tree falls, so let it lie." I may say that all of Walton's citizens that go beyond her bounds into the marts of the great cities for more active business, when they run their earthly course and lay them down in the arms of death's sleep, are brought back to 'finish their rest here beneath the shades of the old Valley by the side of their fathers and mothers, brothers, sisters and friends of long ago. There was started another grave yard on the south side of the Valley, in Mossy Bend years ago, but there are comparatively few buried there in comparison with this old place. I spent days recently among the Valley tombs looking up data for these sketches, and found them very helpful to me. I was very anxious to learn who was the first white person to die in Walton and failed to find it in this Valley yard, but found it in the Mossy Bend burying garden, buried long before it was claimed for a burying place. That first white person who died in Walton was Mrs. Peggie Folks, wife of John Folks, who came with Neill McLendon and Daniel D. Campbell at the first, on the trail way to Walton, to Sam Story's camp at the "Old Place." This Scotch lady died at her home, near the head of a branch that makes up from the south to the Mossy Bend, Free Port and Euchee Anna roads, not far from where these roads intersect each other, and not far from the old McIver or Anderson shop. She died in December, A. D., 1824. For years and years this first death created a great sensation among the aborigines and negroes when they came. It was the first person the Indians had ever seen buried in a coffin and placed down in the ground. This interment was the product of many legends and superstitions among the Indians to which the negroes fell heir when they came and got acquainted with them. Some few of the negroes that remained here after the war hold to these traditions today. This branch head near her home bears the name of the "Bugaboo Head" until this day. These superstitious people claimed that they never pass this "Bugaboo Head" at night, without seeing Peggy Folks walking about it, a thanky-bag on her arm, a yellow bandanna handkerchief about her head and neck, and always carrying a lighted candle in her hand. The Indians claimed that it was her spirit hunting for her body that was buried under the ground, and that she spoke words of warning and comfort to those who were not afraid to stop and talk with her. But these superstitious people that hand down these ghost stories through the generations, have never been known to pass there at night.

These people passed down another legend that afforded much talk in those early days, and was believed in by many of later years. They claimed that they often saw, on the Euchee Anna and Free Port roads, on the hills about the Sand Hill Branches, a "No Headed Dog" that would follow them for a piece. Many claimed to have seen this wonderful dog, and told much about how he would act. So much was said about him that many old and young people would not dare to go along that part of the road after night. Some intelligent people would give ear to this story. My father spurned such talk and would drive out such foolish, unreasonable stories from our young minds; said "he had passed along that road at all hours of the night and had never seen such a creature, and only silly minded people could." But he had a neighbor of the same opinion as he, Peter K, McDonald, his cousin, and one night as he came up from Freeport with his ox team lightly loaded with a supply of dry goods and groceries for himself and neighbors, in passing the haunted place he heard something after him, gave a glancing look backwards and saw through the dim starlight the monster coming after him, running and leaping and reaching out his long arm or paw to catch him. He put whip to his ox team, making all the speed possible, the headless dog keeping right close up to him; when he reached the long slant at the White Branch he made the team go down that with added speed, while he could tell by his backward glances that he was gaining some little on the dog, yet the dog was still stretching out his long fore leg and could almost take hold of his wagon. When he reached the current of the branch, oxen like, he could force them no farther until they drank. When the wagon stopped the dog stopped and he took a bold look backward and found that the no-headed dog that had been following him was a bolt of calico that he had on the hinder part of his wagon which had fallen out, leaving the end securely fastened under some grocery boxes; it unfolded and twisted and jumped after him over the high places in the road making the dog, and the twisted unfolded calico fastened to the lower part of the wagon made his long arm or tongue as he thought, stretching out to catch on to his wagon. This true story put a quietus to the no-headed dog scare. Some time after this there were two men killed along this way, Alexander McKinzie and James Oglesby. The branch heads near their murder take their names, and those who claimed that they did see the mysterious dog, claim now that he was there as an apparition to foretell the death of these men. They can have it so if they like. But the lesson here to the young is that all ghost-like appearances will prove to be nothing if you will walk right straight up to them. The tombstones in the Valley graveyard show that Peter McCaskill, brother to Kenneth McCaskill, born in Scotland in 1793 and died November, 1827, was the first person buried there. And that his sister Nancy Jones and her four children, who sleep close by him followed next, and soon after him. These were buried there about the time the logs were being cut and brought up for the first church, before any wagon roads were cut out from their homes to the place. These first dead were brought there on poles carried on men's shoulders. There was something very mysterious and unaccounted for in the death of these Jones children; they were in health, and one suddenly died. When they returned from the burying of the first, another was dead; on returning from burying the second, a third was dead; and these were followed in no great while by a fourth and their mother. These were the wife and children of Rev. Charley Jones, who went by the affectionate name of "Old Brother Charley Jones." He was a Methodist preacher who married a Scotch Presbyterian wife. He lived east of old Knox Hill. He was a very devout self-sacrificing man of God, preached often in the old Valley log church in the absence of a Presbyterian minister, and was heard gladly by the old Scotch Presbyterians. There is today a dim trail that leads from the Valley church across Panther and Bruces creek on to the Alaqua settlements, that was blazed out by this old servant of the Lord and traveled by him in carrying the precious Word to the Alaqua people. It is known today as "Old Brother Charley Jones'" trail. He was the only Methodist in his day in all this country. He never tried to organize a Methodist church here, he preached to Presbyterians and was satisfied to feed any hungry soul on the bread of eternal life. He survived his family and sleeps now near them in that valley of rest. He honored all their graves with a stone and superscription; no one has honored his grave thus. But even the children of today know where "Old Brother Charley Jones," the faithful pedestrian, itinerant preacher rests from his labors.

Chapter Thirty-Six - Mary Gillis

Nearby these early graves and to the east of them, I came to a stone well moulded with age. On it, in block letters, I found this superscription:

"In memory of
Mary, Daughter of Angus and Catharine Gillis.
Born July 29th, 1835.
Died August 25th, A.D. 1847."

As I read this superscription, the very name of the Scotch lassie, the name of her father and mother, awakened in me the deepest emotions, for these were the identical names of my wife and her parents. Then I remembered that my wife was named for a sister who was taken away in the spring time of life; then fond recollections carried me backward more than a half century to a day in the blossoming spring-time, when I walked with a young friend, a schoolmate of mine at old Knox Hill Academy, a scholarly youth just merging into young manhood. We were walking together on the Ridge Road north of the Academy, beneath the deep shades of these great nutting trees along that highway, where they entwine their branches and mingle their foliage across the road. We came to a turn in the road, when this young man caught me gently by the arm stopping me, then pointed me to a large dogwood tree hard by the road with long arching limbs curving downward and near to the ground, forming a beautiful natural shady canopy to rest under. It was in full blossom then, with just enough of green leaves out to shade and soften the white glare of its waxen flowers. When he saw that I appreciated the beauty of the situation along this ridge, he said: "Near three years ago when I was returning from Prof. Henry's school one evening, my eyes fell upon one of the most bewitching scenes in perfect nature beneath those arching limbs of the then green shaded beauty I ever witnessed or ever expect to see again. It was on an August day just as the loving sun was going down and throwing its purpling "trembling horns" in all their swinging beauty around these limbs that you now see in their white waxen flowers tinted with their starting green foliage. Beneath this beautiful natural canopy of green stood a young maiden with black hair and beaming dark eyes, with a white bottle of water in her arms nearly filled with cool water taken from the gushing spring in the jungle just across the road. She stood as an angel of mercy. At her feet and against the trunk of that tree leaned her sister, resting on her right elbow, a Scotch lassie of thirteen summers. She was gowned in modest Scotch plaids of the Campbell stripes, her long, rich, auburn hair hung in two large, soft braids in front across her left shoulder. Her large, blue pensive eyes sparkled in a face that the smiles of love always adorned. This was to me a picture of health in beauty unadorned by art, a picture that no hand of art can ever reproduce. "Lassies." said I, "you have chosen quite a pretty place for rest this beautiful evening." Then that mouth made to speak kind words opened its ruddy lips, moving over pearly teeth, causing, as I thought, that Scotch like vermilion hue to play around over her lovely cheeks. She answered in the sweetest, calmest tones: "I was so warm and thirsty, I had to stop here and rest while sister went to the spring and brought me a cool drink of water, and it was so cool!" said the thankful soul. I learned at once through these trembling lips that uttered these soft words that it was something like the hectic flush intruding on that fair face. I asked if there was anything that I could do to help them on. Sweet words of thanks came from both lips, saying "Thank you, we will try to make it on in a little while." Their home was far away, but they were stopping with their grandmother near my home, going to the same school with me; they were my own dear, fond school mates. I knew what to do. I hastened on to tell what I saw and thought to their grandparents, and in a little while their grandfather was with them with a vehicle to take them to his home, and the sick one was soon enfolded in the tender arms of a dear, affectionate grandmother. She never reached her dear parental home, but her loved ones were soon with her, bringing all the help that could be found. But typhoid fever had taken hold on her, and as April's sun had melted the white waxen flowers that so beautifully symbolized her pure life, so, now, the fever's heat in these hot August days melts away her sweet mortal life. Her young spirit took wings just as the bright, soft sun began to glint amid the tender blue of the morning. The next day her body was borne to the new Valley cemetery, followed by her many friends and weeping loved ones, all submissively wondering at the providence of God in taking from the home, the school, the community, that tender flower "snatched away in beauty's bloom." But all found comfort in the sentiment of this story. A King had a landscape garden; he employed two florists, assigning them portions in his garden that they might keep it and raise for him the choicest shrubs and flowers until his coming, and then he went away. They were faithful rivals, each doing his best; they planted and raised by the best culture the choicest species of shrubs and flowers. Soon their labors were crowned with rich blooming beauties in a variety of colors and fragrance. It was conceded by all that number "one" raised by far the choicest flowers in fragrance and rare beauty in all the garden; this was even conceded by gardener number "two"; and he was overjoyed at his success, thinking how the King, on his return, would be pleased with its fragrance and extravagant beauty. But this gardener was away for a little while one morning, and on returning found that some one had entered the garden and had plucked and taken away his dearest flower. So he was sorrowful and his anxious heart bled, when he thought of the cruel one who would blast all of his fond hopes. While he was sorrowing so, one approached him and said, "In the beauty of the early morning, when the little birds sang so sweetly and chirped and nestled amid your shrubs and flowers, and while you were away, we saw the King walking through his garden, enjoying its beauties; and when he came to your choicest flower he stopped and drank in its fragrance and beauty; then he smiled and plucked it from the stem and carried it away with him." Then the poor gardener smiled and was glad and exclaimed, "It is well, for it was for him I raised it!" So, too, these sorrowing ones said "It is the Lord, let Him take His own to the prepared mansion." They dug the grave in the east end of the cemetery, among the great spreading trees in the deep shades of the Valley. Just as the dying day was going, just as the setting sun was sinking beneath the purpling west, that casket that held all that was left of that dear one was gently lowered to its resting place, the sod of the Valley softly laid over it, and the rich mould gathered shapely above it while tears flowed freely down furrowed faces and made moist the blanched cheeks of the young that were there. Then with sad hearts we all went to our several homes, leaving that dear sleeping body at rest in the beautiful new home claimed for the dead, beneath the stars of God's great universe, awaiting there the victory of the resurrection. This was the first funeral I had ever attended. The words spoken and the scenes of that yet lingering day went straight to my young heart, impressing me as I had never been before or since; and they are as vivid to my memory now as they were on that eventful, sad occasion. This young Scotch laddie, a lover of poetry and beauty in nature, was Wm. McPherson, a graduate in the first class of old Knox Hill Academy, Walton's first son from the Academy to Oglethorpe College, Georgia, a graduate of the Lebanon law school, of Lebanon, Tenn. It was he that wrote *"Propos de Table"* (Table Talk) that was much read and so very popular in California, where it was written and the characters placed. This book was not only entertaining and amusing, but it had a vein of rich moral thought running through it. It was written in "prose poetry," the language of his every day conversation, the language of his heart and mind, with gushes of exuberant joy and ardent love tingling through it, from beginning to end, disturbed only by bitter disappointments and weird neglect, which always come as incidents of surcharged passions. The critics dealt with this book pro and con, as sane and pointed, as extravagant and falling short of the mark. As Captain of the Walton Guards he became Major of the Battalion when the two companies were formed at Camp Walton. After the war he located at Marianna, Fla., in the law business and married a Miss ____ Baltzell of that town. After the death of his young wife he cast his lot in the far West and sleeps today solitary and alone on the Pacific slopes beneath the golden sands of California.

Lessons Learned

The writer learned that a day spent in this Sacred City in the Valley, though saddening to the heart, is refreshing to the mind and soul. It brings many dear recollections to mind, deeds of kindness done, deeds neglected that might have been done. You can't go away after spending such a day there without being a better man or woman. I saw there that day a stone darkened with age overhung by bridal wreaths. I asked my brother who stood close by to pull the wreaths aside that I might read the superscription, and this is what it said: "James Tinlin. Born in Scotland A.D. 1800. Died at Col. John L. McKinnon's in 1852. Buried away from his Scotia, but in the midst of his Scotch friends." Then we remembered the highly educated young Scotchman our father found in Pensacola, suffering from some pulmonary disease, and brought him home with him, and gave him one of our best bed rooms. How he would recuperate and go back in a few months to his work in the navy yard and return again and again and finally came to stay, to stop here for a rest on his way to his eternal home. We remembered how our mother and sisters would be up with him in the cold winter nights trying with medicines to aid his expectorations, and how very grateful he was.

Then we remembered the grave of George McArthur here, where and how our father found this sick young man and brought him to his home. We were on a week's cow hunt on the bay. Passing near Portland our father spoke to a man coming out from the bayou, who told us of a young man alone in one of the bunks of the steamer "New Boston" then lying for the summer at Portland, who was suffering with high fever. We turned in and found him sure enough alone, no one to hand him so much as a cup of cold water. It was three o'clock in the afternoon, September's sun was pouring its hottest rays against his bunk. He was full of Choctawhatchie river malaria, his fever was high, the Captain and owner of the vessel was away seeking medical help for him, and his nurse had left him; we gave him water and such comforts as we were able to find there, and he was so grateful! Our father asked him if he would not like for him to take him to his home on the farm where he would be well cared for? How gladly he accepted the invitation! The cow hunt was abandoned. We hastened on home, a distance of 18 miles; after reaching home we had a negro man to make ready a wagon, placed a feather bed in it, and the writer was sent with the negro man in the night time, while it was cool and less fatiguing than to come in the hot day. We were back at home with him before the sun was up the next day and he seemed to be none the worse from the trip. The very best medical aid and nursing that could be had was given him, but the fever would not yield, it did its work in spite of medicines. He lingered for several weeks. was patient and thankful to the end, and passed away in peace and his body rests beneath these shades.

Here too was the grave of Hubbard, a Mississippi cavalry soldier, left behind by his command in a low, suffering condition near Euchee Anna. Our father had him brought to his home to be cared for. It was in the dead of the cold winter, they had to keep him on a bed before the open fire place in the parlor to keep him warm he was so nervous; he claimed to be cold through and through. He was quite 'different from the other two slick men, he was ungrateful, unappreciative, hard to wait on. The colored servants who waited on him gave him the name of "growling Hubbard," and when our mother, knowing his nervous prostration, would express sympathy and fears about his recovery, these negro nurses would say, "Don't fear. Missus, he is too contrary to die." But the poor abandoned Confederate soldier had more to annoy him than his nurses thought, and after two months nervous, prostrating suffering, the poor boy died, like many another poor Confederate soldier, away from his command, away from his home and loved ones, leaving the unfinished battles to be fought by others. Now these are just a few incidents of sacrifices in just one family of the early pioneers that crowd upon our memories in this sacred place, and given as lessons for their generations. The like can be told of many other families. Let the lessons from these be impressed in the form of this question. Are we, their descendants, as ready to help the destitute in our land today as our fathers and mothers were in their day? When opportunity brings you face to face with distress, be ever ready to lend the helping hand. And don't forget to launch out and seek opportunities for doing good to your fellows.

Fourth Epoch

Chapter Thirty-Seven - The Civil War

We have dwelt at some length on the third epoch in Walton history. It is pleasant to linger about these delightful days, these ante-bellum hours of peace and plenty and contentment. But these bright Elysian days issuing in joy and gladness of heart, ushered in or were rather harbingers of a pandemonium of days, filled with the destruction of life and property and happiness. Great political agitations are being felt all over our lovely land. National parties are dividing up on political and sectional lines, and new parties are being formed. The dark ominous cloud that had been gathering so long around the political horizon of our country, seems to have settled heavily over our capital and now it begins to spread over our fair land. Sectional feelings run high. These contending parties resort to the ballot box, that had ever been the peaceful quietings in like National commotions. But when it was opened, instead of its restoring the blessings of peace of the ballot box of other days, it proved to be an open Pandora's Box, full of ills. The fourth epoch — the war days are at hand. States begin to secede, the cloud over the capital begins to quiver, flashes of lightning begin to leap from it, deep tones of thunder come out of its blackness. Florida says let's secede and go with the other States and calls a convention of her people. Walton says no, Lincoln will administer the Government in accordance with the Constitution. He is not one of those who would put a strictly literal construction on the declaration, "All men are born free and equal," and then object to giving a literal meaning to the laws and Constitution of our fathers, or to having this declaration interpreted by their doings in the premises. He says clearly, in one of his public addresses: "He (the negro) is not my equal in many respects, certainly not in color, perhaps not in morals or intellectual endowment." You see, he does not claim that the negro is our equal, neither does he believe in social equality. So the mere election of Lincoln by

John Morrison

the people in accordance with the law and the Constitution, gives no good reason for secession, even if it was sectional and not by a plurality of votes. We claim that the Constitution is all right and that we have ever stood by it and the Union, and if any one must go out of the Union let those who have been trampling upon it and the Constitution be driven out. These were the correct and logical views. Walton was a Whig county and was not afraid of Lincoln's administration with his views on slavery. And she easily elected anti-secession delegates to the Convention, by an almost unanimous vote. John Morrison and A. L. McCaskill were elected and instructed to vote against the secession of the State, and they voted as directed to the last, and the Convention gave to Walton the appellation of "Lincoln County." But Florida seceded from the Union, all of the delegates signing the articles of secession except Walton's delegates mentioned above and a few others from West Florida. Let it be remembered here that the question of the State having the right to secede or that the States had grievances that ought to be redressed under the Constitution were not mooted in this election. It was the inexpediency of the act that she opposed. It is not always best to say or do what we know we have a right to say and do. Walton believed with the State of Florida and the other States that a sovereign State that was a State before the Union was formed and which had voluntarily entered the Union, might voluntarily and peaceably withdraw from it, and that we had grievances that ought to be redressed inside of the Union. The difference of opinion was only in the manner of redress. The State said, "by going out of the Union." Walton said, "they can and ought to be redressed in the Union." A Confederate government is being formed at Montgomery, Ala., with a new Constitution and a new flag, as much like the old as two black-eyed peas. In fact these Constitutions were virtually the same, the flag having bars instead of stripes, proving their devotion to and respect for the old. There was a hurrying to and fro over the land, the shadows of the spreading clouds were falling thick about us, war is not only imminent but it has actually begun. The booms of Sumter's cannons are heard through their vibrations from ocean to ocean, from the great lakes to the Mexican Sea. Florida calls for troops. Walton is

Col. A. L. McCaskill

among the very first to respond, in a splendid company of young men, the flower of her land, under Captain Wm. McPherson, First Lieut. C. L. McKinnon, Second Lieut. A. B. McLeod and Third Lieut. H. W. Reddick, to make up the First Florida Regiment. This company was held in reserve as a guard on this Choctawhatchie coast. Henry Hatcher and Iverson Goodwin went on and joined another company in the First Florida Regiment and represented Walton in the battle of Santa Rosa Island and the battle of Shiloh. About the first of July, 1861, this first company under the name of "Walton Guards" was placed on duty on the bay on the Narrows and they called the station "Camp Walton." They were stationed there to watch East Pass entrance and to report the maneuvers of the blockading vessels anchored out in the Gulf near East Pass and to protect the inland waterway leading from Pensacola up the Choctawhatchie Sound, Narrows and up the bay that leads to Fre^ Port in Walton. They remained there for one and a half years. They were armed at first with all kinds of fire arms that they could pick up around their homes, the long Buckhannon rifle, the old flint and steel Indian war musket, single and double-barrel shot gun. the short rifle and the boy-bird gun; the most of these were flint and steel and all muzzle loaders. These soldiers were armed later "to the very teeth" with great Zouave bowie-knives. They seemed to depend on these more than on their snapping guns, that had to be kept primed with fresh power in the pan to make a shot. It is enough to say that this company did excellent service. They kept a gunboat anchored all the time in the Gulf opposite East Pass or opposite their camp. We had a supply schooner that plyed between Camp Walton, Free Port and Pensacola to bring our supplies and mail. As our schooner was passing East Pass one day this blockading war vessel sent out her long boats to capture her. We drove them back with heavy loss, we having the advantage, lost none. Our supply boat was fired on several times from behind the island mounds while passing up and down from Pensacola and Free Port besides the occasion already mentioned, when they shelled us out in the early morning while standing at roll call with batteries brought up from Fort Pickens parked behind the mounds on the island opposite our camps, assisted by the man-of-war ship anchored opposite our station. So very powerful were her guns that they cut off trunks of trees twelve inches in diameter one mile beyond our camp. After this our government sent us a large cannon to answer back to them, which we mounted on a mound in the midst of our camp for action, from which we had a fair sweep over island and gulf. I have often wondered how easily we could have been captured had the enemy known how poorly we were armed at first, and have been impressed with the thought of how much there is in brass, in dare, especially in times of war. To say that we had a good time at Camp Walton, in spite of the strict drill, heavy guard duty and dangers that surrounded us, would but be giving a faint idea of the good time. We were not satisfied with one boat to bring down our relatives and friends to see us, our supplies and mail, we chartered a second schooner. It was a delightful place to spend the summer, had an abundance of choice fish. For the first year these lady relatives and friends furnished us with all our clothing and most of our food supplies from home. At the end of the first year's service, there was a reenlistment of the old Walton Guards and the forming of two new companies.

Chapter Thirty-Eight - Reenlistment — Two Companies

Captain C. L. McKinnon raised a company under the reenlistment with First Lieut. Neill I. McKinnon, Second Lieut. Dave Evins, Third Lieut. Robt. McCallum. Captain A. B. McLeod raised one with First Lieut. H. W. Reddick, Second Lieut. H. T. Wright, Third Lieut. James Cotton. These companies were armed with the very best guns extant. After these companies were organized we began to get the most of our supplies from our headquarters at the Pensacola navy yard. Major McPherson made out a list of camp equipage, provisions, ammunition and clothing, all in his own neat handwriting. We had never drawn any clothing before, and on this list he made application for certain articles and sizes of clothing for new recruits, adding "We are in particular need of these articles, as some of the men are now in almost a state of nudity." He signed it officially, put it in an official envelope, addressed it neatly and officially to the commander of the post, Pensacola Navy Yard, General Samuel Jones. The writer took it down and handed it to the General, who opened and read it and when he had finished reading he threw it down in hot haste into the waste basket, saying, "I will send him nothing. An officer that acknowledges his men, at this day, to be in a state of mutiny is not fit to command a company of monkeys!" I said to him very calmly but with some feeling of pride, "I never heard of any talk of mutiny in the camps up there." He replied, "I'll send a court martial committee up there and have this whole matter investigated!" Then I said to him, "General, will you please let me look at the letter just a moment?" He took the letter from the basket and handed it to me, saying, "It is his closing words." I read them over carefully and said, "General, aren't you mistaken in taking the word 'nudity' for the word 'mutiny?'" I handed him the letter. He read it and said, "Yes it is 'nudity' and it is written plainly, too." Yet he did not have the true soldierly manliness to apologize. The order was promptly filled and we had many a hearty laugh over this little word, and were deeply impressed with the value in a word. I am reminded of this incident now by reading recently a mistake in a word given by Judge Campbell in his "Historical Sketches of Colonial Florida," and give it here for the same reasons he gives it. "To illustrate the vice or virtue there may be in a word or name," he says, "in A. D. 1822 when the legislative council of thirteen appointed by the President met in Pensaloca under W. P. Duval as Governor of Florida and from Kentucky, and on account of yellow fever breaking out; in Pensacola compelled an adjournment to the Fifteen Mile House, among the Acts passed there was one, the title of 'An Act for the Benefit of Indigent Debtors,' was misprinted in the laws of the session so as to read: 'An Act for the relief of Insolent Debtors.' The error destroyed its utility, and no man, it is said, as long as it remained on the statute book ever invoked the relief of its provisions."

We will linger no longer around the pleasant haunts of old Camp Walton, on which a book could be written on the pleasant camp life there that would carry interest to many readers for years, Capt. Reddick has written at large on the "Walton Guards and Camp Walton," which will be of interest. Now we will lead to the more active front, "Young America," the restless young soldier boy, chafing for more active service and fearing lest the war might close before he could show his valor on some big bloody battlefield like Manassas, Bull's Run or Shiloh, is longing for the front. Poor restless, dissatisfied, ambitious, longing, soldier boy! How very soon his longings, his unbridled ambitions were satisfied on many a bloody battlefield. How often he wished for the pleasant shades of old Camp Walton, for his hammock swinging in the grove, for the toothsome fish pulled fresh from the Gulf or Narrows as his fastidious taste indicated, to hear the murmurings of deep waters, to be fanned by the soft gentle breezes fresh from the Gulf stream.

Chapter Thirty-Nine - Leaves Camp Walton

On the 16th day of August, A. D. 1862, we struck camps and bid adieu to the dear Old Camp with its many home-like amenities, for Pensacola Navy Yard. From that day on Walton's earliest soldiers and all who came after them began to see hard army service on every line in the eastern, middle and western armies. The lines were being drawn tight around them, the watchword was "March and Fight." We can't speak so definitely of those who enlisted in battalions and regiments other than ours, the First Florida Regiment, as they were in different parts of the army the most of the time. We must leave this for other writers who are more conversant with their history. After the destroying and evacuation of the Navy Yard at Pensacola, we were stationed for a while at Camp Pringle, on the Escambia river above Pensacola, where our companies suffered much by the introduction of measles into our camp. From there we were sent to Montgomery and stationed for a while. From thence to "Camp Moccasin" on the Tennessee river at Chattanooga, and from there we went on that forced march through Kentucky under General Bragg. On that march we made ready near Mumfordsville and not far from the Mammoth Cave for a night battle with General Rosencrans, but moved on and fought the battle of Perryville in the open field standing on a ridge, while the enemy stood behind a stone fence. General Wm. Miller, then Colonel, commanded our Regiment, General John C. Brown commanded our Brigade and was in our immediate rear until he and his horse were shot down. Walton lost several brave young men in that battle. The writer was shot in the left forearm, ball passing between two bones, shattering them. While he lay suffering on that bloody field he saw General Brown's horse standing in the agonies of a fatal bomb explosion, on his hind legs, and then fall dead to the ground, his master on him badly wounded. It was then that this pertinent question was asked, "Is this the glory of the bloody battlefield we read of in books?" The Confederates won the battle, the Federals were driven from the stone fence and our line advanced. I was helped off the battlefield by my youngest brother, Daniel L. McKinnon and friend John McLean. They got me under the hill in a ravine, where we were sheltered some little from the flying missiles. They had plenty of water to cool my bleeding wound and quench my thirst. I always felt that this water was one of the means in their hands in saving my life. The water was the last thing I remembered until sometime in the night of that day I found myself on a cot in front of the amputating room in a hospital in Harrodsburg. Ky. I was awakened by the groans of the poor sufferers under the amputating knife. Early the next morning I remember my brother coming to me and saying, "They are expecting a battle today and want all the soldiers to be in line. The doctor here says he will see that you are cared for, so I think I had better go to the command and as soon as the battle is over I will get permission and come in and see you." But I never saw him again in Kentucky. Bragg went out through Cumberland Gap and he was taken out with him, and I was left to fall into the hands of the enemy. In the evening of the next day I saw the doctor of my ward going around with a bevy of the ladies of the town, talking to them about the condition of the wounded. When they were by the side of my cot the doctor said to them: "This young man is shot through the arm; his wound is not dangerous, but he is very weak from the loss of blood, and faints when lifted up." As they passed on to the next, one of the ladies stopped and drew near my cot and said to me, "Would you not like to go out to our home here in town and let me take care of you?" I said "Sure I would!" and thanked her right heartily and began to feel better right then. Something like home seemed to be in prospect. She called the doctor back and said to him, "I want you to send this young man to our home and I will see that he gets the best of attention." He told her that it would not be safe to move me for several days, but as soon as I was able to be moved he would send me to her home. In a few days I saw the kind lady coming with four strong men bearing a litter. I was placed on it and borne by these men to her home and up a winding stairway into a quiet, handsomely furnished room opening out on the main street. She furnished me with a splendid negro boy to wait on me. And what a change for a wornout, wounded soldier, taken from the turmoil of battle and hospital, from the stench of human blood, to this pleasant retreat in the home of Miss Mary Herndon to breath pure air and fare like a king!

These good ladies came to the hospital day after day taking to their homes such wounded soldiers as could be moved until their homes were filled, and they never forgot to care for those who had to remain. My lady friend had ever so many young lady friends and relatives, among them the Misses Bettie and Florence Hood, of Danville, Kentucky, nieces of General John B. Hood, two beautiful lovely lassies who called on me with the others while I was a shut-in. When I got up and out I had a nice time returning calls. Miss Herndon through the Trapsnells. who were her relatives, procured a permit, giving me the liberties of the town and surrounding country. I was taken to the Perryville battlefield. Shakertown and other places worth seeing in that blue grass region. And I, wherever I went, received royal or rather homelike treatment, and this with other kindnesses received, brings old Kentucky close to my heart, next to my own dear Land of Flowers. And in passing up and down the steeps of life I look back with a delight to my stay in Harrodsburg as one of the green pages in my life's history. When Dr. C. A. Landrum, of my company, who was wounded in the left leg at Perryville and left with me at Harrodsburg, but not in the same home, were well enough to be moved, they sent us, with other prisoners to Lexington, Ky., and we were crowded into a filthy county jail where negroes had been kept with small pox. Quite a change from our Harrodsburg confinement! In a little while some of the good ladies came to our relief, told us that they would see that we would have better quarters in a little while. And in a short time we were taken from this filthy place to a two-story new building.

The Gillis Brothers

While in these new quarters several ladies called asking if there was any one from Florida in the prison? We told them that we were from Florida. They asked if we knew Murdock and William Gillis, young Confederate soldiers of the Sixth Florida Regiment. We told them we did. Then the fact of their death was broken to us. These ladies said, it can truly be said of them, 'They were pleasant and lovely in their lives and in their death they were not divided.' We were taken from there to Louisville, Ky., and kept there for several days. While there it was reported that we would be taken from there to Vicksburg for exchange. This was good news for us, so in a little while we were taken down the Ohio River to its conjunction with the Mississippi and kept there in the suburbs of Cairo, in a low, wet place with but little shelter, cold drizzly rain or hominy snow falling all the time, no place to make a fire to warm by except out in the open air on the wet ground, no blankets or bedding of any kind to sleep on. In this condition we spent the time there, until one day a "Free Mason" came down and found quite a number of Masons among us, and he went away and in a little while he returned with a dray load of good blankets for us all. This was quite a treat and we blessed him. Notwithstanding these surroundings the soldiers were jolly all the while, and would sit close together around the smokey fire, in the drip, and without the doors with the new blankets pulled close about them, and sing the Confederate National songs such as "Dixie," "My Maryland," and the like.

Chapter Forty - On to Vicksburg

Finally the hoped for news eventuated in placing us on board of the "City of Madison." a large steamer with hundreds of other prisoners. Her great prow turned down the Mississippi, splitting the water in the direction of Vicksburg, making no stops save where she rounded up to some bluff or landing, where the gang-planks were run ashore to take from on board the dead body of some poor oldier for burial, who had made an exchange, we hoped, far better than the one he had in prospect at Vicksburg, that he had reached a mansion of peace beyond the river more glorious than the earthly home of anxious, watching loved ones. As we steamed down the river a collier followed close in our wake, but gave to the breeze no white flag. Our steamer filled up her bunkers once from her supply of coal. The burden of her coal was for General Grant's work changing the course of the Mississippi at Vicksburg. One bright day as we steamed along near the banks on the Arkansas side of the river, we passed a mammoth tree lying on the ground near to and parallel with the river. As we were passing it twelve or fifteen Arkansas soldiers rose up from behind this tree, lifted their broad brimmed hats from their heads and waved them on high giving "Three cheers for Jeff Davis." This was something new to us up there and those of us on deck responded to them with right good cheer; then they sank back behind their tree. Our steamer blew a blast from her whistle, we thought she was cheering with us, but when the collier came up opposite flying no white flag, they greeted her with a fusillade of musketry, driving her to the opposite side and down the river with all the power she could muster, she, too, blowing her whistle with its loudest blasts. The pilot house was filled with shot, the pilot and one man was wounded, the only damage sustained. The Captain told us that these were an independent roving band in Arkansas, that did a great deal of hurt along the river. When our craft steamed up to the dock at Vicksburg we all passed out unmolested, a happy band with our feet planted again in Dixie's land. This was the last trip the "City of Madison" made. She was burned up on the next. We were passed on to Jackson, Miss., where those of us with unhealed wounds received furloughs to our homes until we were able to go to the front. We reached our homes in safety. Words are too weak and poor to express the joy of a soldier at home from the army, the prison, on a furlough. It was but a little while before we were able to return to the army and go on regular duty with our command, stationed at Tullahoma, Tenn. The Sixth Florida Regiment with a Walton County Company in it that was raised by Col. A. D. McLeon and afterwards commanded by Capt. S. D. Cawthon, were in Kentucky with our First Florida Regiment. They came in by way of Big Creek Gap, with Kirby Smith, and all came out by way of Cumberland Gap with Bragg. Walton's soldiers in the First Regiments fought, soon after their return, in the first battle of Murfreesboro with distinction. The First and Third Regiments were moved the following summer to Mississippi and stationed around Jackson and fought in all the battles defending that place, with more loss to the enemy than to them, we fighting most of the time from behind breastworks. We went from there on a forced march to support Vicksburg. We were crossing big Black on our pontoons when the word reached us telling us of its capitulation. We fell back to Canton, then to Jackson, to Morton, and from there back to Tennessee. And we may say, Walton's troops fought in all the battles, from the battle "among the clouds" at Lookout Mountain to Atlanta. Walton's precious blood reddened Missionary Ridge and every mountain top, hill and valley that intervened.

Chapter Forty-One - Battle of Chickamauga

On Friday before the Chickamauga battle our Regiments, First and Third, were placed on the extreme left of our army, without provisions in our haversacks. The Sixth Florida was placed on the right. There was a little grist mill on one of these mountain torrent streams near where we were stationed that turned out flour very slowly. Our commissary man hauled up quite a lot of fine wheat to this mill, turned over the plant to us to grind, bake and eat as fast as we could, for they knew not at what moment the fight might come on. We run this mill day and night, each taking his turn catching the flour fresh from the mill, baking it on heated rocks and eating it while it was yet warm, for a day and night, without catching up with our hunger, when we had to go to the battle to drive back the Federal Cavalry from our source of supply. This incident is called to mind by a true story Col. Chipley always delighted in telling on D. L. McKinnon, who soon after the war commenced the practice of law in Walton. McKinnon had a client, a Mr. Daniels, who rented a little grist mill from a Mr. Henderson, on Alaqua creek for a part of its earnings. Daniels refused to pay the rent and was sued for possession. Henderson was placed upon the stand and stated the contract to the jury. Then came Daniels, whose only plea was, that the mill would not make meal up to the capacity it was represented to him. McKinnon said to him, "Mr. Daniels, state to the jury how much grist this mill would turn out per hour?" He replied, "I have never timed it by the hour." Tell them," said McKinnon, "how much per day?" "I have never timed it by the day," said Daniels. "Well," said McKinnon, "can't you give the jury some idea of its capacity for making grist?" Daniels innocently said, "Well, I went down to the mill early one morning, put up a bushel of corn into the hopper — hoisted the gate and put the mill to grinding. I went back to the mill just before noon — in four or five hours — I had a medium-sized hound dog and I found this dog of mine standing in the meal chest, eating the meal as fast as the mill ground it." Mr. McKinnon said, "Mr. Daniels, how long could this dog have continued to do this?" "I believe sir, he could have done it until he would have starved to death," said Daniels. So, too, we believe our command could have eaten the flour from that Chickamauga mountain mill as fast as it ground it, until we would all have starved to death. It is well to state here that McKinnon had to sue Daniels for his fee, Daniels claiming that it was his understanding that McKinnon was to take part of the damages for his fee. But we were not held at this mill to starve — we were called to the front to keep back the cavalry the next day — Saturday — and fought most of the day on the extreme left of our army, with but little losses in Walton's soldiers. In the deep stillness of that late night, we were moved, by the way we came, from the extreme left to the extreme right of our army. As we plodded along by the little mill, we could hear it knocking away at its grist, the hungry soldiers would break ranks, run by and fill up their haversacks with what had accumulated through the hours we had been away beating back the U. S. cavalry. As we marched on, for miles, to do bloody battle all through that long coming day and well into its night, and when the day began to dawn and the glorious sun with its gentle rays of soft light began to light up the fields and forests that we were passing through — what a sickening, heartrending spectacle in carnage — in bitter death, was presented to our view! The day came to us, just as we were passing through the bloodiest battle-fields of the day before, and as we passed along, there lay on either hand both the soldiers in gray and the soldiers in blue, often close together. There lay dismantled field-pieces, horses and mules, piled up in death all about them. To add to the horrors of this scene of carnage in war, the forests were on fire, burning up the clothing and flesh of our fallen braves. No time for a halt, to protect or do homage to the bodies of these fallen brothers. For the command comes, "Hasten on in a forced march to shed more precious blood" — the gluttonous appetite of cruel civil war is not satisfied. Oh, what a stench in the nostrils of tired, sleepy, hungry soldiers, marching on to ready battle! Shame to our boasted civilized manhood! No wonder delicate, tender woman turn aside and shudders now, at the thought of grim, cruel, civil war! A little after sunrise we were in line of battle, in front of the enemy's entrenched strongholds, ready to charge their works. At the command, the charge was made with heavy loss, without moving them. It was repeated throughout the day, with first one brigade, or division, and then another, with great loss, and no good results. As the sun was passing away several lines of battle were formed in the oak scrub thicket as close up to the enemy's lines as we dared to go. All were commanded to lie down on the ground as flat as flounders and as quiet as beetles, and await orders. As we lay there in this suspense, the sharpshooters' bullets flying thick above our heads, my brother, A. D. McKinnon, whispered to me, "The sun is now gone, there are three lines of battle in our front, and I don't think we will have to charge the works any more today, for before these in front of us get through it will be too dark for us to make a charge.

The Charge That Won

When darkness was on, there came a whispered command down the line to our line first: "Attention, 1st and 3rd Florida Regiments!" We were on our feet in automatic quickness and order, and then we were moved over and just beyond the three lines lying prostrate in our front, who readily forgave heavy tramping upon them in passing to the front. They, too, were brought to attention. Then this whispered order came to all, "At the words, 'forward, march,' let every soldier move to the front in quiet, perfect order, and at the words, 'charge bayonets,' let every man give the Rebel Yell, run with all his might right up to their breastworks, and let no one fire a gun until he is on their works.' These orders were admirably carried out — so said our division commander, Gen, John C. Breckenridge. When the last command was given — our brigade in the lead — was near enough to see the bulk of their breastworks through the deep shadows of the long departing day. The darkness that had come over them, and the consternation of that awful yell, caused the enemy to overshoot us, and we reached their works with loaded guns, while theirs were empty. They thought to do the decent thing — throw theirs down and take to the woods, so the day made glorious, was ours in its close. Worn out, and hungry, we were parked in the thicket, just in the rear of these works near the edge of an old field. Scouts were put out to gather in those who were cut off from their main army, and all through the night and next forenoon, bands of armed and unarmed Union soldiers were brought in, and some came into our lines seeking their commands. Quite a batch of them came to Walton's camps inquiring after their division. They were told that they were in Breckenridge's division, who was pointed out to them a little ways in the grove, sitting on the ground in his shirtsleeves, with his legs doubled in front of him broiling a bit of meat on the live coals. When they realized their mistake, they seemed somewhat relieved to know that they were in his command, and when they had surrendered their arms, they desired to see him more closely. And they were escorted by quite a number of the guard to where he sat on the ground. They gathered anxiously around him — some climbed up trees that stood about him to get a better view. One — a little Irishman — short of stature, being crowded back cried out, "General, will you please stand up so that we may have a good look at you?" The General readily stood up with his broiled bacon on a bit of corn bread in his left hand, his knife in his right, straightening himself up to his manly height, he said, "Well, gentlemen, this is what is left of me." The little Irishman exclaimed, "Yes, and a d—m fine specimen of humanity you are, too! There is not another such a hunk of humanity in our land! I voted for you once, and I want this cursed war over with so that I may vote for you again for president." We cheered and they cheered. The General thanked all and said to them as they retired, "We will take the best care of you we can. I am willing to divide this morsel with you all (the bit of bread and meat in his hand) if you think we can make it go around." They thanked him for the kind offer. Now, all who ever saw this noble man know how very truly the little Irishman appreciated his elegant physique, for he surely was as fine a specimen of humanity as ever animated a human soul, and was as good as his looks. It was an inspiration to look upon his manly, symmetrical form, to look into his intelligent, beaming eyes, sparkling with benignity. We left Henry Hatcher for dead on the field in one of our morning charges — shot in the face. Six months afterwards we got a letter from home stating that he had spent the night with them, and says he was captured three times that day and retaken each time. I never see him or think of this but as a miracle. We remained on this battle ground until we rested and got enough to eat once more. Walton's loss, in killed and wounded, was considerable in Sunday's battles. After this battle the 6th, 7th, and 4th consolidated with the 1st Florida cavalry (dismounted) were put with the 1st and 3rd Florida regiments and were put in one brigade. J. J. Finley was made general and this command was known 'till close of the war as the "Florida Brigade," and after this, the history of Walton's soldiers is practically the same.

Chapter Forty-Two - General Joseph E. Johnston's Battles and Retreats to Atlanta

General Johnston in falling back to Atlanta confronted the enemy in line of battle in every conceivable way, on the hills and in the plains, on the mountain tops and valleys — in the scrub woods and open fields. Some evenings the two armies would be drawn up in lines of battle near each other, with nothing but a little woodland in a ravine intervening; and we would predict that the next day's sun would rise and set in blood. But the next morning would find us far apart and no battle fought. On this retreat to Atlanta, on one occasion, double lines of breastworks, of the two armies, were drawn so close together on the top of the mountains, that it was difficult a little ways to the right or left to tell from which works the "Stars and Bars" or the "Stars and Stripes" waved. They were built so close together that water carriers would pass over through mistake into the wrong lines with their water. These confronting lines, when permitted, would keep up a friendly conversation with each other in an ordinary tone of voice. Yet they would charge each others works, trying to take them, and be mown down like wheat in the field. Then they would have an armistice to bury the dead. After abandoning these works in such close proximity, and manoeuvering and skirmishing around for several days, we fell back into a well prepared, one line breastworks. It was evident to us all that it was laid out by good engineers who knew their duty, who prepared it with a view to our acting on the defensive altogether. It ran almost north and south along a ridge with a deep ravine in front. All the undergrowth was cut down in the ravine and well up on the opposite hill slope, and these were tangled and tied so as to make an almost unapproachable, impregnable line of defense — impossible for the enemy to surprise or reach us alive. Of course, the enemy came up and entrenched on the opposite hill and threw out their picket line in the woodland in their front. We were well pleased with this situation and rested complacently for several days in perfect safety, with no picket line in our front. We kept watch from the ditches, all sleeping on our arms while there. But one afternoon, while the soldiers lay closely in the ditches for protection from sharpshooters' bullets, many of them enjoying sweet sleep, there came an order down the line from our right through the officers, "Put your men in readiness to pass over the breastworks and take the enemy's line in their front." Capt. McKinnon had to awaken from sleep several of his men to give the order and whispered to me as he passed, "I feel that I am awakening these men to go to their deaths." And it was true with very many of them. Just as we were crossing over in front of our works Capt. McKinnon called to me, saying. "Col. McLean is dead, shot through the head!" Shot while moving up the line getting his men ready to pass over to the front — shot by sharpshooters' bullets. He fell here as the first sacrifice of the day's battle — a noble young soldier — my kinsman, my schoolmate for many years at old Knox Hill Academy. There too stood Capt. Saxson, next in rank to Capt. McKinnon, wounded in the head and blood streaming down his face, received while crossing the works. We all rushed down the hill into the ravine and then up the hill into the grove into the very jaws of death, our men falling along every step of the route. There we found the enemy entrenched behind well prepared works, and a strong picket line in pits just in front of them, with commissioned officers in the pits with them. We went close up to their picket line in the grove before we commenced firing on them. Of course, they had all the advantage over us. Our flag-bearer. Sergeant Bazemore, fell at my right with flag and face towards the enemy. A commissioned officer jumped out of the pit, with sword drawn, pointed to the flag, saying to his men in the pit, "Take it! Take it!" I directed John Love McLean to direct his firing line on this officer, and he did and was wounded in return in the thigh, and had to be taken to the rear. Others fired on him, but he seemed to be invulnerable. In the meantime Sergeant Bridgman snatched up the flag and lifted it on high in its place. Bridgman was shot down and the flag fell again. The smoke from the firing of the two armies became so dense that it almost enveloped the place in darkness, which was to our advantage. Lieutenant Stebbins grabbed the flag when Bridgman fell. The order was given to fall back to our breastworks. Stebbins, though badly wounded, tore the flag from its staff, crammed it in his bosom and brought it off. Passing the infirmary corps with many wounded friends and as we were rising to the top of the hill, and very near our works of safety, Capt. Columbus Cobb, from that part of Walton that went to make Santa Rosa county, turned to me and said, "Did you ever hear of such a fool order for the massacre of noble men?" These words had scarcely passed his lips when a minnie ball struck him in the left side, and he fell over on his face a dead man without a struggle. I ran to him, tried to lift him, but soon found that he was gone. Almost safe behind our impregnable breastworks, but lost! The curtains of night were being let down around us as we reached our fortifications. And there were such a running to and fro, up and down the line by the relatives and friends inquiring after their loved ones. The ravine and hillside were being searched under the sable cover of the welcome night, and many brought out. In the midst of this hurrying to and fro in search of loved ones, I heard a voice among those anxious inquirers that I recognized to be the voice of Capt. Cobb's young son, and this was the inquiry he was making, "Can any of you tell me of the whereabouts of my dear father? He was seen after the battle, unwounded, by several, passing up the ravine just in front of us. I searched up and down the ravine, but could not find him. I called to him but no answer. I went up and down the line of works but no one could tell me of him. I went to the hospital tent in our rear and searched among the wounded, but he could not be found there." It was my painful duty to go to the distressed young son and tell him what I knew, and go with him and other friends and members of his company, just a little ways in front of where we stood, in that darksome night and point out the dead body of his dear father, just as I had left it. The son fell upon his father's neck and wept bitterly, saying, "This is why you did not answer when T called so anxiously, so loudly for you!" This was to me one of the most pathetic scenes I witnessed during the war. I myself was among those anxious ones, searching after absent loved ones. I had two brothers, Capt. McKinnon, a younger brother. A. D. McKinnon. and a nephew. John Love McLean, all absent, and for a while all I could learn of them was that they had been seen on the battle-field badly wounded. I learned in the later night-time that they had been taken to the hospital tent and were being cared for. Oh! I shall never forget the sad solitary thoughts that kept vigil in my active mind all through that long, lonely, bloody night! This battle is called by some, "New Hope Church," by others, "Dallas." Early the following morning we were informed that this charge was a mistake — another illustration of the saying, "We did not know that it was loaded" — a wrong, misunderstood order. But let the reader remember here, that its fatal work, its sad results, were just as real as if the order had been genuine, and emanating from the proper headquarters. Beware of mistakes.

In other breastworks near Atlanta on a holy Sabbath evening, as we lay enjoying its quiet, Walton's companies, together with the balance of their regiments, received a compliment, not much coveted in those days. The brigade picket lines in our front had been taken by the enemy. Our division commander, General Bates, ordered our brigade commander to send his best regiment to retake the line. Our regiment was called out. We leaped over our breastworks and in a little while we were in possession of the picket line in our front with but little damage. We remained in this fortified place near Atlanta for some time, driving back the enemy's advances on our works from time to time. It was during our stay here that General Bates was wounded and General John C. Brown of Tennessee was put in his place to command us.

General Brown Cheered

Gen. Brown was a great favorite with the Florida Brigade; it was he that went with us through Kentucky and commanded us in the battle of Perryville. The officers and men were drawn very close to him. Notice was given that he would be around with his staff on a certain morning to inspect the division. Capt. Call Tippins. a tall, stout young man, with exuberant spirits, full of enthusiasm, always finding something good in prospect, and a greater admirer of the General than any of us, went around through the brigade, especially through the 1st Florida Regiment, boosting up the men to give General Brown a rousing cheer, when he came around to inspect reminding them of his kindness, his gentleness on the Kentucky march, how he fell wounded by our side at Perryville, that he would appreciate the compliment and that it would be well for us in the afterwards. All willingly assented, and agreed that it would be the very thing for the occasion. Now, old soldiers can appreciate how indifferent, how very contrary soldiers in the ditches in those days could be when they tried — hollowing and cheering when they should be silent and keeping silent when they should cheer. On the approach of the General and his staff, Capt. Tippins had Dr. Landrum and myself to stand with him in front of our regiment when the party was opposite, the Captain lifted his "flint and steel" cap, whirled it around his head, proposing the three cheers for General John C. Brown, and whooped with about all the power he could command, and that was great. Dr. Landrum and I, the only ones joining — he gave the second whoop and Landrum dropped out, I alone joining him; he gave the third, and it was more strenuous, if possible, than the others, and it went ringing down alone through the quiet forest. General Brown lifted his hat modestly and rode on. It was hard to say which of the two, the General or the Captain, we were the sorriest for. The Captain did not see the General when he lifted his hat; he had turned his back on him before the last whoop was out of his mouth, and commenced abusing the brigade in general, the 1st Florida Regiment especially, venting the greatest power of his spleen on Dr. Landrum and myself. He was in a condition to fight the whole brigade, if they had come out to him. He said, "You all have disgraced yourselves and are not fit to be called Confederate soldiers." Turning to Landrum and myself, he said, "You two stood with me here and promised to lead with me in the cheer and didn't do it." Landrum spoke up and told him he cheered the first time and dropped out, seeing no one else was going to join him. I told him — I assured him — that I joined him in the first and second whoops. He declared that no one joined him in the third and last whoop. Landrum said to him, "You are mistaken, Captain. I saw Statam join you in the third." Now, Statam had lost his voice and could not speak above a whisper. This started the Captain anew and about this time several came running up from the 6th Florida Regiment that lay well back in the grove, under the hill, in reserve, asking who was shot, as several of their friends had been shot walking about the front line. The Captain answered quickly, "No one is shot, but a set of fool men here have disgraced themselves and ought to be shot." It was but a little while before we had the Captain in good humor. He is a good, jolly soul, and can't stay mad with any one long. I have had many hearty laughs from crowds in and around Pensacola and other places, telling this true joke in his presence and enjoy it today when memory brings it up. The poverty of the

English language renders it too inefficient to set up this story in its true risibleness as it happened there on that day. Only those who heard it and witnessed the scene can fully appreciate it.

Chapter Forty-Three - General Joseph E. Johnston is superseded by General John B. Hood, Who Goes in Rear of General Sherman

After many days of worrying in the ditches around Atlanta, trying to keep back the enemy in arms — resorting to every means possible, to keep our bodies rid of the loathsome vermin that were annoying us quite as much as the armed forces, boiling and washing our bedding and clothing of every description from day to day, when there came a partial relief from an unexpected source, and with many regrets, General Johnston, a great favorite with our army, was superseded by General Hood, who takes us out of the ditches into the open, on a forced march to go in rear of General Sherman. On our way we found a federal garrison stationed at Decatur. In the night-time we surrounded them with a picket line, who dug ditches for their protection through the following day and held them in until the army passed by.

General Pat Cleborne Addresses His Men

At Powder Springs we serenaded General Cleborne and he spoke to us at some length, explaining to us the purpose of the rear move — the forced march — the result, if it succeeded, the consequences if it failed. He urged every man to do his whole duty, to stand firm by the righteous cause they had espoused. He pictured to us Ireland in its downfallen and trampled condition and told us if we failed our condition would be much worse than that of Ireland's, as long as that spirit of hate and revenge lived in the North. In closing his address that night he turned his face towards the skies and with all the fervenc}'^ of his soul he exclaimed. "If this cause that is so dear to my heart is doomed to fail, I pray heaven may let me fall with it, while my face is toward the enemy and my arm battling for that which I know to be right. It was one of the most stirring patriotic speeches I ever listened to. Early the next morning, we moved on with quick steps and buoyant hearts, feeling as free as animals loosed from their cages. The roads were rocky, and over hills and mountains we moved so rapidly it was difficult for commissary wagons to forage for us, and keep up so as to supply us at night. The soles of the men's shoes were being worn through against the sharp rocks. In the last days of the march, the butchers would go ahead, kill and butcher the meat along the road the army was to pass, and hand it in hunks out to the men as they passed to take it in their haversacks to cook and eat in the camp when they stopped at night. In some instances the beef was just killed by the side of the road, hide stripped from it and the men had to cut off pieces in passing by. Many of them would cut soles for their shoes from the green hide and put them inside of their shoes with the flesh side down to protect their feet from the sharp rocks. Others whose shoes were about gone, made themselves shoes out of these green beef skins, sewing them with whangs cut from the raw hide, which served them for a while, in keeping their bleeding feet from the cruel, sharp rocks.

Chapter Forty-Four - The Battle of Franklin

It is early in the evening before the battle. We are nearing Franklin, Tenn., marching by the flank through an open valley, to take our position on the line of battle — the enemy is firing cannon shot and shell at us as we pass, from a clump of trees on a lofty mountain top to our right — the missiles falling at one time short of us, and then over our heads. General Hood is being abused for being reckless in having us exposed to that open fire, while he and his staff were in secure quarters. In a little while the General and his staff ride by us, turn to the right in the direction of the firing, riding out of sight into the woods that covered the artillery, to where he had his picket line thrown out, that he might locate the position of his line of battle around Franklin. Nothing more was said about his "bomb-proof security." The battle was fought well into the night and was a dear but complete victory for the Confederates — the enemy fleeing in confusion. The boys called this battle "Hoods Killing." It was the bloodiest battle fought during the war — more men killed in proportion to those engaged than in any other battle, and more generals killed. What a bloody scene that battle-field presented the next morning! The enemy gone — I go to find the body of my friend, Luther Fisher, another one of my schoolmates at old Knox Hill. He is not far from where General Cleborne fell, who had passed the enemy's works, and after having had two horses shot from under him, and while driving them back. There the General — that ideal officer and soldier — lay surrounded by his friends in tears, ready to bear his body away for burial. His sword, no doubt, in his hand when he fell, and his face turned toward the enemy, while he battled for his cause. How truly, how literally true was that prayer answered made at Powder Springs. General Hood sits in Franklin on a veranda with his elbow resting on a table, his hand supporting his head, and as he looks on the depleted ranks as they pass, the torn rifled white and blue flags, representing regiments not a great deal bigger than companies of the day before, and when he thinks of his noble generals who fell in that battle, great tears rolled down his florid, weatherbeaten face. We hasten on to take up the railroad and fight the second battle of Murfreesboro. After accomplishing this mission, the army hastens on to Nashville; and the writer, in charge of the "Bare-footed Brigade," is to follow as a rear guard. In a little while one of General Forrest's staff officers, with his courier, comes in haste to us, with orders to form a line of battle along the

Western edge of a field close up to the woods, running north and south; when formed the scattering cavalry formed on our left, and we presented quite a formidable front to the enemy at a distance across the field, and saved a part of General Forrest's cavalry from being bagged. The body of the army had hastened on to Nashville, Tenn., and laid out a line of battle under very poor engineering. We went into these works in the late night-time on Dec. __, 1864, and when the day dawned, private soldiers familiar with lines of battle pointed out defects that could be, and were taken advantage of by the enemy, in enfilading our lines, and which cost us several lives to remedy. The day opened up with one continuous roar of cannon and fusillades of musketry that lasted from early morning until well onto evening — the enemy charging our works with double lines, first at one place and then at another, trying to make a breach in them; but were driven back with great loss each time, until the evening was well-nigh gone, when they concentrated their artillery firing on the very top of the mountain to our left, and kept up for a time the most terrific firing of the war. They had amassed their infantry under the cover of this firing, made a charge with a triple line of battle and broke our line on the very peak of the mountain. The triple line extended as far down the mountain as the front of the Florida Brigade, and we were driving them back with great jubilation from our front when private Robt. Holley turned his face towards me to reload, grabbed me by the right arm, with a grasp I long felt, and said, "Look at the U.S. flag on our breastworks!" I looked to my left and there it was, our ditches empty, the men escaping through the mountain woodlands; I turned to our rear and they were going pell-mell through an open field, to gain a dense grove just beyond, the federal army disorderly following. The officers that came into the field with their men from the mountain top, where the line was first broken, signaled to us who were left in their rear in the ditches, with their handkerchiefs not to shoot. Our men in the valley saw the breach in our line before we saw it and escaped beyond the field to their rear. In a jiffy the Federal army was coming in from right, left and front, while the bullets were whistling over our heads from every direction. They cried, "Don't shoot! Don't shoot!" They jumped into the ditches with us, and when the bullets quit flying over us, an officer said to me, "Let me have your sword; let's all get out of the ditches and go to the rear." We had gone but a little ways to the rear, when I heard a call to me for help, out of the woodland to our left. I knew the voice, it was my relative, my old schoolmate, one of Walton's soldiers from the 6th Regiment that fought to our left, on the slope of the mountain — Lieut. Archibald G. Morrison. I ran to him without thinking to ask permission. But the officer followed close by. He asked the officer to let me remain with him. He was asked, "Is he your brother?" He replied, "He is my relative, and I beg of you to leave him with me." He left me with him and went on with the rest. We were then alone for a little while, save the dead and dying. He was shot after he had surrendered his sword and had gone some distance to the rear — through mistake we hoped. He lay suffering with his head in my lap, with his hands pressed to the pit of his stomach — he thought he was struck in front. I examined and found no incision there at all, and felt encouraged and spoke encouraging words to him; told him that I thought it was the contusion of a shell or a minnie ball that struck him and all would be well in a little while. Then the captain of the provost guard came up with his band of men, a nice, genteel, courteous man, with a kind heart in him. He inquired into the whole situation, expressed regrets, especially at having been wounded by mistake, after he had surrendered. While he was with us I made a more thorough examination, and found that he had been shot in the right side, well to the back, and that it must have been the ball resting in his breast that caused the pain there. The captain left two of his men to guard us with instructions, "As soon as he is able to move on, take them to Nashville and deliver them to the command there," and then passed on to the front. In a little while, a part of the army which seemed to have had no part in the day's battle, came on, marching by the flank, and as they passed by, some of them said tormenting things to us, and asked truculent questions of us. One, I remember, said, "We got you piled up, ha? Just say the Lord's prayer and put your trust in Abraham Lincoln and you will come out all right." This brought a great laugh from his comrades — he was the smart Alec of his band. How savage such advice to a dying man! Not many months after this, Abraham Lincoln lay bleeding and dying from the hands of an assassin, with his head in the lap of a lady, as helpless as my friend lay with his in mine. Oh, how foolish it would have been for him to have put his trust in this great man — in any man! No, my friend had his trust stayed on a higher and better rock — the Rock of Ages. And as the smoky day died out of the skies, with declining hope, my friend, realizing fully his condition, spoke a few kind words of sweet remembrance for his mother and then said to me, "I had hoped that it might have been different with me in the end; but it is all right." And with that dying day, there came to him from on high a voice saying, "You have stayed long enough in this mountain; come up higher." And he passed on higher up the mountain, even to the beautiful Mount of God. I had the guard to go with me to our breastworks to where I knew there were pick and spade and went to work digging the grave at once on that mountain side, head resting by one of the great mountain oaks that had withstood the storms for ages. I picked and dug in the rock all that cold, bleak December night before I got it deep enough; neither of the guard offering to help, and I too proud to ask them. While it was yet dark in that early morning and the grave ready, I had to ask them to take hold of the corners of the blanket and help me to lower the body into the grave. They did this very readily and gently. I gathered the soft mould and then the rock over the grave, marked it, as best I could, rolling down a stone to the head, planting the mattock there by it at the head and the spade at the feet, and cut his initials on the tree; and then my work was over. I had done all that I could. The sun was well up in the trees, so I stopped for a little rest. I shall never forget the stillness — the painful silence, that reigned supreme in that mountain forest — coming after the din of battle, the groans of the wounded and dying, the noise of the ambulances as they went rolling to and fro through the night, bearing away the wounded and the dying, and the commands of men moving the dead and wounded down a steep place in the mountain to reach the ambulance. I surveyed well the situation amid this silence, and thought then, if I were among the spared, and even had an opportunity, I could and would come to this sacred spot.

Visits Nashville's Battle Ground

(While in Louisville, Ky., in A. D. 1896 attending the Confederate Reunion with A. G. Campbell and my three oldest daughters, we arranged on our return to stop over at Nashville and visit the grave of my friend and relative. We ordered a carriage from a livery there, with a driver that could take us along Hood's old line of battle. We got what we ordered, and started in the early morning, but when we got there we found the topography of that section so changed, by the felling of trees, building of fences and macadamized roads that it was impossible to designate the sacred spot. In passing through Franklin a gentleman of that town pointed out to us an academy built on the very spot where Gen. Pat Cleborne fell.) Now, this short December day was going by as this silent survey and soliloquy was going on with me — when the officer in charge of the infirmary corps came to us and told the sergeant — one of the men who held me in charge — to take me to Nashville and deliver me to the officer in charge of the penitentiary. The day was well spent when we started. We met all along the way, quite a lot of scattering cavalrymen. One called to the guard saying, "Why don't you take his hat and shoes and let him go in bare? That is the way they do us." He would not have gotten much had he obeyed. Another stopped and insisted that the guard search me, and if he found money, take it and divide up with him. I had some money and this speech put me on my guard and I placed it as securely on my person as I could. It was in the late evening when we reached the suburbs of the city; we stopped at the first grocery store we came to, the guard bought crackers and cheese and divided with me, without asking if I had money to pay for a lunch. He did for me just what I intended doing for him had I not been warned. I feared nothing from him for he treated me gentlemanly all the time. This was the first I ate since noon the day before, and I certainly appreciated it, especially coming as it did.

Chapter Forty-Five - Lady Sympathizers

When we got well up into the city, walking along on the sidewalk, two pretty young Southern ladies, dressed in black, joined us, walking close by my side for some distance giving sympathy and asking many pertinent questions about the battle of the day before, and the army left at Atlanta, that they were very much interested in, all of which, I was able and gratified to answer satisfactorily. As we passed up with this delightful company, to me, jostled about with the throng of passers-by, we met the "Officer of the Day," who stopped us and told the guard not to allow any further conversation with the prisoner. Like a good soldier, he obeyed, telling me not to engage in further conversation with the ladies. We moved on, the ladies continuing to walk closely and silently by me. We had gone but a little ways, when the same officer halted the guard, saying, "Take the prisoner off the pavement and carry him up the street." As we went up the street, these ladies walked on the outside of the pavement close up to the curbing, opposite to, and near us, for several blocks, until we turned to go into the prison. There was more to me in their silent walk, their anxious look of sympathy, than all the words of encouragement they had spoken. Their bright cherry faces beaming with Southern beauty, grace and love, sent cheer into my sad, discouraged heart, kindling a flame there, that burned afresh through my bleak prison life and brings cheer, even today, when sweet recollections call them up. No one can know, without experiencing it, the power of good in sympathy under such circumstances as these. Oh, how buoyant declining hope did become, with such silent bewitching sympathy from our Southern beauties. They had gotten my name and regiment. I intended getting their full address, but was cut off by that censorious officer. The guard delivered me to the officer at the entrance of the penitentiary. When ushered in, I was surprised to find so many political prisoners in there and among them were some of the first ladies of Tennessee, for speaking what they called, "disrespectful words" to officers. Was surprised to find Lieut. Neill L McKinnon from our company there. Thought he had escaped.

Chapter Forty-Six - To Johnson's Island Prison in Lake Erie

The next day they sent all the commissioned officers to Johnson's Island prison, opposite Sandusky City, Ohio. We changed cars in Louisville, Ky., and while there, in the streets, the sympathizing ladies came right into our ranks, giving us open words of cheer and encouragement for our cause, and were only driven back to the pavements at the point of the Federal bayonets. And then they never ceased to express sympathy while we remained there. Our next stop was at Indianapolis, Ind. While grouped under the car shed, among those who wanted to look at us, was a slender cross-eyed fellow dressed in a Sergeant's U. S. uniform. We readily recognized him to be G. A. Rebb, once the adjutant of our regiment, who deserted us on Bragg's march through Kentucky. We all called out to him, "deserter, sneak, scalawag," and he hurried away through the crowd, and the Federal soldiers enquired more into his history. We are standing on the water front in Sandusky City early on Christmas morning. December's surly blast is coming strong across the frozen lake cutting our defenceless faces and poorly clad bodies. Both the outer and inner soles of our shoes were worn through, and in this condition we were moved on to the ice, facing a stiff Norther, while it snowed or sleeted just enough to make the ice more difficult to walk on. Never did men inexperienced have such a time walking on ice. We would slip and fall, and the first part of our bodies to meet the ice would be our heads and shoulders, which were beaten blue with heavy licks. We reached the Island prison alive, after a time, in this bruised, frozen condition, and lived, but only through the support of our strength-giving God. I can but look on this march over that frozen lake, on that severe day, as a miracle of life preservation. Lieut. McKinnon, my cousin, and I, were put in block No. 11. We found the men living on scant rations in retaliation for the scant rations at Andersonville, Ga. We entered the prison hungry, and remained hungry dreaming of something to eat, while we stayed there, until after the surrender. While all suffered with hunger it was harder with some than with others. It took more to keep some than others, and there were some who could not, or would not divide their ten days' rations up into ten parts, so as to have some each day, but would eat and be without in the end, and go about in a woeful condition. When we were in such want Congress only lacked a few votes of cutting these stinted rations smaller. Capt. Wilson from Arkansas, but a native of Kentucky headed a list of men who swore with an oath, that if the bill cutting the rations became a law, and was put into execution they would go in a body and charge the walls to make their escape or be killed, rather than starve to death. And we all knew that they would have done it, for they were becoming reckless as it was. Of course the subject of something to eat was the all absorbing subject for discussion in the prison at this time. One morning after the sergeant had finished our roll call and we were awaiting the drum beat to disband, this subject was being discussed, when the sergeant remarked, "These men you see on guard duty came in from Andersonville prison two days ago, they saw the rations issued to you yesterday and said it was twice as much as they got at Andersonville." Then Capt. Wilson spoke up with a loud voice and said, "They are d__d liars and the very fact that they are there on duty proves it, for you know, no men could do guard duty on less rations than we receive here." We realized in this prison, how very difficult it is to get men and keep them on an equality in this world. It does seem to me if there was a place in this world where men could be placed and kept on an equality in material matters, it would be on a water or ice bound island prison like this and too, at a time, when retaliation, like this was on. Yet we can't say all fared alike here in getting rations as strict as they were in retaliating. Some controlled money through friends outside and succeeded in getting the guard to smuggle in something to eat. Some got boxes in on the sick list through their physician and in other ways. Such a prison is the place to study and know men, and we were glad to have learned here that there were so many unselfish men cooped up together on this island. And when we think of how many kinds of people it takes to make our world, we have reason to be thankful that we get along together as well as we do. Dr. G. P. Henry, Capt. J. T. Stubbs, Lieut. Rice and Capt. Angus McMillan were prisoners there with me. While our bodies were poorly clad and fed, our minds and souls were richly fed. We had plenty of good books and splendid opportunities in literature and Bible study. Dr. J. L. Girardeau, a Presbyterian minister and army chaplain from North Carolina was a prisoner with us and did splendid work there, teaching a Bible class and preaching on the Sabbaths. I never enjoyed any thing in a religious way so much as I did his teachings there. They were antidotes for hunger for a little while. The prison life was not an idle life. There were real geniuses there. A great deal was done there in the way of art in drawing pictures and making ingenious toys. It did look like it would be impossible for one to make his escape from such a prison yet there were some constantly making their escape.

The winter is gone on the Island, the ice is being broken up by the winds and sun and piled in great heaps against the spiling driven by Commodore Perry on the Sandusky side. The migrating birds are returning from my dear Southern home by the Mexican gulf, from Florida's lovely shores where they went to escape the rigors of the severe winters in the cold North. And how I wished that I had wings like they, that I might fly away and be with loved ones. The days are lengthening out and growing hotter and hotter as they lengthen. The mail steamer is making her regular daily trips back and forth from Sandusky City along the line we came over on frozen water, but like the birds, these mails bring no glad news from our homes. But one day as we sat in the quiet solitude of the evening in our prison home, with our faces like the Jew's, homeward turned, we saw the mail steamer coming across the lake, with the stars and stripes flying at high mast, with yards of red, white and blue bunting running from stem to stern on either side encircling the whole boat, and with lesser flags flying all about the steamer. We knew that it was bringing news, bad news for us. We awaited its arrival with bated breath. It landed at the dock on the outside, and there went up a shout of triumph from the crowd that gathered there. And the news was soon broken to us — "General Lee had surrendered at Appomattox." This sad intelligence fell like a cyclone on our unprepared ears. It presaged the downfall of the Confederacy and introduced new topics for discussion. That night Sandusky City was painted red. Skyrockets and fireworks of every description leaped up into the black skies, dispelling the darkness, while a continual roar of artillery jarred the earth. As we stood in groups looking and listening to this jubilation outside, over our downfall, one remarked, "If it is thus in this little city what is it in the great cities all over this Northern country? Thousands and thousands of dollars are being spent in this night's revelry." Dr. J. L. Girardeau standing in the group, said, "Yes. and here we are, their prisoners, in actual need of the daily bread of life. I look for God to bring this nation into mourning for this night's extravagant, hilarious rejoicings." The all absorbing question about something to eat is relegated to the background for a while and what is to be done with the prisoners is brought to the front. Some advancing tragic ideas, others treating it flippantly, and some with indifference, while others gave it cool sober thought. Quite a lot of us fell back on the hope that the scattered army might rally around Kirby Smith and make a stand in the Trans Mississippi. While these matters were uppermost in the minds for discussion and all waiting and watching anxiously for every mail to bring some grounds to base our hopes upon, yet each mail brought darker prospects for our hope to rest upon.

Lincoln Assassinated

Late one evening we saw the U. S. mail boat steaming over from the city in quite a different attire to that presented in her coming a few days before. Instead of the symbols of joy and glory, we find those of sorrow and mourning. Instead of the flag of the union waving from the topmost mast, it swings at half-mast, expressive of grief. Instead of the bunting in its bright National colors — red, white and blue — the deep black crape expressive of sorrow takes its place, encircling the entire steamer in its graceful draping folds. Instead of the shout of victory when she rounded up to the outside wharf as before, men stood with bowed heads in silence. It was evident to us all that something sad had come to the nation. But none could divine what it was. Soon after the landing, a courier came around to every block telling us, "At the beat of the drum you are ordered to assemble yourselves in front of the great gate, and General Hill, commander of the post, will address you from the elevated stand." That was all he knew to tell us. We readily assembled ourselves as ordered. After addressing himself to us, he read this telegram in substance: "Last night as President Lincoln sat with his family in a private box in 'Ford's Theatre' in this city he was shot to death by an assassin — J. Wilkes Booth — who is being pursued by great forces." One can well imagine how this unexpected news fell upon our anxious ears and minds in these dark days. After reading the dispatch. General Hill made a short speech in which he paid deserved tribute to the fallen President and said to us, "That while we were prisoners of war, he did not look upon us as assassins, that he knew that there were excellent men before him, who in their hearts condemned this act, as he did." He forbade any expression or demonstration in any way of joy over this death by the prisoners; forbade any gathering in groups over the campus for conversation; ordered that the lights must be turned out promptly at 8 o'clock — at the tap of the drum — and said,

"If any of these orders were violated the guards on the wall were directed to fire into the violators." Every man of us went straight to his own place — to his own block.

A Tragedy Averted in Block No. 11.

When we of block No. 11 were seated in quietude for a moment, those who seemed to have taken in the situation more clearly and understood Abraham Lincoln, Andy Johnson and those in charge of the affairs of the government best, engaged in an undertone discussion of our situation. Some said in substance, of Abraham Lincoln, on that occasion, what President Jefferson Davis said of him years afterwards. One said in substance. "The assassination of President Lincoln last night, next to the surrender of General Lee, was the worst blow the South has ever had. Had Lincoln lived and our cause failed, as it seems it must, no man would have dealt more justly with our people than he. He was one of the best of men, had a good pure heart in him. All of his public documents ring with the milk of human kindness, and none of them are burdened with the abuse of a single Southern man, not even his great Gettysburg speech. I often meditate on his two inaugural addresses, their honest pleadings, so plain and so earnest, so clear and fair, his conscientious convictions of duty. "You have no oath registered in heaven to destroy the government, while I have the most sacred one to preserve, protect and defend it." Such are some of his plain earnest pleadings, and it gives me pain to know that he is gone, and see the government go into the hands of others who are, and always have been, full of hate for the South. Another said, "I know Andy Johnson well, personally, and you will find none of this vindictive spirit in him, he too, is kind hearted and forgiving, and would prove a friend to the South, and I would as lief have him as Lincoln." And yet another spoke up in muffled tones and said, "He may be all this, but he will never stand in with his party, he will have no power nor influence, the South will be sure to suffer under his administration. You will not find in him that bold, kind, conscientious, high toned Christian gentleman that we would have had in Mr. Lincoln; his death at this time, is the greatest slam that could have come on us. It may be the cause of our having to remain in this prison for a year or two and I think it well for us — the prisoners on this island — to come together and make a public expression of sorrow for his death." The bold, reckless Capt, Wilson sat quietly listening to all these commendations. I could see him swelling up all the while. This was more than he could stand. He jumped upon his feet with his eyes sparkling with fire, with his finger pointing to those who had been doing the talking and said in no suppressed tones, "Why men, I am astonished at you, surprised at your sycophancy. At such obsequious, cringing sympathy as you express it here, you could not have said more in praise, or expressed more sympathy for our own President Davis had he been killed last night (a whispering voice said, close to the door, "You don't understand.)" "I do understand, I have listened to every word said, I have been here longer than any of you — since the fall of Fort Pillow — and am willing to stay here ten times that long for the work of last night. I am shedding no tears, I am glad." A voice said, "Captain, please don't speak so loud, you know our orders?" "Yes, I heard them, what do I care for their bullets? Let them shoot. There are some of us here who had rather be shot down and die here, than to live to go home and withstand that reeking revengeful hate that has ever burned in the hearts of these sycophants in power." (A watch was put on the outside of the door to report the approach of any Federal.) Several of his friends gathered around him insisting that he would not talk so loud, but with little effect. "Where is that conscientious observance of his oath recorded in heaven when he swore he would protect the constitution and then freed by proclamation all the slaves in the South before he had been in office three years? And too, when he said, 'I will not interfere with slavery where it exists in the States.'" A voice said, "But you don't understand this freeing of the negroes." "Yes, I do, but I can't understand how he could have been such a Christian saint as you would have him be, and then find him at such times as these, sitting up with his family in a special box in the most popular theatre in the Capital City. Don't you think if he had been such an one as you would have him be, it would have been more befitting for him to have been at home on his knees in his closet, or bowed with his family around the home altar, asking his God for wisdom to help him deal justly with our overpowered suffering people?" (The man outside keeping watch at the door reports that the officer is coming with guard to be mounted for the night. Every man is on his feet, some indifferent, a few with the nod of approval, others anxious, all in the end agreeing that enough had been said at that time, that we were in danger of being fired into, that the retaliating, revengeful spirit that obtained in the minds of the army at that time, would make them too ready and anxious for an occasion to fire into us and this was evidenced a few nights later when our block was fired into, when there was a little delay in turning off the lights at the tap of the drum. Capt. Wilson's friends quieted him down, begging in behalf of the dear defenseless home ones — mothers and children — to desist. So a tragedy was barely averted and there were no more eulogies passed in our block on either Mr. Lincoln or Mr. Johnson while Capt. Wilson remained there, but he was among the very first to go. Time rolled on making history fast outside. They began to administer the amnesty oath and sending us to our homes in the order of our capture. Walton's prisoners were among the very last to go from our prison. On the 14th of July we left on the steamer for Sandusky City. The day was so hot, no wind blowing, so we came near being suffocated with heat along the very same route we liked to have frozen, walking and crawling over the ice, six months before. We came over on Saturday evening, had to stop over in the city until Monday. I went to the Presbyterian Church — was received kindly. In passing through Dayton, Ohio, the home of Valandingham — we were detained there some time. I asked one who came up to where we were if Mr. Valandingham was in town? He answered abruptly: "We don't keep the run of such d__d rascals as he." I replied, "We love such Ohioans as he and S. S. Cox." He answered back: "I would suppose so." When we reached Louisville, Ky., the good ladies of that town had tables spread and sumptuously fed the hungry Confederate soldiers as they passed on daily from their prisons to their homes, and when the whistle blew for starting, they placed themselves automatically at the car steps with open pocket books and as each soldier entered, place a piece of silver money in their hand to help them on home. "God bless the good ladies in our Southland" went up from every lip. Forty-five miles of the railroad track was destroyed north of Atlanta. That distance had to be made through sand, heat and dust. From Eufaula, Ala., we had to make our way through the country, but we found relatives and friends to help us on home. Oh. what endearing words, home, mother, father, sister, brother, relative, friend! How they do stir our hearts, loom up in our minds after the turmoil of war is over, with our backs turned on isolated prisons when every step brings us nearer and nearer to them. At home! All of us at home. Brought safely through all the phases incident to a bloody cruel civil war. Who can express the joy, the gladness, the gratitude of such a home coming. When one spoke to my father about the war robbing him, he would always say "No. it was my children that were robbed, I have enough to do me as long as I want to live. Really, it was Angus Gillis. John Morrison, Mrs. Daniel G. McLean and persons like these who lost their sons who were robbed.

Walton Hears News of Surrender Beneath Historic Oak

In the closing days of the war the mail service was very irregular and unreliable on account of deserters that roamed up and down the Choctawhatchie river and bay. These would meet the postman in crossing the river, or on the highway as it suited them and they would rifle the mail bags, taking what would profit or interest them. In the last days the mails were carried from Old Knox Hill to Marianna by private arrangements. The mail pouches were never under lock and key. These were no barriers along this route. Friends in Marianna would take out the m.ost important matters and have the carrier secure it about his person or saddle and friends at Knox Hill would do the same on return to Marianna. Mr. Newton, when he first came to the Hill, among his first transplanting of trees, replanted a nice oak in rear of the Academy, in the boys playground,

Kenneth McCaskill

outside of the back gate. This noble oak was the boys "Home Base Tree." It grew through all these years to be a great oak, spreading its branches out in every direction, offering a most delightful and profound shade for a cool rest on the top of this high hill. It was here in these last days, beneath these hospitable shades, that the old Valley Scotchmen and sometimes the anxious mothers and daughters, would come once a week in the evening time, and lounge about on the green sward beneath the shades of this generous oak tree, with throbbing hearts and with anxious eyes running down the stretches toward the East, to catch the first glimpse of the postman coming up the hill with his good or evil tidings from the front. One evening as these McLeans, McPhersons, McKenzies, McDonalds, Campbells, Douglasses, Gunns, Rays and others from a distance, among whom was Dr. Charles McKinnon, a surgeon of the Confederate army at home in Mossy Bend on furlough — all stood beneath these shades, the postman rode up, handed over the mail pouch, and while they sat around examining this mail matter, he dismounted, took his knife from his pocket, ripped open a small sack that was neatly and securely placed between two of his saddle cloths, took a newspaper from it and passed it on to these gentlemen, saying, "This paper Judge Bush in Marianna placed here, and charged me 'that I see that you get it.'" The paper was handed over to Dr. McKinnon who was requested to read it aloud. He read in a full distinct voice as follows: "General Lee Has Surrendered — Our Cause Lost."

He read on to the end, with the editor's comments. When through the paper fell from his hands to the ground, and they all sat, with heads down for several moments, as silent as Jobs' comforters. Dr. McKinnon lifts his head, the silence is broken by his exclaiming: "Gentlemen, we as a Southern people are politically, irredeemably damned!" Some may claim that he said the wrong thing when he did speak, as did Job's comforters, when they broke their silence, but in the dark bitter days of reconstruction, we thought how very advisedly he had spoken on that sad occasion. Within the boundary lines that inscribe the territory that makes up the Walton of today, she sent out four infantry companies and one cavalry company under Capt. J. B. Hutto. Besides these, she furnished many men for other companies, and when the necessities demanded, she raised a full sized infantry company made up of old men and boys — "The Home Guard" — and armed them with the same guns that she sent out her first company with — "The Walton Guards." These were commanded by Capt. John Gillis, an elder in the Presbyterian Church in the Valley. These did excellent service in the closing months of the war among the thieving deserters. Walton sent out more men in proportion to her population than any other county and our State sent out more in proportion to her population than any other State.

Chapter Forty-Seven - Walton's Soldiers at Home

The war at the front is over and all of Walton's soldiers whose lives had been spared are at home. But they find it far from being over in the rear — along our sea coast line. They find a reflex influence along this line, a cloud hanging over them that beglooms the joy of their home coming. The Federal raids through west Florida that were so cruel and devastating, were not to be compared with these deserters' night grabbing raids. They commenced concentrating in West Florida and South Alabama with headquarters in Walton more than a year before the war closed, committing high-handed outrages all over this region. They got to doing so badly that some Mississippi cavalry had to come in after and were more depredating than ever. They secreted themselves near Dr. A. D. McKinnon's home at night and shot him down; thinking he was dead they ran off leaving his wife alone with her little children and negro servants. She had to send a negro man twenty-five miles for a doctor. This gang made a raid in the day time on Elba, Ala., and were killed, routed and wounded, those that escaped in the streets and fled to the bay were overtaken, brought out and hung. A boy — Frank Bullard — stood behind a China tree in the streets of Elba and killed two of these on horseback, when he was only fourteen years old. Clark commanded this gang and was the man that ordered Dr. McKinnon shot, and before he was hung he confessed and said, "I don't know why I ordered him killed unless the devil was in me." They agreed with him that it was the devil and swung him up. Rhodes with his lieutenant, Dick Kerlee, moved on the home of Kenneth McCaskill in the Valley — father of our J. J. McCaskill. Before they entered the house Kenneth and his young son, John J., escaped in the grove with their double barreled guns and fired on them in the dark. John loading while his father shot at them. Finally Kerlee said to Mrs. McCaskill, "If you don't make your husband quit shooting us, I will fire the house." Kenneth said, "Set it on fire! It will make a better light to shoot by." Then they broke for their horses and they turned loose on them with both barrels of each gun, wounding Kerlee and two of the others. McCaskill cried to them as they ran for life, "I will get you yet!" They had nothing but little shot to shoot them with. At the close of the war in the days of settling down and cleaning up the raiders, Kenneth was chosen captain or leader of the regulating band in bringing back stolen property and the like. And about the first thing he did, was to make his word good to Kerlee. He came up with him at his home, put a

John J. McCaskill

rope around his neck, put him in a wagon, drove between the two gate posts, tied the rope to the cross piece and drove from under him leaving him swinging in the air. He then put the rope around his father-in-law and got him in the wagon and ready to drive from under him, when his age and the pleadings of those around, touched his heart and he spared his life, telling him "Quit your meanness." The people in the Valley hearing that he was spared said, "What a pity, what a pity!" Those who know nothing of the threats and doings of these raiders in the Valley and surrounding country may think this cruel, but it was the only thing to do to down them; and those who know nothing of the inwardness of this Old Scotch Pioneer, may look upon him, as having been a stern, hard-hearted man, full of revenge in dealing with these desperate raiding deserters in putting them in and keeping them in their places, but he was one of our most peaceable citizens, a kindhearted, sympathetic, loving husband and father, ever ready to lend a helping hand where help was needed. He followed all his days the simple farm life, looking after his stock and home. Raised up a large family of sons and daughters on his Valley farm. After the close of the civil war. his son, J. J. McCaskill. like many other young men struck out to developing the dormant resources of Walton. With unbridled energy he plunged into her timber with mills, boats and a mercantile business and has gotten more out of it than any other man has, leaving the lands in a better condition for farming than they were at the first. These East Alabama deserters came down and raided Mossy Bend. Some of the men, and women, dressed in men's clothing, came to Capt. J. B. Hutto's near Euchee Anna and robbed his home of everything, leaving his sick wife without a mouthful to eat, and she with eight little children, two of them twins two months old. Rhoad's gang came to Angus Gillis's in L'. S. uniform and took ofif loads of bedding and provisions: he recognized several of them as some of his neighbors disguised and they came the next day and abused the ones that did the robbing; and yet they dared not tell them that they knew that it was themselves that did it; but there did come a day when they told them of it, and they had to bring back the stolen property. My brother A. D. McKinnon and I went after some of our stolen property over Boggy bayou and thought we were going to have trouble. We did have trouble in East Alabama, the stronghold of the raider band, had to take a yoke of oxen by force from one of them. He swore he would come up with us when he was armed and we were unarmed. He got his band together and followed us twenty-five miles. Providentially, we got to Campbellton, Fla., and were safe before they could overtake us. Sure enough three or four months after this he came with three more armed men on me unarmed at Freeport, Fla., but again, providentially, I met them, and overcame them, and sent them back home. The first raid that came into Walton under Federal authority was something on the order of these deserters' raids. A dash in the night time, a grabbing of things easily carried off, and the taking of things that a decent company would not bother. In fact it was headed by deserters from our army who had been officered by the Federal government. Capt. Joe Carrol, who went to school with us at Knox Hill, a pleasant social fellow, but without a bit of character. He surrounded Col. McKinnon's house in the night time, after killing the guard dogs, took his wounded son, Alex. D., who was at home on crutches — all the spoils he could gather in the house — one wagon load — a horse and buggy, the wounded prisoner — two negro men on the Colonel's fine horses, and two negro women in the wagon. Carrol answered, to some extent, for this raid after the war.

Chapter Forty-Eight - The Ashboth Raid

General Ashboth, an old Hungarian, left the Pensacola Navy Yard on his raid through Walton and intervening counties to Marianna on September 21st, handed his steamer and troops of horsemen and infantry on the East shore of East bay, marched through that unfrequented, desolate country and on the 22nd he came to the home of Lafayette Cawthon's, took him and brother. That night he camped on the grounds where the Chatauqua Auditorium in DeFuniak Springs now stands. On the 23rd he came to Euchee Anna, camped there with his headquarters at the home of Giles Bowers. On the 24th he sent a squad to take the Euchee Anna prisoners and those that he had gathered up on his way, to Freeport where he had his steamer to meet them and carry them across the bay to Point Washington, to meet him on his return from Marianna. While at Euchee Anna he sent out squads of men into the country gathering up the old men and boys and putting them in the little old twostory hewn log jail. He sent out some of his negro troops that acted disgracefully. He sent a Captain with a squad of white men and negroes to the home of Col. McKinnon south of Euchee Anna, three miles away. These made a clean sweep of negroes, horses, mules, oxen, turkeys, chickens, corn, meat and everything they could find to eat. The wagons were driven in front of the big "smoke house" door and were loaded with bacon and beef as long as it would lie on them, they dug up the big lard barrels out of the ground and placed them on the wagons. Other wagons were being loaded at the cribs with corn, peas and fodder. They did not leave a single thing to eat for the family. In passing through the house for booty the Captain spied a large sword hanging on the wall and here occurred the episode of the sword given by Miss Brevard in her history of Florida. They did not ask the negroes if they wanted to go, they ordered them to hitch up the teams and make ready to go. They took all of them save Aunt Harriet that had been the wife of Jim Crow, Indian Chief of the Euchees, her youngest daughter, little yellow Flora, a house girl of 15 years and little George, these gave them the dodge. When they had all gone, one of my sisters and Aunt Harriet followed them a little ways to learn which road they had gone and to see if they could learn any thing of a sick brother that was at home and had spent the night with a neighbor. They had gone but a little ways before they found a big side of bacon that they could not lift. Then they saw the brother coming, who had been beckoned away from the dangers at the house by one of the negro men at the lot. With his help the meat was taken home. Father and mother made glad for the safety of their sick son. Our dear sick mother said, "It could have been so much worse." Buzzing quiet and cutting sadness reigned supreme around our once dear happy home and the busy, hilarious negro quarters. Ears of corn wasted in loading were gathered by the brother, carried to the grist mill, ground into meal and this and the side of meat made the meals for the family and for the sick mother until the milch cows that thought to stay away, came home. Mr. Alex. Johnson, a neighbor of the Colonel's sent him a nice mare to ride around. In a little while the deserters took her. This raid left an old broken down horse, a stack of bones. He would not fatten, but when rested was full of life. He was called "Old Abe" and was a good saddler and woods horse. He was kept in the pasture the most of the time. The deserters could not bridle him. He was not tempting to them. They sent a squad of men to the Misses McDonalds, two miles south of Euchee Anna, to take their sick brother, Archibald L. McDonald. They surrounded the house before they knew that they were there. His sisters lifted one of the floor planks and let him slip through into the clay hole in front of the chimney, made in taking clay out to build the chimney with, it was a large double pen-split log house with hall running through it. When they made a search of the house and found he had eluded them, they stopped there the most of that day and night living on their chickens and eggs, shooting the chickens down in the yard and over Archy in the hole. Fortunately the chickens were as scared of Archy in the hole as they were of the Yankees with their guns, and would never stop near the hole, but on the opposite side from the Yankee. But when they went to leave, they made a clean sweep of ducks, turkeys and chickens, and in shooting an old rooster over Archy under the house, they only wounded him and he flopped and jumped about under there and Archy thought every minute he would be on him in the hole, but before he got in Mr. Yank crawled under and got him, saying "D__n you, I have got you!" His sisters thought they had Archy. When this band left with their booty, the sisters lifted the plank and let Archy out, and his black hair was about as gray as it is today. He, only, can describe the suspense in that hole when the bullets were flying over him, and the wounded rooster flopping and jumping toward him.

Euchee Anna Prison

These are some of the names of those who were crowded in that little prison and kept in there a night and a part of two days: The Bowerses, McLeans, McCallums, Kay, Col. George W. Walker, a Kentuckian by birth and the Campbells. Dr. D. L. Campbell of De Funiak was of them. It will interest you to hear him give a description of the prison life there, especially that pertaining to Col. Walker who was a wonderful character in this country, an uncompromising Union man, the very soul of character, tall, lean, straight with eagle piercing eyes. Never spoke but with emphasis and positiveness. Was a great smoker of the pipe, walking up and down the floor while he smoked, in deep thought. He was respected and admired by all Waltonians. Crowded in this little prison without pipe and no room to walk up and down; his noble pet horse, his best companion, taken from him; the doctor says in this nervous, irritable condition he broke loose with such invectives as he had never heard before from him, winding up every speech with. "The U. S. has come to a d__d low pass when she had to pick up this dirty old foreigner, this d__d Hungarian hog to command her armies, to slobber over decent people!" This scene and treatment made a strong Southern sympathizer of him. Never more did curses fall from his lips on secessionists. Before leaving Euchee Anna the General had these prisoners drawn up in line in the bottom between Bowers' and the town. He rode up and down on Col. McKinnon's fine pacing stallion that Carrol had stolen and taken to him, then rode off leaving them standing there in suspense not knowing whether they would have to go to Fort Pickens or not, but he had already culled out those he would send there. After a while they all broke ranks and went to their homes. The army went on to Marianna by Angus Gillis.' Taking negroes, mules and horses and everything they could find to eat. They passed out of Walton and through Holmes, leaving a black trail behind them and on to Marianna and back to their steamer at Point Washington and then down to Fort Pickens with their prisoners. We will let the State publicist tell of them there. It was this last Yankee raid that put a new devil and new energy in the organized deserters and they had no common sense to back them. The most of their skilled leaders were killed out. So these fool raiders, who came to feel that the "bottom rail was on top" to stay, and every thing had to go their way, had to be attended to without gloves, teaching those that stole, must steal no more, and that stolen property must be returned to the proper owners. There was neither law nor order in the country. The leader of the gang that robbed the Mossy Bend people was overtaken and a rope had to be placed around his neck and thrown over a limb before he would point out the stolen goods or tell who were his accomplices. After disclosing and being released, he sent to Gen'l. Ashboth and

Angus C. Douglass

reported his treatment, who promised that he would send up a company of negro soldiers, have the offenders arrested and brought down to him and placed in Fort Pickens. The citizens were deeply moved by this threat, remembering the depredations and outrages committed by some of his negro troops when he was stationed at Euchee Anna on his raid. They call a mass meeting of the citizens and select a committee of old men; Capt. Berry, father of Rev. George Berry, John Morrison, Giles Bowers, Wesley Bowers, Angus Douglass and one young man, J. L. McKinnon, Jr.

Chapter Forty-Nine - Committee Sent

On reaching the Navy Yard the committee consulted as to what we would say and as to how we would say it. It was the consensus of opinion that nothing harsh was to be said. I was chosen to do the talking. We went into his office and were met at the outer door by his orderly. I said to him, "We are a delegation from Walton County who want to have an interview with the General." He was gone but a little while when he returned and ushered us into the General's presence. A great big bungling, rough looking fellow with his head all bound around with wide strips of white cloth, through which the mollifying salves on his wounds had penetrated and were running down the furrows on his red cheeks. I introduced myself and the other gentlemen. We were given seats around the table. I stated our mission in full, giving facts as they were. He flew all to pieces, spoke in a rage through his broken English for quite a while insultingly. He said in part: "You of the South gathered yourselves together and tried to destroy the best government in the world, and the world showed you that you couldn't do it. I came across the waters to help the good people of the North over here to guarantee freedom to the poor negro and look here (pointing to his wounded head) what you rebellious people did for me at Marianna while trying to free them; this may yet be the giving of my life for the freedom of this poor abused race (this poor (?) old hypocrite did die of his wounds in a little while and we could but rejoice at the news.) You must not put ropes around my men's necks in any such threatening manner, who, when they saw they were wrong, fled to me for protection and to stand by and help me to lift the ropes from off the necks of their poor oppressed brothers in black." My young heart surged within me, so did the old men's at such vain talk. When we knew, too, if the old hypocrite had been such a patriot and humanitarian as he would have us believe, he could have found subjects in countries nearer his home, in greater need than in ours. But we did not dare speak a word of this in our contentions if we hoped to gain anything by our interview. When he let up a little so that I could put in a word I said, "General, the war is over. I have just returned from a Northern prison. I have taken the amnesty oath and am as much a citizen of the U. S. as the President. I have sworn to obey and protect the Constitution and laws of the U. S. and mean to do it. We have no Governor, no officer of the law, and therefore the laws can't be strictly executed in our county. I told him what the deserters were claiming, threatening and doing up there, how they were trying to stir up our quiet satisfied negroes. Called his attention to the assaulted mother and daughter living north of Euchee Anna, who came to his headquarters while there and made complaint to him about the treatment of two of his negro soldiers, one a Corporal, the other a Sergeant, in his army. That they were able, readily to identify them, yet they went unpunished. That the negro bucks up there were treating it as a good practical joke and that the deserters up there were using this to put the very devil in them. I showed him what a curse it would entail on the community up there if he stationed negro troop in that section; that it could but bring the saddest results of shame and death, and that I did not believe U. S. government would tolerate such abuses, and if they were sent up there the committee would go right on to Washington and carry the whole matter before President Johnson. I showed that this man complaining was a deserter from both armies and had been a raiding deserter for more than a year. All this made him think. It was evident he did not want to be reported to President Johnson with the proof of his indifference at Euchee Anna. When he learned of a truth that the man complaining was a double deserter and raider, he calmed down and the interview ended by his promising us that he would send no troops at all up, and asked us that we would assist him in keeping order up there and he would help us. We bid him good-bye — went home and made our people proud with our success. Things had pretty well settled down when the hanging of the negro at Knox Hill happened and some of the negroes called on General Ashboth and he sent up a company of white and one of negro troops, stationing them at Euchee Anna. We knew that their coming was inevitable and made no effort to stay it. Some of the Knox Hill boys got out of the way. I remained at home as though nothing had happened. The second morning after the day they camped at Euchee Anna, an officer with a little squad of men hailed at our front gate. A servant (girl answered. I was up stairs, heard them ask her if the younger John L. McKinnon was at home. She told them I was. They told her to tell him that he was wanted at the gate. I reported at once. (I think he was surprised, thought I had gotten out of the way.) The Captain introduced himself as Capt. Merry of Company — and introduced those with him. I asked them to dismount and come in. He said, 'T am up here investigating the hanging of that negro at Knox Hill some time ago and learn that you were connected with it, and we want to know what you have to say about it?" I said again, "Dismount, come into the house and I will tell you all I know about it." We all went in and when seated in the parlor the Captain said, "Now, we wish you to give us a full statement of the whole affair?" I did this and told him there never had been in all the days of slavery an attempt at such a deed, and that I veritably believed that it was that unpunished crime above Euchee Anna that General Ashboth let go without a notice, that moved that boy to this awful deed. That I had known the boy all his life; that he belonged to a near relative of mine and all this made it hard for me to deal with him as we did. That we had no officers or law and we knew by the cases mentioned that we could hope for no help from Gen. Ashboth, if we went to him with cases of this sort; that the protection of our mothers, sisters and neighbor women, demanded of us that this incarnate brute should not go at large and that we could see no other way out of it, but to do just as we did, and under the same condition we don't see how we could do differently now. I was glad to hear him say, "Neither can I." After asking me a few questions pertaining to the matter, that I answered promptly, he said, "I believe every word you say. Much that you have told is corroborated by statements from some of the older and better negroes in that settlement." We had them to stop and take dinner with us for which they showed appreciation. He was a fine looking gentleman with a kind open face. When leaving he said, "I will keep strict control over these negro troops while here and if they bother you over here I will stop them." We were good friends while he stopped here. This was the winding up of Federal troops in old Walton.

Chapter Fifty - Reclaiming Property and Settling Deserters

The endangering of life, the time spent in the gathering up and restoring stolen property to the proper owners, the settling down and keeping the roving raiders in their proper places amounted to but little commercially, but from a moral, social standpoint we see them as teachers, pregnant with great lessons in character building. This severe handling had to be resorted to; they could not be reformed or put in, or kept in their proper places by other process. They soon learned that if the South did fail in the great struggle at arms, surrendering them, if she had acknowledged her armies overpowered and accepted the arbitrament of the Union Sword that she struggled against, there was no surrender of character, no cringing humility, no acknowledgement of dishonor, no obsequious words of apology for anything that had been said or done, to any body, any State or government. She did the very best she could against odds to establish what she believed to be an ideal government; and her people were just as honest, just as conscientious then and now, in doing this, as the Northern statesmen and soldiers felt that they were right in hindering it. They believed as truly, that they had a moral and legal right to withdraw from the Union and establish their Confederate government, as our forefathers believed they had a right to withdraw from the British government and establish this Republic. The bellum situation in Walton having been leveled up and men settled down in their proper spheres; her young soldiery came together and discussed commercial problems under the post-bellum regime. Instead of the two main anti-bellum industries — agricultural farming and stock raising — they found their Walton full of resources to develop. There is the ranging timber business, the logging business, steam saw mill building and operatings, sail and steam boat building and operatings, and the improved mercantile business on bay and rivers.

1. D. G. Gunn.   2. Prof. C. C. Gunn.   3. Colin C. Gunn

Young men embarked in these enterprises with energy, honesty and succeeded in spite of political conditions, in spite of reconstruction outrages, because there was plenty of money loose in our country to develop its resources. The North was flooded with Lincoln's green-back money, the best money ever made; the war closed, peace opened the doors that kept it shut in — money unrestrained by graft legislation — turned loose to be free — seeks and finds its level like water unrestrained finds its level. The "Aurora," a heavy timbered, thick planked, round knuckled, shallow draft, side wheel steamer — the first steam boat built in Walton — built at Freeport by "McKinnon Bros." for the trade between Pensacola, Fla. and Geneva, Ala., touching at the many intervening points along that route. She ran successfully there for four seasons, navigating the river in its natural state and coming out in the end alive, the only steamer that did before the "Government cleanout." She actually gave the river a pretty good "cleanout" before the government took hold. She found up this river, hanging on some of the worst snags, all of the anti-bellum steamers. "The 8th of January," the "Julian," the "Mary Clifton," the "New Boston" as living warnings to all steamers who would dare to navigate these waters. The "Aurora" left these waters to ply 'between Key West and Havana. In the beginning of the developing of these resources, conditions, politically, began to show up propitiously. Law and order began to assert their rights. Under the Lincoln reconstruction regime, Walton is becoming her former self, a State election is called, Hon. David S. Walker, a near relative of Gol. George W. Walker, is elected Governor. Walton sends as her representatives in this post-bellum government, John Morrison, Daniel G. Gunn and John L. McKinnon, Jr. When the legislature met to inaugurate the newly elected Governor we found in the Executive chair that grand old man, Hon. Wm. Marvin, of N. Y., exercising the functions of provisional Governor. He steps down nobly, Gov. Walker steps up gracefully, manfully. This legislative body was able to compete with any the State ever had. The State elected its representatives to Congress, the legislature their U. S. Senators who were never admitted Those in charge of the U. S. government at Washington were not in accord with Mr. Lincoln's plan of reconstruction. This newly organized, reconstructed State government enacted wholesome laws and moved on under a bright sky under the most flattering auspices. Yet in the very start there was a murmuring of dissatisfaction among the abolition fanatics, saying, "The negro has no voice in this new start, he must be enfranchised."

Chapter Fifty-One - The Carpetbag Negro Rule of Reconstruction

This State government under Gov. Walker moved on in peace and quiet and all is loyal, progressive and lovely for two years. Then comes the reconstruction, negro rule that darkened the splendid azure sheen of our political and moral sky, a darkness as black as erebus, leaving a stain that permeated the inner nature so deep that it will require years and years to wipe out. Harrison Reed a carpetbagger, is our Governor. Not a mean man at heart, was an intelligent, a devout Presbyterian, but a weakling, pliable in the hands of ill designing men. Not like the carpetbaggers in the main, but they, with the negroes, were largely in the majority. Old Walton held her full white representatives through all the days of reconstruction, which meant something to her, and the State. Walton bounded as today, together with Santa Rosa, formerly a part of Walton, sent A. L. McCaskill as their Senator. John L. McKinnon, Jr., D. L. McKinnon, George Berry and Angus McMillon as their representatives. Holmes, formerly a part of Walton with Washington, sent A. D. McKinnon as their Senator and W. F. Green and Thos. Hanner as their representatives. We stood as a solid phalanx working harmoniously together and with others through all those bitter days. One side of the legislative hall was crowded with black faces dotted about with a few white carpetbag faces scattered among them. Here as in the army and prison we were still taking lessons in patience or "just letting patience have her perfect work." All sorts of subterfuges were resorted to by this mongrel crowd to carry out their plans, the story of these belong to the State to bring out. Just two incidents in which Walton figures in, are worthy of mentioning. To have the organization of the Senate what the vilest of them would have it, they had Senator McCaskill arrested taken before the U. S. court in Jacksonville for trial of a crime that they had not a scintilla of evidence of his guilt, and turned him loose, without a trial as soon as the Senate was organized. After the death of their second Governor, Ossian B. Hart, a native Floridian, Marcellus L. Stearns became Governor. The matter of the reorganization of the House of Representatives was being considered. There was a breach between the majority of the negroes and the carpetbaggers. The negroes wanted to elect one of themselves Speaker and other attaches. The carpetbaggers did not want a negro no more than we did, they wanted to elect Col. Martin Speaker. The house had for chaplain a great big ignorant, greasy black negro, with a big mouth that was always saying ugly, mean things. He was becoming more and more intolerable to our side of the House. While this breach was at its worst and the carpetbaggers in a dilemma, one of our friends at the R. R. Depot came up and told us that this Chaplain said in his hearing, while standing in the midst of a crowd of his fellows, and was cheered by them, 'T hope to see the day when I shall have the power to cut every slave-holder's throat from ear to ear!" This moved us to feelings of desperation. Threats of assassination and Kuklucking were being made. Walton's representative went to Speaker Stearns, told him what dangers were brewing and that something must be done quick to stay it, or there would be serious, bloody trouble, that the whites would not put up with this man any longer and proposed to him that if they would give the white side of the house the Chaplain they would go with them and elect Col. Martin Speaker. The Governor was a one-armed Union soldier and wanted to be fair, he said it was an outrage and must be remedied. He said if the whites would select some decent colored man that would be acceptable, they would join in the proposition, but they would not be able to elect both Speaker and Chaplain without the help of the whites. We found Rev. Henry Call, now a citizen of DeFuniak, a decent colored man with some intelligence, who was acceptable to all, and we at once elected Martin Speaker and Call Chaplain and stayed a tragedy; the old Chaplain left town by request for parts unknown. This little episode was fruitful for good in the afterwards. This kind of legislation went on, growing worse and worse from 1868 to 1877. Then the real white people raised up in all their might all over the State and said, "We can and must free ourselves from this negro-carpetbaggism. "George W. Drew was nominated for Governor. There was a mighty effort put forth all over the State. Walton was in the forefront, all who could speak or exercise any influence went to work in earnest, early and late. Hon. A. L. McCaskill and I spoke in every precinct in Walton and many in Santa Rosa visited pretty much every home and saw that all white men were registered properly. The carpetbaggers followed close behind us with their best speakers in negro precincts, W. J. Purman. Hamelton and Dickson, with their headquarters at Marianna. were the campaigners through Walton. They made extravagant, rash promises to the negroes, reminding themselves no doubt of the old rhyme:

"Much to promise and little to give
Causes the fools in comfort to live."

"The forty acres and the mule," was their leading promise to the end. The whites attended all of their meetings when they knew of them, and would take them up on their rash, foolish promises; but they would hold secret, night meetings, and say things that they would not dare say in the presence of the whites. They were good speakers and educated as to books, but bankrupts as to character. They called an open advertised meeting at Euchee Anna in the open day time, pretty much every negro voter was there. This was called their "Grand Rally Meeting." The white voters were there in force, the meeting was held in the old courthouse in the southern part of the town. They had to be checked up several times in their extravagant statements. They lead us to believe they wanted their opponents to reply when they were through. But when they finished, they had a tacit understanding with the negroes to meet them for private instructions, and they went out in a body in the direction of the hotel where they had stopped, not by the street way, but direct through a grove that intervened, and when they were well in the grove and near the hotel they stopped. Hamilton, a tall, stout, rawboney man of fair complexion, light hair and 'blue eyes weighing about two hundred pounds, 38 years old, a college athlete in appearance, stood talking to the negroes as they gathered around him in the grove. The white voters who moved on to the business part of town by the street way, saw that he had stopped and was talking with the negroes. Bill Bell, a farmer from Knox Hill, a full match in build, weight, and years, for Hamilton, with dark complexion, black hair and dark eagle piercing eyes, said, "Men we have had enough of this today, and those negroes have had enough, let's go over there and send these rascals over the river and the negroes home, where they belong?" "All right" came from everybody. They walked up to the circle. Bell in the lead, while Hamilton was yet speaking. Bell with his right hand on the left shoulder of one negro, his left on the right of another, made a breach and enlarged the circle, walked right up in front of Hamilton and said in loud unmistakable tones, using severe ugly adjectives. "See here. Hamilton, these negroes have had enough of this stuff today, you are fixing them up to be put under the ground. You were allowed to say too much in yonder building, you can't sneak out here in these bushes and stir up the devil in them, and let me tell you right here, if you know what is best for you, you had better cross the river and crawl up in your hole." Hamilton straightened himself up boastingly with an air of bravery, and he was brave with his big crowd of negroes around him and said. "I am a free born American citizen exercising the right of free speech and don't want to be disturbed in this way." "You are." said Bell. "a free born American jackass risking the dangers of a free fight!" "You are more of a jackass than I am," said Hamilton. As these words fell upon Bell's ears, he dealt a blow with his right fist directly in Hamilton's breast that staggered him. It was promptly returned and while these blows and fencings were flying swiftly there went up a cry from the white voters, "A fair fight, a fair fight!" They clenched each other then and went at it right. The negroes indiscriminately took to the woods, running pell-mell in every direction. Purman and their negro driver made for the hotel, got their horses and were ready on the ground in a little while to go for the river. Bell proved more than his equal in a clenched wrestle. Hamilton realizing his situation cried out, "Am I left alone, have they all deserted me?" It was then the white voters laid hold on them, loosed their hold on each other, pulled them apart and there they stood unexhausted in front of each other, with their faces scratched a little, the greatest damage done being to their Sunday clothes. Hamilton got into the carriage with Purman and the negro driver and they went down the Douglass Ferry road, the negro driving with such flying speed through the sand and dust that flew so thick and high above their heads, that they were hid from view. When they got to the ferry it was night. They urged Mr. Campbell to help them across that night, that they might be safe. When they had told him what had befallen them that day at Euchee Anna, he told them that it would not be safe to try crossing the river at night and that he knew all of those men and would guarantee their safety with him that night, that all they wanted was for them to let the negroes alone. They stopped until morning in security and passed over the river, and that was the last of carpetbaggism in Walton. The most remarkable and creditable thing In this whole affair was, that there was neither knife or pistol drawn during the encounter, notwithstanding in these times, and on such occasions men went armed to the teeth. But it took more than this to drive them out of Marianna. It took the shooting up of Col. McClellan, the killing of his dear daughter, the most lovely, the most beautiful, innocent and the most winsome of Marianna's fair daughters. This done, too, by black trained assassins, who took shelter under the great oak trees by the side walk and shot to death this sweet innocent daughter, as she sat on the veranda in the evening tide, musing on the beauties in Nature — in sky and trees before her — and while her young heart dilated with the bright prospects just ahead, in the near future, when the incubus of reconstruction would be swept away. Think, too, she fell a lifeless corpse in the arms of her dear wounded father, who was not able to hold her up in that trying hour. This was not a Walton tragedy but we are constrained to mention it here, for there were Walton boys there who helped to avenge the heartless deed. Some time, someone, will tell Jackson County's dark story of carpetbag reign and do justice to this sad story.

The "ides of March" comes — every white voter is in his place. Vehicles are provided and men ready to bring in the sick, the lame, the halt and the blind to the polls. Walton's full vote is cast. Other counties followed suit. Drew is elected Governor of Florida. There went up a shout from the land, "carpetbagism is stabbed to the heart and practically dead in Florida. Died, too, in the arms of the military and with 'but little sympathy from them." But it left its shame in our land that the blood of bulls and goats are not able to blot out. A shout of triumph went up to heaven, to Him to whom vengeance belongs. Oh, how well we remember unto this day the ear-splitting, joyful shout that rang throughout our fair State. This day of gladness, of promised peace in Walton was far more gladsome, than the promised peace after Appomattox that was so slow in coming. The latter was a victory of the power of the sword over us. and was grinding; the former a victory of the ballot over them and was jubilating. So these carpetbaggers, like the Arabs, folded their tents and silently stole away, leaving us alone with our affairs. The gates of Janus shut. The people rejoice. Men having a mind to work, worked. Money unrestrained by legislation, in the hands of the common people, moves around crowning every honest effort of the laborer with success. Walton's people were never more prosperous in their efforts to develop her resources than they were in the first two decades that followed the close of the war. Their energy in developing her resources had but to beckon to this unrestrained capital, when it came and was satisfied, and they enriched. But in the midst of this prosperity and satisfaction among the masses there went up a howl, "There is too much money in circulation!" This howl did not come from the laborers, the soldiers that bore the brunt of the Union Army, neither did it come from the Confederates that lost all, nor from the farmer or any manual laborer. It started in London, was caught up in Wall Street, heralded by the bankers, corporationist and was answered by paid congressional representatives.

Chapter Fifty-Two - Sorrow and Progress

But with all these advantages and good cheer it seems in the Divine plan not to let Walton rest too securely too long in this cheering work lest she might become too proud, too much elated, overjoyed. Two brutish negroes, Streeter and Monk, came down the river from Alabama and in the early night time entered the store of McKinnon and McCullough at Freeport. to rob it. While Monk kept watch outside Streeter entered with club and most brutally clubbed to death Ezery Moore, their clerk, a noble young man, the friend of every body. Streeter only found fifty cents, escaped through a window leaving his bloody tracks behind him. He was pursued by great forces, captured above Geneva, Ala., and brought back to Freeport. Monk was captured on the ground. They both had a trial, acknowledged guilt, and were put to death. Greed for money tempts men to risk their lives, throw away their characters and lose their souls. Oh, what a price these poor brutes paid for that fifty cents that they were never permitted to spend! This bold, open, bloody tragedy, on a good inoffensive young man, stirred the women of Walton as nothing else ever had. They shuddered with fear for the safety of their homes and persons. In 1875 the U. S. government called for bids to put steam mail service between Freeport and Pensacola touching at intermediate points, for twice each week, for four years. The writer was the successful bidder. He went to New Orleans, purchased a commodious little steamship adapted to the work. She was put on the line of work and made successful trips. Captain John Watson was the master of her in the last years, a worthy young man, faithful to duty; no curses or strong drink ever passed his lips. He was an excellent steamboat manager, giving satisfaction to all. As he turned into Point Washington one night the steamer's new boilers blew up, killing him. He died at Point Washington a few hours later. He had a barge in tow and a lot of passengers; he and they were placed on board of barge and poled into the Point. This sad news was broken to me just as I was getting out of bed early on the Sabbath morning. I shall never forget the shock of this sad news. My first thought was to go and carry the news to his young wife and children. I started, went a little ways, and found that I was not equal to the task. I turned back and had some of our tenderhearted ladies to go with their soft words and break the sad news to her. I turned and went in haste with others and brought the body home. It was in the gloaming of that holy day when we reached his home. His weeping wife 'who exclaimed, "Oh, that he could but look natural as in other days!" The next day we laid him at rest in the cemetery. After all these years that have gone, this event is just as fresh in my mind as it was on that sad day. How it must have lingered in the mind and probed the heart of the wife and mother, all these years in her reticent widowhood.

Fifth Epoch

Chapter Fifty-Three - The Projection of the P. and A. Rail Road

What the Civil War lacked in stirring up and scattering abroad those of the old Scotch Valley people from their well-made nests, the P. and A. Division of the L. and N. R. R. about accomplished. It acted as though it was a great bomb shell dropped down in the midst of the Valley, crushing, rooting up and driving the old Scotch settlers in every direction, leaving only enough there for seed. We trust this stirring up and driving away, was for some good. For it 'broke up, to some extent, one of the plainest, simplest, most social, and truly religious communities in Walton. You will find today, the descendants of these early Scotch Pioneers among the leading business men and best church workers in Pensacola and Jacksonville and intervening towns along the R. R., and in Geneva and Florala, Ala, And we are astonished on close investigation, how many of these descendants are in these towns. The Presbyterian churches in De Funiak, Freeport, Mossy Bend, Florala and Geneva are to some extent, products of the Valley Church. Time may yet show what we stated in the beginning. Walton never needed any R. R. with her water courses improved as they could and should, and may yet be. We are told that we would never have had our beautiful De Funiak Springs, that has always been a prohibition town had we had no R. R. That may be. But think of it in the not very far off future when the Pea River with all its tributaries will .be turned near Geneva, down by De Funiak into the Choctawhatchie bay and the palatial interwaterway steamers coming direct from New Orleans by Mobile, Pensacola, De Funiak and Geneva and on to Elba and no telling how much farther beyond. And the rich bottoms of the Choctawhatchie reclaimed, the river shortened by being straightened and made more navigable. These things are coming fast.

Chapter Fifty-Four - De Funiak Springs

At the first, this town was called "Lake De Funiak," then "De Funiak Springs," in honor of Mr. De Funiak of Lousivlle, Ky., a prominent L. and N. R. R. manager, named not for his money, but for his noble character. Col. Chipley, one of the founders and a great admirer of the place, proposed the change, as visitors were saying "What a pretty little lake on the top of this hill!" When the change is made they will say "What a pretty big round spring boiling up on the top of this high plateau." This town is situated in the High Lands of Western, Fla., on the foot hills of the Appalachians in the center of Walton and Western Florida, 300 feet above sea level. In approaching this beautiful little table land, in the center of which its great Springs boil up in a perfect circle of one mile in circumference, around which the town is artistically laid off and built. All is upward. One broad boulevard on the rimmed circle, conforming to the Spring circle. The gentle slopes to the Spring making a beautiful park filled with oaks and the tall waving pines. Other streets converging into this broad, graded, circular boulevard on the top of plateau. Then comes Crescent street in a semi-circle, starting some distance east of the Spring from Main street, that runs east and west, and south of the R. R., passing in a semicircle through Poets' corner and circling around west of the Spring and back to the R. R. You will, on every approach to its great Spring have to ascend quite a hill; For Big Sandy, Bruces and Alaqua creeks all head up around this plateau, and it is thought that they have a subterranean source or feeders. This topographic lay of the town shows how well Nature has provided for its drainage, making it healthful and beautiful for situation.

The Soil Around De Funiak

While the ground on which De Funiak is built, is so very desiraible, it is of the poorest in Walton, Yet it's astonishing how it will respond so readily and so abundantly to agricultural tillage and commercial help in this oxygenic-nitrogenious clime, when warmed up into assimilation by the warm winds from off our gulf stream. This soil becomes gardens of blooming roses and fields of bending cereals, with the right kind of help.

The Crowning Work

When the Great Master Builder finished the Land of Flowers, He stood upon this highland plateau and took one ravishing view of His work, its stretches of indented sea shores, washed by the great gulf and broad Atlantic, its winding rivers and rivulets, its lakes and lakelets, its mammoth mineral springs, gushing up from immeasurable depths; He was pleased with the work and said, "I will crown this beauty, we have enough of squares and triangles, so I will place my great compass on this beautiful eminence and strike a circle just one mile in circumference and scoop it out with my own hands, forming a rim around the basin and fill it with springs of pure limpid water, gushing from beneath the bedded rocks, to cheer the heart and slake the thirst of man and beast, and let man embellish it as he likes."

The Planting of the Town

This town is truly the product of faith. Let the honor of its founding and institutions rest where they belong; clearly stated facts, truth in its sovereignty, and broad catholic views of the surroundings are promoters to this end. When the steamer "C. Fisher" was making her regular trips in the early 70s, between Pensacola and Freeport, Col. T. T. Wright, then the leading dry goods merchant in Pensacola, acquired much knowledge from different sources, about the aborigines, the Valley Scotch Pioneers, the Knox Hill School and Mr. John Newton's work up there in Walton. He became very much interested in the history of them, proposed that funds be raised to build a Memorial Hall in the Valley, where annual meetings could be held, music and speakers procured and people from a distance be invited to come and do honor to these early settlers, and keep the flame of progressive education alive in Walton, and bring about a better National feeling. He got no encouragement in this enterprise, no account of the inaccessibility of the place, the Euchee Valley and Knox Hill being 15 and 18 miles respectively, from Freeport, the nearest point of public conveyance. The survey of the P. and A. division of the L. & N. R. R. was being made. Col T. T. Wright, Col. W. D. Chipley and Maj. W. J. VanKirk were along, and camped on the slopes around the spring, under the shelter of the great pines. It was a beautiful star lit night and the moon was in its virgin beauty — they saw this gem of waters at its best — they laid themselves down on the green sward along its gentle slopes, and while the stars twinkled in reflections on its placid bosom, and the tall pines acted as sentinels above, lulling them to rest with the murmurings to their long accetalious foliage; they dreamed dreams and saw visions of coming prospects. And when they were awakened and refreshed in the morning, Col. Chipley, the enterprising builder said, "The R. R. must come 'by this beautiful lake and we must make this a splendid winter resort." Col. Wright, the Scotch-Irish thinker, said, "Yes, and let us build at least one tabernacle here in honor of the Euchee Valley Scotch Presbyterians, and their great teacher, John Newton, who love and appreciate each other so much." And Major W. J. VanKirk, "the blue stocking" Scotch Presbyterian, said, "Yes, and let us make this an educational center, let us establish a Presbyterian College here. I have no heirs, I will make it my heir." (VanKirk was worth $100,000.00 at that time.) And as soon as the R. R. was through and in operation, he made this offer through the Valley Church to the Florida Presbytery, offering too, 40 acres of land at Lake Stanley for the college grounds. Trustees were elected, the enterprise put in motion, when an unexpected and a most outrageous move swept the Major's property from him, as if by a tornado. So this noble enterprise fell through. And it is due him, to say here, notwithstanding his great losses, he made good his promise, "If you will furnish the wood work for the Presbyterian Church, I will have the brick work done." So the little brick church, nestling by the spring beneath the beautiful magnolias pines and oaks in Chipley Park today, stands as a reminder of his Scotch Presbyterian genrosity. These men moved at once to break the ground, to build themselves handsome homes on the spring circle. The Murray Cawthon home, as it now stands, the Levi Plank's, moved back in the corner of Magnolia and Third streets, and now Dr. Cawthon's home, and the Gray building, now M. A. Warren's home improved in the corner of Main and 2nd street, were the very first dwellings built in this town.

Prof. W. C. Eddie, Levi Plank, St., and C. C. Banfill were the first to come to us from the North country. Chipley, Wright, VanKirk and Bonfill put their heads and shoulders together and made a strong quartette to start off with, for town building. They seemed to have unbounded faith in the future prospects of the place, and so expressed themselves, wherever they went, instilling this faith in those with whom they came in contact. Meet them where you would, it was, "Winter resort, educational center, college town, the logical center on R. R. for the county capital." Col. Wright would ever urge his long cherished pet scheme, the building of a tabernacle for the gathering in of the clans, for the mingling and intermingling of people from all over this great country of ours, so as to foster the education established and bring about better political, moral and social relations between the people at large. This suggestion was made long before the Chautauqua was ever mentioned. And in the fullness of time they came in their richest expectations. We dare say, there is not a town South of this fading imaginary "Mason and Dixon" line, in which there is a broader, a more catholic spirit, especially among the veterans of the two armies of the late war as was evidenced not a great while ago on Sabbath evening, when our oldest Union soldier, a pioneer veteran of the place died and his pallbearers to take his body to its last resting place were, at his own request, three each, of the oldest Union and Confederate veterans of this place. We have learned to appreciate each other better in these latter days. Some of my best friends are from the North. We ask not "Where are you from," but "What are you?" This spirit of faith in our founders, seemed to take hold on people from its incipiency. These advantages in prospect come to the front in every discussion, as the best place on the R. R. for a town, and they asserted their claims with effect; of course there were jealous ones in opposition, but this soon vanished into thin air. These four enterprising men's elegant homes, buttressed their declared faith. And while they were building, others came and built, the writer being among the very first to come and build, and the question was often put to him, "Why did you come to this place?" and the answer has invariably been, "For Church and School advantages," notwithstanding there was not a Church nor School building in the place. But he is glad to say, he has already enjoyed these privileges beyond his most earnest expectations.

Chapter Fifty-Five - The Florida Chautauqua Established

The Times Union had this bit of information in its news column, "Dr. A. H. Gillett with a party are touring in Florida looking out for a suitable locality for a winter Chautauqua and will return to Jacksonville on the 12th inst." A meeting of citizens was called at once and C. C. Banfill was sent to Jacksonville to meet the party and try and induce them to come to De Funiak before locating. Dr. Gillett and Rev. C. C. McLean returned with him. It rained and it poured for several days, no depot save a box car switched off, no hotel but a few scattering dwellings to offer any sort of accommodations. They looked over the grounds between showers and held an interview with the land owners and were very much pleased with the situation and prospects ahead. So, in a little while all the arrangements were consummated for the Florida Winter Chautauqua to have its home here. The managers prepared a pine plank 14 inches by 14 feet long, painted it snow white, and had these words printed on it in large coal black letters: The Florida Chautauqua — First Annual Session will open Feb. the 10th to March the 9th, A.D. 1885. This board was fastened up on a tree in the northeast corner of Chipley Park, just across the street, west from M. M. Morrison's home, where it could be easily seen and read by the passersby, both on the dirt and R. R. This announcement may be termed "the open beginning of the Florida Chautauqua in De Funiak Springs." The name and what it meant was much discussed and gave it much publicity far and near, few had ever heard of the name, much less of what it now stood for. The Chautauqua Hotel and Tabernacle were begun then, and both rushed through, to be ready for the opening. Col. Wright's long called-for tabernacle for the gathering in of the clans of old Walton, for the intermingling of the people and fostering morals and Christian education here, with the National Chautauqua idea that he felt must bring about broader moral ideas and social relations throughout our land, is about to be realized. One of the leading farmers and business men of Walton said to Mr. Bonfill. "It is foolish to build such a mammoth hotel here, it will never be filled up." Mr. Banfill said, "Why, sir, we expect to build as much more to it in less than five years." And the second year they built on to it the north wing and three weeks 'before the next assembly convened every room with a fire place, was taken up.

The Opening Morning

When the 10th of February, 1885 came, about 50 of us, men, women and children, came together on the front seats, and the different classes as advertised were arranged, and teachers, places, and times of meetings assigned. The teachers were of the very best class in all the departments. Rev. Frank Russell, D. D., was instructor in the S. S. Normal. He had a large interesting class, who hated to give him up, and who felt wiser and better for having sat at his feet. And so it was in all of the schools. The first opening evening found about 100 of us bunched together on either side of the middle aisle. At the close of the evening exercise, Prof. W. F. Sherwin, of the Conservatory of Music, from Boston, came to the front with the program in his hand and said, "After I had signed my contract for my services here as Chorus Director, with Dr. Gillett, he sent me this program. I looked over it carefully, took my pencil, put down the R. R. fare of every individual connected with it, to De Funiak and back home, the hotel bill of each, the cost of the talent as I knew it to be with us, and added something for contingencies, struck a line and made the addition, and found that it footed up $11,000.00. I wrote at once to Dr. Gillett, asked him what was the population of the City of De Funiak, that he proposed to render this program in? He answered me promptly "'Only a few hundred.'" I was astonished and when I came and saw the few houses around in these woods, I was the more astonished. But since I came and learned more, I find that you need just such an institution as this located permanently in these splendid grounds, around this lovely little lake. And the Northern tourists need it too, so that they may drop down here and escape the rigors of the cold North and be fanned by the warm, soft, gentle breezes, fresh from off your Mexican Gulf stream. I learn too that there are business men, moneyed men who realize that you need this institution. But let me tell you here on this opening night, that if you want this institution here, you can have it, it depends upon your attitude towards it, and not upon this man or that man, nor upon these moneyed men, but upon you in this little growing town, just now in its embryo. Put your heads and shoulders together — work and pull together and I will guarantee that you can have this institution here as long as it will be a blessing to you. Every one of you go home tonight, write to your relatives and friends and tell them what a good thing you have here, and ask them to come and see and you will be surprised how many will come to see and stay. Speak a word here and there, urging everybody to come; even if they come only as so many sacks of salt, they can't help but absorb some of the good things out of this matchless program." The people had a mind in those days to follow good advice and they wote and they came to see, and stayed — they came to listen and to learn, neither darkness, rain or cold kept them back. Those at a distance often brought their dinners and stayed until after supper. The days were full in class work and Tabernacle exercises; and no one could afford to miss any of these good things. And before this first session closed, the Tabernacle was full on Saturdays. This institution has had its ups and downs, as all worthy enterprises have. It has always had good friends to stand by it. In its earliest days the L. & N. R. R. with its friends stood by it and held the bag. In later days they wanted some one else to bear the brunt of the burden, and it was rolled upon Hon. Wallace Bruce's shoulders and he and his family has stood by it nobly. Their business tact, their travel and association with such institutions, together with their industry, their diversified knowledge and indomitable energy make them a little Chautauqua within themselves. And it may be said, that it was under their management that the institution was first set upon its own feet, where it could stand alone. He had no financial help outside of its earnings, until the past year, when monied friends, especially De Funiakers, came to him with gifts to help build the splendid Auditorium and "Hall of Brotherhood," that we now have, that was to cost $18,000.00 but will cost $28,000.00 by the time it is finished up. The L. & N. has continued all these years, a close friend to this enterprise and to the people along its line, from Pensacola to River Junction in giving them an outing from their routine farm work once a week for six or eight weeks each year in a R. R. Assembly Ticket to all the exercises in the Florida Chautauqua Tabernacle during the day, from any point along that line, for the small sum of eighty-five cents. All should be very thankful for such golden opportunities to visit relatives and friends for a nominal sum, in addition to the other advantages. We find this paralleled nowhere else. We look on these Saturday excursions, as one of the crowning features of the Chautauqua. And yet, you hear "Selfish Greed," lifting up its puny voice in disapproval. "These had better stay at home on their farms, with their wives and children, where they belong," not willing that they may see and hear things that will give them cheer in their isolated farm homes through the long summer days, but rather see them serfs, chained to the soil, coming up annually with their tax money and to buy a pittance for their families. If you would have a good happy, thrifty community, you must work to give them advantages, to bring them in contact with the best things extant. Some of Chautauqua's best friends have passed under the shadows. Dr. Gillett, Banfill, Chipley and VanKirk. Col. Wright was allowed to leave here when he might have been retained, with his marvelous foresight and resourcefulness in developing and crystallizing town utilities and beauties. But his forces were not fully appreciated until he had gone; so the towns in Tennessee and South Florida got the benefits that might have been ours.

Chapter Fifty-Six - Schools

Prof. C. C. Gunn, a descendant of the early pioneers, one of the first graduates of Knox Hill Academy, was the one that opened the stream of education, that now runs so free and fresh through this little town, and is destined to 'become a river of knowledge enlightening the minds and souls of those who will drink of it, as it flows on. This first school was taught in a little round log house, north of the R. R. in what is now known as "Happy Hollow." The second was taught by Prof. W. C. Eddy in East End and on Main Street in a neat little frame building, belonging to Dr. D. L. Campbell. This school lasted several months. John L. McKinnon taught the third on the grounds now occupied by the Public School, in a large frame house and now moved off the grounds and used as the residence of P. W. Bloodsworth, Esq. This school continued for near three years and is now turned into a regular Public School, with splendid buildings, a large two-story, commodious, modern brick building, with excellent grades from primary up through to "High School Grades." The Northern M. E. Church and their friends organized a school under the name of "The McCormic Institute;" built quite a large handsome two-story frame building in Chipley Park a little east of the Presbyterian Church, brought down teachers and put them to work. In less than two years' time a storm came, blew down the building and put a stop to this educational enterprise.

The Normal School

The State of Florida was out on a hunt for a home for her White State Normal. We invite her to come and see? She comes and finds enchanting grounds here, in the home of the Florida Chautauqua, and a booming Public School. The grounds are tendered, she accepts and the State Normal on these grounds is established here and does splendid work, increasing in numbers until it becomes the most representative public school in the State, with a curriculum that did honor to our best Normals. And after it had been taught here, successfully for seventeen consecutive years, giving general satisfaction, the Legislature of politicians met in Tallahassee and took it away from us without giving a single good legitimate reason for so doing. Not long after the furniture was moved out of the buildings Rev. F. L. Higdon then pastor of the Presbyterian Church at De Funiak Springs, came in a little early to the Wednesday evening prayer meeting, sat down by the writer and said, "If there is one thing above another in a religious educational way, that we do need in this section, it is a religious high School or College, and this Normal School property is an ideal locality for such an institution and our Church ought to take steps at once to procure the property for this purpose, before the State disposes of it." I told him that I had never thought of it and did not know that we were able to take hold of such a mammoth enterprise as that. He presented these views to others, and in a little while the old Scotch Presbyterians were in a meeting together with their friends, the money raised and the property purchased for the purpose proposed. An Academic School, leading up to Collegiate work was organized under the auspices of our Florida Presbytery with a corps of teachers under the name of Palmer College. And J. W. Waldin, D. D., of Athens, Georgia, was elected unanimously its president. He went to work at once in West Florida and South Alabama, to raise funds to equip and run it until it could be gotten on its own legs. He found many friends regardless of denominations who responded with their substance. He procured an excellent body of teachers. G. Clyde Fisher, A. B., of Miami University, was chosen as principal. The fourth year with Rev. Lynn R. Walker, president, will soon close, as the most successful year. The progress has been upward all the time notwithstanding the dark financial clouds that have been overshadowing our commercial interests. The College is now a legally incorporated institution. We have evident reasons for believing that the Lord has owned and blessed this enterprise and will hold it up. This gives us faith to ask and trust Him to give us strength and wisdom to stand by it more faithfully.

Chapter Fifty-Seven - Churches in De Funiak

The Presbyterians were the first to organize a Church here and the first to start a Church building. We put a solid brick foundation down on which the present superstructure now stands, that cost us $358.00 and paid for it, our money gave out. There were but few of us here, and we were poor indeed, and did not want to go in debt, so we had to stop for a while. Rev. R. Q. Baker was on the commission that organized the Church here, was its first pastor for a long time, and gave good material help in the Church building. Rev. Johnson from Toronto, Canada, was the second pastor for some months. The Northern M. E. Church came in, organized and pushed through their Church building and got into it just a little before we got into ours. The Episcopal Church was the next to be built, then the Southern Methodist, then the Universalist, and then the Baptist. So we have six splendid church buildings in our town besides the many colored churches. The first building of the Northern Methodist Church was burned down in one of the many conflagrations we used to have before our waterworks were established, they put up a better building on same grounds, and the Northern and Southern Methodist have united and they all worship in the Northern Church building. The Southern M. E. Church building is occupied now by the "Christians." Rev. E. E. Erwin, of North Carolina was the third pastor of the De Funiak Presbyterian Church. Rev. L. F. Higdon, the next, then Rev. John Stanley Thomas and J. W. Waldon, D. D., president of Palmer College supplied the pulpit for one year in the absence of a pastor. Rev. Lynn R. Walker, president of Palmer College, is now the regular pastor.

Chapter Fifty-Eight - Walton's Daughters

The glory of Walton has ever been in her daughters. The heroism of these daughters of the two wars — Indian and Civil — which is akin to Godliness, may never be fully appreciated. The pen of the historian is too circumscribed to take in and picture to the world their intrinsic worth in all of the varied departments of their lives. But they did stand out as bright promotories in the minds and hearts of the soldiery of those days; for it was they who gave them good cheer in the sinking despondent days, and set them up on the rock again. The pioneer fathers and mothers of Walton held advanced thoughts in regard to the education and spheres of their daughters in society; and had them educated in the broadest sense in the schools Had them brought on in the classes with the sons of toil; for these old Scotch educators had long learned, that if you educate a boy you will give to the world an educated man to help it; but if you educate a daughter, the world will have an educated family to help humanity. It seems too as though they must have had some premonitions as to what awaited them in the future — a time when the butterflies of fashion, the mothers of brainless dudes, the waxen dolls of life, could not withstand the heat and toil of the day. They wanted their daughters to have some other protection, other than their beauty and mere superficial accomplishments. Anacreon, 450 years before Christ, in reciting the means of defense bestowed by nature on man and beasts, the fowls of the air and the fishes of the sea, asks: "What for the helpless woman has she more?" And he answers his own question thus:

"Beauty falls to woman's share
Armed with this she need not fear
Flame, nor sword, nor dart, nor spear."

But the sturdy old Scotch pioneers of Walton wanted their daughters to have something else, more lasting than their shifting, fading beauty, and sought to give them equal opportunities with their sons in the fields of mental activities. And when the tug of war came, the sad twisting days that wrung men's souls, we find them ready to help and comfort their weary mothers in their never ending toil, receiving in return gushes of praise from that well of love that ever springs fresh and pure in an overburdened mother's heart. And in the strength of their modest retirement, their trenchant pens reached out in earnest pleadings to the front of battle, holding back brothers and friends from universal corruption; while their eloquent tongues were to the disturbed peace at home, as oil to the surging waves. Their training seems to have fitted them for all the emergencies of the times. It is universally conceded that woman bore more than half the burdens of life, and yet, it is rarely you hear of them leading in a strike to throw off these burdens, or for higher wages. For self-sacrifice, endurance, purity of heart, faithfulness and devotion to duty they are, by far man's superiors. One has truly said, "Whilst labor is the strength of a country, its civilization and refinement are in exact proportion to the love and respect entertained for woman." Walton has ever shown the profoundest love and deepest respect for her daughters. And how could she do otherwise, when she remembers the sacrifices they made for, and how they held up the hearts and .hands of her soldiery at the front, through these four long unparalleled years of Civil War. And, too, how they stood always ready to fold the returning soldier brothers in their lovely arms in victory or in defeat. The writer remembers unto this day, a night ride through the Valley, when at home on furlough, when the sound of the distaff was scarcely ever out of the hearing of his ears, when the swift moving shuttle, the bang of the weavers beam, the buzz of the spindle, and the merry laughter of working maidens, made the music of the long evenings as well as that of the early morn and toilsome day. These implements of cloth making were wielded not only by the trained arms of colored maidens enured to constant work, but these were helped by the cheer and deft hands of their mistresses, whose fingers -were better schooled in striking sweet notes on stringed instruments. But none of these things worried these daughters. It was the charge of their loved ones at the front, the dread of deserters and coast raiders to rob them. It was such carking cares as these that piled up "Pelion on Ossia," that well nigh crushed their young lives out of them, and not the manual labor they did, nor dread of the negro, in whose power they were, for they had never been tampered with, and ever remained obedient and respectful. Dr. George Fisher, "Walton's first physician, who was robbed and driven to Geneva, Ala., by the deserters, was brutally murdered there by another band of these raiders from East Alabama. His wife and dependent daughters were left to struggle for their living by manual labor under these dark forebodings that overshadowed them. These accomplished daughters, like many other Confederate daughters in these days, went to work and supported the home at the spindle and loom, and by gardening, without a murmur, while their mother kept the home in order. In those days there came a rain storm — a cloud burst, that over-flooded the banks of the three rivers there, driving out all the inhabitants of the town, even carrying some of the dwellings across the river without wrecking them. It was the greatest flood in all the history of the place and is known as the "Lincoln Freshet." The waters stood for several days six or eight feet in the dwellings that were not swept away. When the waters had subsided so that the homes could be entered by rowboats, friends took the Misses Fishers into their drowned home to see what was left. Miss Mary a sweet, beautiful and admirable young lassie in the bloom of young girlhood, a paragon of excellencies and a prodigy in music, was the owner of the beautiful piano in the home; she loved it as some dear friend, it was a solace to them in their lonely hours, and lightened and cheered their labors; she could make it talk cheer to them about their Florida home that they had been driven from, the absent brothers at the front and about their dear departed, sacrificed father, who was so cruelly murdered. It was the great comfort in the home for them all. When the row-boat landed at their home, the young ladies leaped from it with a hurriedness befitting their anxieties; they came first to the parlor, Miss Mary in the lead opened the door, hurried anxiously to her piano, ran her trained fingers over the bright shining keys, but no response, it was dumb — as silent as death. Folding her arms across the keys with her head resting upon them, she baptized it anew with her tears, while her young heart pounded like a hammer in her generous bosom. Her disappointments, her griefs were assuaged by the mollifying words of her sisters and companions and she was herself again. After looking through the parlor at other damages they all agreed that things might have been worse. They entered next the working or spinning room. Miss Mary in the lead. On opening the door the first thing that greeted her was the old big spinning wheel standing before her in a juxtaposition, with broach on spindle, band properly adjusted, both on little spool and great rim wheel, just as she had left it, in perfect order for work and it seemed to say, "Here I am none the worse from the flood, take hold, go to work, forget the soft melodies of your piano and play on me the humble buzzing wheel songs that are keeping time in these stirring days with your Dixie songs." This was tantalizing, more than she could bear, looking about her she spied a hatchet, seized it with a "Carry Nation" grip, and dealt blows on its head and ears, unspindling and disbanding it, saying, "I shall find a more congenial companion in the future to gain a livelihood with than you." And she did, and is among the first ladies of the land raising up sons and daughters to call her blessed.

Chapter Fifty-Nine - The Monument

Walton's daughters were the first to organize a Memorial Society to commemorate in marble, her Confederate dead — her fallen worth — the glory of her sacrifices. They were the first to erect a monument in stone to a fallen Confederate soldier. Soon after the deserters and scalawags were made to know their places and were settled down in them, and while the dark clouds of carpetbaggism were gathering over us, her daughters met at Euchee Anna and organized themselves into a "Ladies' Memorial Association" with Miss Jeannette I. McKinnon president, the object of which, was to erect a monument in marble in honor of Walton's Confederate dead. Notwithstanding the burden that had borne down on their shoulders for four years they cheerfully took up this new work and went on to it in every laudable way to raise funds for its consummation; and this, too, in the face of the disclaimers to such right, through the Northern press. These ladies said, "We will build this monument of marble to their memory, they can pull it down and destroy it if they like; but we have one erected in our hearts and minds that they can't tear down nor mutilate." Sometime after they went to work the ladies of Tallahassee organized a State Memorial Association to build a memorial monument for the State's Confederate dead. Miss Bessie Brown, daughter of ex-Gov. Thos. Brown, was the president. All of the counties were asked to organize and join in with them to accomplish this end. Walton already organized and at work acquiesced in the call. A little more than a year after this State move the writer went up to Tallahassee and the Walton ladies sent by him $250.00 to be turned over to the State Association. He could find no one in Tallahassee to take charge of the money so he drove out to Bellaire, Gov. Brown's suburban home, met Miss Brown, the president and tendered the money. She hesitated and called the Governor and after ventilating the whole matter found that the Association had never materialized. Walton was the only one that came up to time and it was the consensus of opinion that this money be returned to the Walton Association to be used as they liked. The Governor said the trouble in the way was that there were such bad feelings brewing in the North that they thought it best to do nothing to stir up more feeling and they thought best to drop the organization. The money was returned to the Walton Association. They had passed on all these matters more than a year before, so they moved right on with more energy than ever to accomplish their ends. But this sidetracking at Tallahassee provoked in them an earnest desire to know more about governmental affairs, international laws, states' rights and belligerency; more about the men on both sides that led in State affairs, and war matters; who were the bulldozers and who the toadies, before, during and since the war. They requested some of the young soldiers to read up "with them and become informed on these subjects and invited them to deliver addresses before their societies from time to time, giving data that would help lead up to broader education. They entered as truly, and as fully upon this campaign of education, as ever our political parties entered upon their campaign in a Presidential year, and stayed in it until they had learned that some of the leading Northern Statesmen had gone mad in vindictive hate towards the South and were seeking, in the way of reconstruction, to humiliate and fasten all sorts of hardships upon them. For these they could but entertain the profoundest disgust. On the other hand they found the little two by four Southern Statesmen and Editors fondling generously and with sycophancy, coddling with these obdurate radical Northern Statesmen heaping fulsome praise on President Lincoln and his administration and turning their backs on President Davis and wantonly criticising his administration in defeat. Why some of these little Georgia fellows went so far as to condemn their own Senator, Ben Hill, for defending our rights in his famous speech on the arena of the U. S. Senate, in his tilt with Senator Blaine — the only place left us to set ourselves right before the world. The constant persuasions of these little pusillanimous fellows were "non-resistance, forbearance, submission, humility." Now for these little fellows they held the supremest contempt, the deepest disgust. Their campaign of education led them up to believe that President Jefferson Davis and President Abraham Lincoln were both good men in their several places; that they were honest in their concepts of duty, and that they were loyally and morally active in the discharge of the same. They believed that Davis deserved as much honor and glory for what he did in following his convictions in the years of the civil war, as President Lincoln deserved for what he did, and that the Confederate Soldier's name should and would stand as high on the roll of honor and fame as the Union soldier's. And any well drawn parallel, impartially gotten up, will show that these ladies were correct in their conclusions. So in the light of this education, Walton's lovely daughters move on steadfastly to build a time-lasting monument in marble, to their fallen braves, to honor their sacred memories and sacrifices. It was erected at first at the Valley Church then moved to Euchee Anna, the county site, as a more appropriate place, where it stands today as a monument of love in pure white marble, plain and unique in its modest dignity. Yet it effectually presents their work of gratitude for their fallen worth, to the eyes of the passersby, keeps alive sentiments that they cherished and shows their constant regard for the principles that they sacrificed their lives. It is no Bunker Hill Monument, with its shaft rising skyward, "piercing the clouds to meet the sun in his coming, so that the earliest light of the morning might gild it, and parting day linger and play on its summit." It has no broad entablatures resting upon its capital, with inscriptions of great generals, battles won and independence gained, but it stands there in its modest dignity representing heroes fallen in battles won, as much as it stands for that glorious "Lost Cause." Its apex is a human hand, with its index finger pointing skyward, beyond the rolling clouds, beyond the trembling stars and beyond the gild of the sun; alluring to a haven of rest beyond the stretch of the eye where there is no need of the sun where the Son of Righteousness gives light, glory and honor and a due recompense of reward to all the deserving ones. They have these tender lines engraved on one of the faces of the shaft:

> When the Spirit free deserts the body as it must
> What matters where the lifeless form dissolves itself again to dust.
> 'Twere sweet indeed to close our eyes with those we cherish near;
> And wafted upward by their sighs, soar to some calmer sphere.
> But whether on the scaffold high, or in the battle van
> The fittest place where're man can die is where he dies for man.

On another face is this superscription:

To the memory of the Confederate dead of Walton County, Florida. Erected by the "Ladies of Walton County Female Memorial Association."

A. D. 1871.
Col. Angus D. McLean, 6th Fla. Vols.

Capt. Murdoch Gillis, 6th Fla. Vols.	H. Kemp	Ed McCullough
Calvin McLean,	H. Wright	E. Wright
Capt. Daniel D. McLean, 7th Fla. Vols.	H. Busby	Hugh McRae
Daniel Moore,	J. Ward	H. Henderson
Lieutenant James McLean, Fla. Vols.	John Moore	Wm. C. Morrison
D. P. McDonald,	John Gent	Wm. Welsh
Lieutenant Archibald G. D. McDonald,	John Crawford	W. C. Gillis
Morrison, Fla. Vols.	M. P. Morrison	Wm. McRae
Lieutenant M. C. McRae, Fla. Vols.	Modison M. Reddick	Wm. Cawthon
D. McQuage.	Martin Reddick	Wm. Thornton
Lieutenant James McClelland. Fla. Vols.	N. Wm. Gillis	Wm. Brooks
D. K. McDonald,	Ned Marshal	Wm. Gomilion
Angus D. Gillis,	Pascal Barnett	Wm. Tiner
D. P. Gillis	Robert McSween	W. Anders
A. L. McCollum,	R. Holly	Wm. Kemp
Daniel McIver	Randal McRae	Wm. Wethington
Abram Konde D. Silcox	Rice Williamson	Wm. C. Campbell
A. Ward	Stephe Milton	Zion Tolie
Angus Gordon	S. Cotton	J. Bobb
B. Blount	Thos. Tiner	J. Silcox
B. Sylcox	Josh Gleason	J. Wright
Colen G. Ray, Jr.	John P. McLeod	Jack Loundy
C, L. McDonald	J. Barnett	J. Nelson
	J. Gomilion	John Williams
	John L. McLean	Joel Brown
	J. L. Anderson	John McLeod
	J. Rooks	Joel Marshel
	Daniel K. McLean	James Evins
	E. Gomilion	John Kinenton

J. Wright	Murdoch Gillis	John Brown
Lockland D. McLean	J. Sanders	Jessa Brooks
John Welsh	Malcom Gillis	

At the time this monument was erected, its cost and freight was very near as much as some of our State's more pretentious monuments cost later. The ladies of the Association agreed to have it moved to De Funiak Springs as this is the County Site now.

Chapter Sixty - Gov. David S. Walker's Tribute to Walton's Daughters

When reconstruction was at its highest pitch and carpetbaggery at its lowest, meanest efforts and our State's best orators were canvassing with a desperate effort for political ascendency over the negroes and carpetbaggers. On reaching Walton they found a big. well-cooked barbecued dinner and the largest collection of people to hear them that ever assembled on a like occasion. Ex-Gov. Walker was among the speakers, and when he stepped from the carriage "The Daughters of the Confederacy" being better acquainted with him than any of the others, gathered around him and engaged for several minutes in conversation with him, and handed him a small, white, slim box about 16 inches long. When he examined its contents he followed the other speakers to the stand and placed the strange little box on the table. The Governor was the first speaker introduced. He was slender, erect and above the medium height, with a fairly large round head, covered with thick iron gray hair; with piercing gray eyes in a lean thoughtful face; a chin and mouth betokening courage and inflexible resolution. His personality was exceedingly dignified and imposing. When he stepped forward and straightened himself up to his full height all eyes were fastened upon him. Then he lifted the strange box from the table in his left hand and said, "Noble fellow citizens of Old Walton! hear me a few moments in behalf of your generous 'Daughters of the Confederacy.' Seven years ago they met out on the green, made the stars and bars with their own lovely fingers, took down the stars and stripes from yonder Liberty Pole and hoisted the then new flag — Stars and Bars — to its place and gave it to the breeze as their pledge and support to the States action of withdrawing from the Union of States, to establish a Confederacy of States in which you hoped to find peace and tranquility. Four years later when in the providence of God your cause failed and you made an honorable surrender and new allegiance to the old flag, they took down the flag of the Confederacy in which their fond hopes were wrapped, in honor to, and indorsement of, your action and as a proof of their own allegiance to the powers that be. And today, a few years later it was their gracious hands that made and hoisted yonder Stars and Stripes to the top of that same liberty pole and they and it are saying with you and with me, that as it floats there in the breeze in its glory, "it represents a white man's government, and that the ill designing carpetbagger and ignorant negro must get out and give place to just such a government. That the red days of reconstruction must come to the bitter end!" I was sorry for a moment after reaching here today to find these live Daughters of the Confederacy with their bright minds and pure hearts staggering under some strange apparition that came to them in their patriotic work today, but which to me is the glory of this day. as they and you must understand. They tell me that in the early morn when they went out on the green, where they sat years ago in a circle and made the Confederate flag, that as they sat in this early morn in a like circle on the same spot, with the white, red and blue bunting spread in their laps, and as they were laying and stitching its folds together, to form that beautiful flag that flutters yonder in the breeze, there came on swift wings from his aerie home nearby, a large, dark, grey, bald eagle — one of these heraldic birds — symbol of American power and liberty. In passing he poised in midair above their heads, uttered a loud shriek and dropped this wing feather (taking it from the box) on the flag in their laps, and then mounted up on quick pinions to greet the morning's coming sun. This moved this noble little bevy of ladies to wonderland. They tell me that they fear this may be a dark bad omen; that they finished the flag, hoisted it to its place but when they look on it and discuss the incident attending its making, they fear it presages yet more bitter days in reconstruction; that the loud shriek uttered was still ringing in their ears, reminding them of that shriek uttered, that they read of at the 'Downfall of Poland' when the poet tells us 'Freedom shrieked as Kosciusko fell.' But said the Governor, lifting the wing feather on high, this gray pinion brings to me anything else but gloom. It is the omen of liberty, the symbol of victory, and we will make it, with its history, the tocsin to move men to action in these fearful days. My dear worthy lady friends, let not your hearts be further troubled. This gray plume gives us new hope with live, ardent expectations, and a more indomitable energy in this campaign. I shall carry this plume with me all over our downtrodden State and lift it on high as your trophy of victory to be won, to move any lagging brother to activity. Be sure that it presages success to us. This bird never witnesses failure. That awakening cry, the dropped plume, and the mount upward, signals "awake to duty; there's help! arise above encroachments. You shall see this feather, your hope on the fatal dart, your live faith, that winged the shaft, your energy in action, that shall quiver in the carpetbagger's heart, sending him to where he belongs. Then in sentiment you can appreciate and say a literal truth, with but little interpolation, with the poet who sings,

"So the struck eagle stretched upon the plain;
No more through rolling clouds to soar again,
Viewed his own feathers on the fatal dart,
And winged the shaft that quivered in his heart."

Then the Governor turned to the men, eulogizing Walton's Daughters for their faithful work during and since the war and showed them how great their shame would be if they failed in this crucial time to measure up to the full statue of men for the time. This speech, in substance, was made all over the State. Men were moved to action as they were never moved before. The move won and the State was saved. Drew was elected Governor, the carpetbagger driven from our country and there came great rejoicings and peace. Walton is keeping pace today with our Nation in its strides upwards in these stringent, scientific literary cultured days of poesy, and holding up its pristine virtues. It is up now to the poet, the very flower of eloquence to tell of these days as they come and go. The object of these pages is to tell of the prosaic, matter of fact, commonplace, love impelling days of long ago, when the latch string ever hung on the outside of the door, when we were so rich and thought ourselves so poor those days, the thought of which, makes our hearts revel in the sentiments of J. Whitcomb Riley's poem:

> Pap's got his patent right, rich as all creation:
> But where's the peace and comfort that we all had before?
> Le's go a-visitin' back to Griggsby's Station —
> Back to where we use to be so happy and so poor!

> "Le's go a-visiting back to Griggsby's Station,
> Back where the latch-string's a-hanging from the door'
> And ever' neighbor round the place is dear as a relation,
> Back to where we use to be so happy and so poor!"

We can't hope to please everybody in these sketches, as we have sought to do justice to every individual, community, class and institution connected with Walton's history and we find some who are never satisfied with justice — with truth. Now, if the truths labored for in these pages, be crushed to earth and fail, in due time, to rise again — then they deserve to go to the waste basket. We will be satisfied if these true stories of prosperity and decadence — of peace and of war — of plenty and of want — and of joy — love — sorrow and gladness, that run through Walton's varied history, will help some in the ways of right, and none be turned from or hindered in these shining paths.

Address of Welcome on Veterans' Day at the Florida Chautauqua on March the 13th, A. D. 1909

By the Author.

Fellow Comrades:

Our commander, General Pasco, in having me speak the welcoming words today, gave me to understand, that it did not require the commanding voice of oratory, nor the persuasive speech of eloquent words, neither was it necessary to dip one's tongue in the fountain of the Muses, to welcome a confederate soldier. But, says he, "it needs only the simple language of the heart, just true heart words." It was only then, I felt I might be able to make you feel at home with us, on this occasion, as my heart is always in tune with, and in sympathy for the Confederate soldier. For I know well of his motives, his grievances, his sacrifices. To some here, your bent forms, your empty sleeves, your halted steps coming down these aisles, may be suggestive of uncouthness. But to us, who remember the cause through which these came, they are grace, beauty and love. Your persecuted cause, that the world now calls "The Lost Cause," made resistless appeals to your manhood. To be sure, it sifted out the insincere and cowardly, but it left you a force of men the stronger for the winnowing. And brought out all that is noble and most daring in you. It struck open the deeps in your souls. No men could have been more sincere in the righteousness and justice of a cause, than you were in the one you espoused. Then shall we say of a truth, ours is a "Lost Cause?" "Nothing is settled until it is settled right." We know our grievances were settled by the power of the sword, and time has shown us how very unjust and unsatisfactory the arbitrament of the sword has been in the past. Now, near half a century has passed, and the problems of those days are the unsolved problems of today. "Courage yet," writes James Renwick, the soul of the Cameronian Societies in the days of the Covenant and Killing Times. "Courage yet, for all that has come and gone. The loss of men is not the loss of the cause. What is the matter tho' we all fall? The cause shall not fall." We see a rock in mid ocean, with its modest form high above the dashing waves, as a beacon light to those who would navigate treacherous seas; inviting the storm tossed ones to take rest on its firm foundations. We see the waves of every sea leaping upon and lashing it. And in the course of time, we find this beacon rock wasting itself away, beating back the angry waves. This rock is not lost, it is resting there on its granite bed, while the waves roll on; and maybe some day when the waters recede from the earth, or in some cosmic disturbances it may be the first to lift its broader form to bring light and give protection around. So, too, in a political or governmental sense, we see a little Republic, born out of contentions and disturbances, modestly lifting itself up and taking its place among the Nations of the world. It, too, has a firm foundation on which to build — a constitution that eliminated the evils and interjected the good found in other governments. With a splendid code of laws enacted, guaranteeing self-government. Yet this little Republic had hardly taken its place on the roll of Republics, before the Nations about began to leap upon and continued to pound upon it, until it wore itself out driving them back. And my fellow comrades, you are here today as the representatives, the exponents of that little Republic — as the resultant — the residuum, if you please, of all that pounding. And your ardent support, all these years to the overpowering government, speaks in noble terms of your patriotism — your loyalty to the same. We feel that we voice the heart sentiments of every one here, when we say, in defending this little Republic, we did nothing that we are ashamed of, one that needs an apology for. None but the coward or degenerate sons would dare say less. We know that we deserve as much respect from the world at large, for standing by our convictions, as those do who opposed us and will be satisfied with nothing less. We acknowledged that we were overpowered, or whipped if you please, but not debauched. The agonies that we know of — the blood that we saw flow, must stand for something. As the years roll on, in the course of human events, there may come a time in our governmental affairs, when "Mercy and truth are met together: righteousness and peace have kissed each other" — when -'truth crushed to the ground shall rise again." When the principles of State Sovereignty of Liberty (and not chattel slavery as some would have believe) that were so dear to us, and for which we fought and gave the best blood in our land, shall come to the front, assert themselves, and make this old Republic — so long as God will have it stand — by far the best government on the globe. Fellow Comrades — we do welcome you here with all our hearts, and to all the good things in our town; and hope through all the years that are going to be yours in this world, we may find you able to come up here annually, that we may have sweet fellowship one with another.

Just a few minutes longer with you here, that I may say a word about a noble soldier friend, whose name is on my mind more than any other. Sometimes I think he is the most pitiable of all others, and yet the most cheerful. He is not with us today as he would like to be. He is a shut-in. He has always been very close to me, we were raised together. We entered the army together, in the first company from Walton — did picket duty on many a line and fought shoulder to shoulder over many a battle field. Went on long marches together — with General Bragg through Kentucky, and fought the battle of Perryville. With General Breckenridge, through Mississippi as far as Big Black, and fought the battles around Jackson. With General Hood through Tennessee in rear of General Sherman, and fought the battles of Franklin, 2nd Murfreesboro and Nashville, where we were captured in the ditches, imprisoned in Northern prisons and lived to return to our home at the close of the war. We fought in every skirmish in our front, and every set battle from Chattanooga to Atlanta. We were young, stout and strong, and weren't able to miss any of this "all hell work." The 22nd day of June A. D. 1864 has ever been a memorial day with us, Johnson's army was fortified behind works on the top of the mountain — Sherman's entrenched in his front, in the valley below. When it was well dark on the evening of the 21st I went with this friend in charge of the picket guard from our Regiment, to relieve the line of pickets in our front — for there was no security of life in approaching that line, save under the cover of darkness. We relieved two picket posts, of dead men, and sent their bodies to the rear. Our orders were to keep a continuous firing night and day, to prevent the advance of the enemy. With the next days dawn, there commenced an artillery battle over our heads that continued through the day. Some of the charges of our own guns, miscarried and the missiles came leaping down the mountain, one carried away the rails we had gathered through the night and piled up in our front as protection from the sharpshooters' bullets. In the middle of the second night we received orders to vacate quietly and fall back to our commands. We fell back to the ditches and found them empty, and it was after daylight before we came up with our command behind other works, prepared in advance. And from that long perilous day, June 22nd A.D. 1864, the longest day in the calendar — that in which our lives were in jeopardy, and we kept safely — we have never forgotten its anniversary, nor to be thinkful for our preservation. We commemorate it in some way — if not together in festivities, we remember it by dropping a letter or a postal card on the run, as a reminder. Now, we wanted you to know something of this noble Confederate veteran in our midst. And while he is being well cared for by relatives and friends, he deserves the deepest sympathy and the most fervent prayers of every old veteran that loves obedience and duty — Northern or Southern. He is not only a shut-in, but his manly form is fast giving way, under the power of diseases contracted in the army, and he is living in a world of darkness, brought on by faithful soldier services. His name is Sergeant Malcom P. McLean, of Euchee Anna, Florida.

www.ingramcontent.com/pod-product-compliance
Lightning Source LLC
LaVergne TN
LVHW011418080426
835512LV00005B/133